English Poetic Theory, 1825-1865

Princeton Studies in English, No. 29

English Poetic Theory

1825-1865

BY ALBA H. WARREN, JR.

1966

OCTAGON BOOKS, INC.

New York

Reprinted 1966
by special arrangement with Princeton University Press

OCTAGON BOOKS, INC.
175 FIFTH AVENUE
NEW YORK, N.Y. 10010

LIBRARY OF CONGRESS CATALOG CARD NUMBER: 66-18052

Printed in U.S.A. by
NOBLE OFFSET PRINTERS, INC.
NEW YORK 3, N. Y.

Foreword

IN SPITE of modern refinements in psychology and semantics, and of more precise techniques of literary analysis, contemporary criticism has been signally unsuccessful in its attempts to reassess the virtues and vices of nineteenth century poetry. There is an initial failure in sympathy, of course, but perhaps one of the chief reasons is our partial understanding of nineteenth century theories of poetry. We know something, if not enough, about romantic theory, and something about the theory of art for art's sake at the end of the century. We know very little, however, about the lively speculation of the middle years in books and periodicals, prefaces, essays, and letters.

English Poetic Theory, 1825-1865 explores this neglected chapter in the history of criticism in breadth and depth. A wide selection of critical documents, reflecting on, defending, consolidating, developing, and striking out from, romantic theory and practice, was brought together for examination, and the results of a systematic analysis of this material are presented at the beginning of the book in the form of a critical manifesto for the period. The clauses of the manifesto are then substantiated by citation and close analysis of representative statements illustrating characteristic solutions of the various problems with which Early Victorian (this tag, while not strictly accurate, has been used throughout for convenience) poetic theory is concerned, the relations between poetry and science, between poetry and nature, the end of poetry, the function of imagery, for example. The topical introduction thus attempts to make accessible the general drift and the more interesting ideas of Early Victorian criticism in a panoramic view. Nine sections follow, presenting nine critical statements by memorable critics and poets of the period, Newman, Keble, Mill, Carlyle, Hunt, Browning, Dallas, Arnold, and Ruskin. These sections are an attempt at *explication de texte* by means of quotation, paraphrase, and running commentary, for the purpose of simplifying, explaining, highlighting, comparing, contrasting, and relating the important observations of each document to both the letter and the spirit of the criticism of the age. It might be noted that considerations of unity have unfortunately made It necessary to limit the discussion of Arnold and Ruskin rather closely to the specific period covered by the study. A concluding chapter on the substance of Early Victorian poetic theory summarizes the argument of the book for easy reference, emphasizes the basic assumptions of the critics: for instance, that poetry is primarily a matter of insight into reality, a matter of moral values; that it is primarily concerned with truth and the communication of truth; that it is primarily to be found in content or emotion; and suggests some of the implications of Early Victorian poetic theory for the modern critic whose standards are exclusively aesthetic and formal.

This is the place to thank my patient friends Donald A. Stauffer and Franklin Gary for their knowing guidance and helpful suggestion, and particularly for their confidence in time of despair. I want to thank Dudley Johnson for his comments on the body of the manuscript, and other good friends, who will recognize themselves in the description, for all sorts of impositions which have to do with the troubles of writing a book and which are not necessarily concerned with matters of text. And at the end I want to remember Asher Estey Hinds, my teacher who also became a friend, and who is unhappily not here to shame me with his unsparing perfectionism for the deficiencies of this book.

Princeton, 1949

ALBA H. WARREN, JR.

Contents

English Poetic Theory, 1825-1865

1. The Topics of English Poetic Theory, 1825-1865

Criticism

THE PERIOD of creative activity that dates roughly from the *Lyrical Ballads* to the death of Byron was succeeded by a period of critical reflection and assessment. The new period was not wanting in poetry and it witnessed the rise of the Victorian novel, but it was also notable for an access of criticism which reached its climax in Matthew Arnold. Arnold, writing in 1865, was certain of the value of the critical endeavor; it was second only to the creative activity itself, and its function was to provide intellectual situations in which the creative artist could work: but if Arnold was able to write of the critical office at all in philosophic terms, it was because he had in front of him a quantity of responsible criticism from which to generalize.

Criticism of the period between 1825 and 1865 was not a concerted effort. There was no center for educated opinion in England such as Arnold found in the French Academy; the romantics had cast off rules and standards, and the new critics recognized few common aims. Besides this, criticism had a wide variety of functions to perform. It had to defend poetry itself from the utilitarians and the practical-minded politicians, businessmen, and social reformers. It had to convey information to a public avid for facts and resorting to book clubs and circulating libraries in a way it never had before. It had to meet the growing demand for reading matter in the newspapers and in a dozen new periodicals and reviews. Furthermore, in respect of its materials, the body of romantic poetry and beliefs, criticism was also faced with a threefold task: to analyze and consolidate the romantic achievement, to evaluate its practice and its theory, and to spread the word in all the corners of England. One forgets that the real appreciation of Keats and Shelley dates from the middle of the century.

The new criticism lacked the homogeneity that might have

been expected of it. The state of criticism was chaotic, infected with purely personal opinion, and, to use Matthew Arnold's term, capricious. But there was a common critical attitude which held that poetry was serious and that the business of writing about poetry was earnest. There was no truce with the dilettante, for the new critics stood with Wordsworth against the men "who talk of Poetry as of a matter of amusement and idle pleasure; who will converse with us as gravely about a *taste* for Poetry, as they express it, as if it were a thing as indifferent as a taste for rope-dancing, or Frontiniac or Sherry." It was the critics themselves, in fact, who pointed out the confusion of critical aim in their own times, and if there was any one thing common to their efforts, it was the attempt to get to the bottom of poetry, to draw up laws and principles, to put poetry on a scientific footing.

The spirit of science was expressed in criticism in a notable succession of documents dealing with poetic theory. Criticism was convinced that a proper application of the deductive and inductive methods of science to the question "What is Poetry?" would reveal a logical structure as satisfying to the mind as any of the scientific studies. "However opinion may vary," wrote one critic in 1854, "as to the comparative merits of our present poets and those of other times, it will on all sides be admitted that the aesthetic principles, upon which poetry itself is based, are now much more generally understood than in any former period. It is a mistake to define poetry merely as an art. It is such only in the endless instances of its application to practice. But in its dependence upon principles of human nature, rather than upon rules,—and in its existence antecedent to, not springing from experience, it partakes of the nature of science."[1] There were critics who resented and resisted the encroachment of science, of course—Carlyle, to name only one—but even these went on with the analysis of the poetic mainsprings in their own way.

The materials of criticism in the period from 1825 to 1865

[1] *The London Quarterly Review*, II, 1854, pp. 440-41.

are largely derivative. If criticism had a tone of its own, a tone of serious and earnest inquiry, it is hard to find any original invention or discovery, freshness or enthusiasm: the period is "post-romantic" rather than anything else. There were conservative elements; academic critics like Newman and Keble retained something of the neoclassic spirit; the school of taste represented by Lord Jeffrey lasted on well into the middle of the century; and the partisan and sectarian criticism of the great reviews and some of the lesser ones did not disappear at once. There were critics who still contended that poetry had nothing to do with locomotives and the electric telegraph. Generally, however, the more thoughtful criticism accepted the body of stimulating ideas provided by Wordsworth and Coleridge in England and Goethe and Schiller in Germany, and set to work to make use of what they found.

It is probably true that the Early Victorians knew more about poetic theory than any of their predecessors. In the first place they had a greater quantity of empirical data, and again they had a wider perspective, coming after the two movements of classicism and romanticism. But over and above all this the interest in speculation led to a review and a revaluation of the theory of poetry in general from Plato to Shelley. Of the ancients Aristotle is naturally the most frequently referred to. His theory of imitation is misunderstood and generally "modified" in the attempt to make room for the expression of emotion, or it is completely discarded as commonplace and officious if not impossible and misleading. Bacon is undoubtedly the first Elizabethan, and he is usually mentioned in connection with Aristotle as holding the opposite theory of poetry; but Sidney, Puttenham, and others are equally well-known. Neoclassical theory is represented in the period by Sir Joshua Reynolds, who is universally discredited along with Burke, Kames, Archibald Alison, and a little later, Dugald Stewart. The primary sources of post-romantic ideas are, of course, Wordsworth and Coleridge. From one or the other, sometimes from both, the critics derived their inspiration, their matter, and their method, and for many of the critics Coleridge was the medium of information on the German poets and philosophers.

The majority of poetic illustrations can be found in four poets, Dante, Shakespeare, Milton, and Wordsworth, while examples of malpractice are taken principally from Pope and Young in the eighteenth, and Byron and Shelley in the nineteenth century. The attitude towards Byron is an extremely interesting one; admiration for his assertive personality struggles with a moral disapproval of his life and "gloomy scepticism," which is transferred to his poetry. At intervals of every ten years some critic will remark that Byron's influence is on the wane, but Arnold's preface in 1881 attests a persistent popularity.

The period of criticism from 1825 to 1865 was marked by the endeavor to formulate laws and principles of poetry. From the body of available critical material a certain number of key terms can be abstracted which might stand for the fundamental concepts of post-romantic theory—genius, insight, fact or reality, truth and sincerity. All of these terms apply to the nature of poetry as an essence or spirit rather than to the nature of poetry as an art, and accurately reflect a primary stress in theory on content rather than the medium. More often than not the word poetry means the poetical—the poetry of life, the poetry of architecture, the poetry of childhood, and even the poetry of science. It is perhaps possible to give the key terms a further expansion in the form of a "creed," which, allowing for a wide disagreement on any number of the articles, might still be accepted as a basic belief by a majority of the writers on theory. The articles of such a manifesto might read as follows:

1. Poetry is a science with ascertainable laws, which, if correctly formulated, will be universally valid in the sense in which the laws of science are valid.
2. Poetry is what the genius says or makes.
3. The organ of genius is insight.
4. The quality of insight depends on the moral perception of the genius.

5. The object of poetry is truth.
6. Beauty is the outward manifestation of truth.
7. The matter of poetry is fact or reality, physical, moral, and spiritual.
8. Poetry must have a practical end, preferably moral, whatever its immediate object.
9. Poetry must contain great ideas.
10. Any subject is fit for poetry if it is treated imaginatively. This includes ordinary feelings, steam engines, and "the grand subject."
11. The form of poetry is determined by the imagination as it expresses itself in imagery or measured language.
12. Style, the "body" of poetry, is directly related to the poet's moral being.
13. The models the poet will follow are Homer, Dante, Shakespeare, Milton, and Wordsworth.
14. Poetry is the greatest of all the arts.

The formulation of articles in this manner must not suggest a unanimity of critical opinion which simply does not exist. Such a table represents at best an ideal theory for the period, but if handled lightly and with full awareness of its typical defects, it can be useful to mark weight and trend and shift in connection with the analyses of specific problems that follow, in which the oppositions or the attempts at synthesis in any given case are presented as a summary statement of the complete view.

Poetry and Science

The relation of poetry and science in post-romantic criticism was a many-sided one. Science, as the word was used in connection with poetry, might have any one of a dozen meanings. It might stand quite simply for any activity of the reason, or for rationalism, logic, the process of analysis, deductive and inductive, for philosophy, materialism, utilitarianism, or for the particular disciplines of biology, geology, botany, politics, or economics. A critic could use any selection and interpretation of these to prove that the spirit of science was hostile to poetry, that poetry and science were striving towards the same goal by different means, that poetry was a science, that poetry made the truths of science more impressive; all of these could be proved as well as their contraries.

The most significant of these relationships is the antithesis between poetry and science as modes of discourse. The antithesis was posed in *The Critique of Judgment* in terms of Kant's distinction between the reason and the understanding. "In order to decide whether anything is beautiful or not," Kant wrote, "we refer the representation, not by the Understanding to the Object for cognition but, by the Imagination (perhaps in conjunction with the Understanding) to the subject, and its feeling of pleasure or pain."[2] Coleridge's definition of a poem as "that species of composition, which is opposed to works of science, by proposing for its *immediate* object pleasure, not truth,"[3] is a transposition of the Kantian statement, and in this form it became accessible to English criticism through the *Biographia Literaria*. Thus George Brimley in "Poetry and Criticism" (1855) places the distinction between poetry and science, not in the materials, but in the faculties which apprehend and operate upon the materials. "The understanding takes any object presented through the consciousness, and proceeds to analyze it into separate qualities, to name it and refer it to a class of objects with which it possesses certain of its qualities in common." The imagination on the other hand "takes the same object that we supposed before presented to the understanding;—as by chemical attraction it lays hold on precisely that part of the phenomenon which the understanding rejects, passing lightly over and taking little heed of that which the understanding was in quest of."[4]

The distinction between science and poetry had another

[2] *Kant Selections*, edited by T. M. Greene, New York, 1929, p. 375.
[3] *Biographia Literaria*, edited by J. Shawcross, Oxford, 1907, II, 10.
[4] George Brimley, *Essays*, London, 1882, "Poetry and Criticism," pp. 191, 193.

source in criticism, however, where it took a somewhat different form. This was Wordsworth's Preface of 1802. Wordsworth, unlike Coleridge, was a sensationalist; for him, to know was to feel, and poetry itself was a kind of knowledge as objective as science. The antithesis between poetry and science is based on a difference in materials and the use to which the knowledge is put. "The knowledge both of the Poet and the Man of science is pleasure; but the knowledge of the one cleaves to us as a necessary part of our existence, our natural and inalienable inheritance; the other is a personal and individual acquisition, slow to come to us, and by no habitual and direct sympathy connecting us with our fellow-beings."[5] The materials of poetry are universals, human and emotional values, and the object is "general" truth. The materials of science, on the other hand, are particular facts considered apart from their relation to the human emotions, and the object is truth, local and particular. Because the appeal of science is to knowledge specifically acquired by the individual, it is unsocial and uncommunicative, while poetry "binds together by passion and knowledge the vast empire of human society." Wordsworth's formulation of the antithesis is followed by Leigh Hunt who writes, "Poetry begins where matter of fact or of science ceases to be merely such, and to exhibit a further truth, that is to say, the connection it has with the world of emotion, and its power to produce imaginative pleasure";[6] and by John Ruskin, who says that the object of poetry and science is truth—in one case truth of fact plus truth of emotion, in the other mere truth of fact.

The distinction according to ends is made by John Stuart Mill and by George Moir in his "Treatise on Poetry" (1839). Mill declares that the object of poetry is to act on the emotions, thus differentiating it from its logical opposite as Wordsworth had said; and Moir, relying on the authority of Coleridge, makes the end of science "to instruct, to dis-

[5] *Wordsworth's Literary Criticism*, edited by N. C. Smith, London, 1905, p. 27.
[6] Leigh Hunt, *Imagination and Fancy*, New York, 1845, p. 3.

cover, and to communicate truth," while the end of poetry is to give "immediate Pleasure."[7]

Coventry Patmore in "The Ethics of Art" (1849) writes that the artistic is the antithesis of the scientific, for its materials are phenomena and "the First Cause" as distinguished from the exclusive preoccupation of science with second causes. "Donne writes very poetically—

> 'We have added to the world Virginia, and sent
> Two new stars lately to the firmament.'

Here the phenomena—that is to say, the facts considered only in their effects, and apart from the method of their origin—are alone regarded; and the mind delights in beholding the simple result of a couple of scientific discoveries conveyed in its simplest possible form."[8]

Patmore's distinction is primarily one of materials, but it also involves the mode in which the materials are regarded. The distinction in mode is perhaps the more valuable; it was made by Mill and Brimley, and with telling effect by David Masson in "Two Theories of Poetry" (1853).

> Let the universe of all accumulated existence inner and outer, material and mental, up to the present moment, lie under one like a sea, and there are two ways in which it may be intellectually dealt with and brooded over. On the one hand, the intellect of man may brood over it inquiringly, striving to penetrate beneath it, to understand the system of laws by which its multitudinous atoms are held together, to master the mystery of its pulsations and sequences. This is the mood of the man of science. On the other hand, the intellect of man may brood over it creatively, careless how it is held together, or whether it is held together at all, and regarding it only as a great accumulation of material to be submitted farther to the

[7] George Moir, *Treatises on Poetry, Modern Romance, and Rhetoric; Being the Articles under those Heads, Contributed to the Encyclopaedia Britannica, Seventh Edition*, Edinburgh, 1839, p. 2.
[8] *The British Quarterly Review*, x, 1849, p. 446.

operation of a combining energy, and lashed and beaten up into new existences.[9]

The antithesis between science and poetry is a critical commonplace of post-romantic theory. It is the natural point of departure in all theories which attempt a definition of the poetic essence, and the relationship is explored in all its facets, ends, materials, mode, faculty, function, and appeal. Its original formulation by Coleridge and Wordsworth is generally acknowledged by the critics, who add little if anything of their own. There is nothing in the later criticism to compare with Wordsworth's statement that "Poetry is the breath and finer spirit of all knowledge; it is the impassioned expression which is in the countenance of all Science."

Poetry and Truth

The problem of artistic truth which was raised in romantic criticism by the assimilation of the end of poetry to that of science provoked a wealth of interesting speculation. "Aristotle, I have been told, has said, that Poetry is the most philosophic of all writing," Wordsworth wrote in 1802, "it is so: its object is truth, not individual and local, but general and operative; not standing upon external testimony, but carried alive into the heart by passion; truth which is its own testimony, which gives competence and confidence to the tribunal to which it appeals, and receives them from the same tribunal."[10] Commenting on this passage in the *Biographia Literaria*, Coleridge contends that by making truth rather than pleasure the immediate object of poetry Wordsworth has destroyed "the main fundamental distinction, not only between a poem and prose, but even between philosophy and works of fiction."[11]

Wordsworth and Coleridge represent the dichotomy between imitation and creation, representation and expression, objective and subjective truth, which is characteristic of post-romantic criticism. The opposition was dramatized as a

[9] *The North British Review*, xix, 1853, p. 165.
[10] *Op. cit.*, p. 25. [11] *Op. cit.*, ii, 104.

conflict between the theories of Aristotle and Bacon. "Aristotle makes the essence of poetry to consist in its being imitative and truthful;" says David Masson, "Bacon in its being creative and fantastical."[12] Masson remarks that it would be possible to extend the Aristotelian theory and make it correspond with the Baconian, although in reality the two theories are antithetical. "If both are true, it is because the theorists tilt at the opposite sides of the shield." As a matter of fact, neither theory is held strictly in the period, and there was more than one attempt at synthesis. In the *Westminster Review* for 1858, for instance, a critic writes that all great poets are many-sided. "Their poetry is both *mimesis* and *poesis*. They illustrate both the Aristotelian and Baconian theory of poetry, as well as much more."[13]

The Aristotelian, the realist or the "concrete idealist" (the terms are synonymous in Early Victorian criticism), finds his truths in nature and reproduces them in the medium of language. The truths of poetry are thus universals, and poetry is true in the sense that it represents these universals accurately. The correspondence of the imitation with reality is an objective one. In the nineteenth century the doctrine of "characteristic truth" takes the place of the Aristotelian universals. The essence of the object for artistic purposes is its characteristic form or type, and it is this characteristic type which the artist represents. Of the Aristotelians, John Ruskin with his "naturalist" ideal was by far the most consistent and influential. Ruskin preached the exact representation of facts or truths of nature without generalization or selection, and without the intrusion of arbitrary moral or emotional peculiarities that belong to the artistic temperament. Truth is the object of art, and only so much beauty is allowed in the representation as is consistent with truth. Coventry Patmore in "The Ethics of Art" (1849), Walter Bagehot in "Pure, Ornate, and Grotesque Art in English Poetry" (1864)—Bagehot invents the word "literatesque" for the characteristic type in literature—and Aubrey De Vere

[12] *Op. cit.*, p. 161.
[13] *The Westminster Review*, LXIX, 1858, p. 122.

in his reviews of Sir Henry Taylor's minor poetry, are all more or less followers of Ruskin.

The Baconian, in contrast to the Aristotelian, believes that poetry is the product of a tendency in the mind to assimilate objective reality to its own emotional and intellectual needs. "Poetry," Bacon had written in the *Advancement of Learning*, "doth raise and erect the mind, by submitting the shows of things to the desires of the mind."[14] If poetry is true for the Baconian, its truth does not necessarily consist in a correspondence with external reality, but is rather in the coherence of the mental process itself; its criterion is subjective. Bryan Waller Procter's essay "On English Poetry" presents the case for the Baconians in its purest form. Poetry, he says, is "a thing created by the mind, and not merely copied either from nature, or facts in any shape." It has no existence in nature, although it finds its materials there, for if it did, it would be mimetic and not creative. The truth of poetry is a truth of imagination and its criterion is therefore imaginative. "However it may be true in itself (and it ought to be true), as a compound image or signification of consistent ideas, it must not be in all respects *literally* true."[15] Poetry is true according to the subjective logic of the imagination. John Stuart Mill, for whom poetry is a peculiar manner of associating ideas, E. S. Dallas, David Masson, and Sydney Dobell in his lecture on "The Nature of Poetry" (1857), in which poetry is the perfect expression of a perfect mind, are all Baconians.

One of the most ornate of the analyses of poetic truth in the criticism of the period is contained in Aubrey De Vere's review of Sir Henry Taylor's minor poems in 1849. De Vere breaks up the notion of poetic truth into a number of separate categories, truth of nature, truth of character, truth of sentiment and thought, truth of passion, truth of style, truth

[14] *Bacon's Advancement of Learning*, Oxford, The World's Classics, 1929, p. 90.

[15] B. W. Procter, *Essays and Tales in Prose by Barry Cornwall*, 2 vols., Boston, 1853, "On English Poetry (1825)," II, 131.

of diction, truth of observation, and truth of keeping; and he discusses each one in some detail.

Truth of nature, "that practical Truth which constitutes reality" in poetry, is contrasted with abstract thought on the one hand, and with "the miscreations of morbid passion, capricious fancy, or fashionable convention" on the other. De Vere's definition of truth of nature derives directly from Ruskin, and perhaps indirectly from Carlyle, and it represents a larger interpretation of the "truth of fact" which plays such an important part in the transcendental poetic theories of both Carlyle and Ruskin. In these theories nature reveals its mysteries only to the gifted eye of the genius. Here the genius does not select and arrange the materials of nature according to some "internal formative principle," but rather he subjects himself to nature, allows nature to speak for itself, and follows "the footsteps of truth whithersoever it goes."[16]

Truth of keeping is the most comprehensive of the various kinds of poetic truth in De Vere's analysis. It includes at once the organic unity of the poem, a unity determined "not by external rule, but inwardly, by the imagination, which conceived the poem originally, and conceived it as a whole," and the higher unity of the poet's total being, in which the work of art is regarded as the unified product of the whole man. The theory of poetry as the expression of the whole man derives from Goethe and was invoked by most of the post-romantic critics, by Hunt, Ruskin, and Dobell, to name only three. Truth of keeping attests the individuality of the artist, the verisimilitude of his representation of reality, and the moral and intellectual self-possession of the artist who produces the work of art.

The dichotomy between the Aristotelians and the Baconians has by no means been resolved in modern aesthetic speculation. A satisfactory solution will probably not be reached until the problem is properly formulated, and here

[16] *The Edinburgh Review*, LXXXIX, 1849, "Taylor's *Eve of the Conquest*," p. 364.

it seems, the various and ingenious speculations of the Early Victorians may have some contribution to make.

Poetry and Nature

Science in dealing with nature is determined by the structure of external reality. Poetry, on the other hand, if it is to be more than a mere transcript of reality, a photographic image of nature, must provide for the operation of the human mind on its materials. Thus some stand on the relation of poetry and nature is fundamental in any poetic theory. The problem, at least as old as Plato and Aristotle, can be formulated in a number of ways, but two of these should suffice as a background for the solutions offered by nineteenth century criticism. Does the poet reproduce an exact mental image of reality in the medium of language, or does he represent the results of a process of mental abstraction from the detail of nature? Does the poet perceive values in and behind nature, distinct from his own consciousness, or does he, by projecting the forms of his own consciousness, create a nature of his own? The answers to these questions in Early Victorian criticism were, broadly speaking, three, and they were suggested by answers which had been given in the previous criticism of the neoclassic and romantic periods.

The neoclassic theory of art as it was drawn up by Sir Joshua Reynolds advocated the imitation of "central forms," which had no real existence in nature, but which were "generalized" from nature according to a standard of beauty or natural perfection in the mind of the artist. The nature represented in art was a "general" nature, nature divested of all its local and particular traits and all its accidental deformities. This is the normative or perfectionist theory of art.

Reynolds' doctrine of central forms was categorically rejected by Wordsworth in favor of a "realist" interpretation of nature in art. Wordsworth held that the human mind was exquisitely fitted to the external world, and the external world to the individual mind. Here nature is divinized and beauty as one of its properties is held inviolable.

Beauty—a living Presence of the earth,
Surpassing the most fair ideal Forms
Which craft of delicate Spirits hath composed
From earth's materials.[17]

The artist, then, according to Wordsworth will reproduce the forms of nature as they are in reality, since the creative process lies in "the blended might" of mind and matter. In the same way the poet will imitate the passions of men, and while the imitation must necessarily fall short of the actual expression of the passions in life, its value lies in its close resemblance to reality.[18]

Coleridge also rejected the doctrine of central forms, but he held that poetry was "ideal," "that it avoids and excludes all *accident*; that its apparent individualities of rank, character, or occupation must be *representative* of a class."[19] Coleridge differs from Reynolds in holding that the ideal of poetry is "an involution of the universal in the individual."[20] A similar position was taken by Hazlitt in his papers "On the Imitation of Nature" and "On the Ideal." "In general," Hazlitt writes, "we would be understood to mean, that the ideal is not a voluntary fiction of the brain, a fanciful piece of patch-work, a compromise between innumerable deformities, (as if we could form a perfect idea of beauty though we had never seen any such thing,) but a preference for what is fine in nature to what is less so. There is nothing fine in art but what is taken almost immediately and entirely from what is finer in nature."[21]

These three fundamental positions, the perfectionist, the realist, and the idealist, are all represented in Early Victorian poetic theory. The positions are by no means consistently held, however, and nature mysticism of one kind or another

---

[17] Wordsworth, *The Recluse*, London, 1888.

[18] "Here is the new version of Imitation, and I think that it is the best so far." T. S. Eliot, *The Use of Poetry and the Use of Criticism*, London, 1933, p. 75.

[19] *Op. cit.*, II, 33-34.

[20] *Ibid.*, p. 159.

[21] *The Collected Works of William Hazlitt*, edited by A. R. Waller and Arnold Glover, 12 vols., London, 1904, XI, 228.

adds to the complication; but in spite of the confused think-
ing on the subject and the even more confused phraseology,
it is possible to distinguish the main outlines of the various
theories.

Ironically enough, John Henry Newman in "Poetry, with
Reference to Aristotle's Poetics" presents an unmistakable
perfectionist attitude towards nature. The poet must gen-
eralize from nature, he says, according to the eternal forms
of beauty in his mind, divesting nature of all local and in-
dividual peculiarities, and purifying and refining its grosser
elements. Poetry is also the perfection of the actual for Bryan
Waller Procter, who contends that poetry is ideal, because
unlike history and biography, it arranges facts according to
an intellectual principle for the purposes of beauty and
morality.

The "naturalist ideal" of John Ruskin contrasts with the
normative ideal of Newman and Procter. "It is naturalist,"
says Ruskin, "because studied from nature, and ideal, be-
cause it is mentally arranged in a certain manner."[22] The
poet's mind, however, is merely a mirror, and the poet an
accurate scribe of his vision. "The work of these great ideal-
ists is, therefore, always universal; not because it is *not por-
trait*, but because it is *complete* portrait down to the heart,
which is the same in all ages: and the work of the mean
idealists is *not* universal, not because it is portrait, but be-
cause it is *half* portrait,—of the outside, the manners and
the dress, not of the heart."[23] Ruskin's realist attitude towards
nature is variously interpreted by Aubrey De Vere, Coven-
try Patmore, and Walter Bagehot. Two sentences from Pat-
more's article on "The Ethics of Art" may help to illuminate
the theory.

There are faces, forms, characters, landscapes, and skies,
which are not to be excelled by art; but such high natural
revelations confine themselves wonderfully to the eye of
the born artist, and require to be clothed anew by him, in

[22] *The Works of John Ruskin*, edited by E. T. Cook and A. Wedder-
burn, London, 1904, v, *Modern Painters*, III, 113.
[23] *Ibid.*, pp. 127-28.

order to become visible to the common gaze. In this kind of imitation, however, the ideal is still at work: the artist detects and selects the essential, rejecting non-essentials; the faculty of such detection and selection being of a piece with the mind's creative power.[24]

The Coleridgeans of post-romantic criticism present an equally impressive front. They include James Montgomery, author of *Lectures on Poetry* (1833), E. S. Dallas, and David Masson. Masson writes that the key word in poetic theory is imagination, for poetry is undoubtedly creation, not imitation, and the poet is properly a creator.

> The poet is emphatically the man who continues the work of creation; who forms, fashions, combines, imagines; who breathes his own spirit into things; who conditions the universe anew according to his whim and pleasure; who bestows heads of brass on men when he likes, and sees beautiful women with arms of azure; who walks amid Nature's appearances, divorcing them, rematching them, interweaving them, starting at every step, as it were, a flock of white-winged phantasies that fly and flutter into the heaven of the future.[25]

Historically, the realist theory of the relation of art and nature is by far the most interesting. It had little effect on the practice of poetry beyond the feeble attempts of Wordsworth's imitators to reproduce his unadorned manner and a poem or two like Rossetti's "My Sister's Sleep" with its careful detail, but its repercussions in other fields were exciting. In painting the factual drawing of the Pre-Raphaelite Brotherhood, and in the novel the realistic narrative of Thackeray and George Eliot can be taken as practical illustrations of the theory of imitation in art.

Imagination and Fancy

The mind in its dealings with nature for artistic purposes makes use of the faculty of imagination. As the image-mak-

[24] *Op. cit.*, p. 445. [25] *Op. cit.*, p. 165.

ing faculty of the mind, imagination can have either or both of two functions according to definition: it can image the real, in which case its function is reproductive, or it can image the unreal or fantastic, in which case its function is productive. Neoclassical criticism tended to confine the imagination to its productive activity, and regarded its operation in poetry as one of combining and associating images. Kant, however, in making the imagination a mediator between reason and understanding, included both functions in his definition, which was used by Coleridge and Wordsworth in formulating their theories of imagination and fancy for English criticism.

Coleridge, primarily interested in the metaphysical implications of the theory, equated the imagination and reason, and made it the creative, originating function of the mind which deals with wholes; and he equated the understanding with fancy, differing from imagination in kind, a noncreative, associative faculty of the mind which deals with parts. Wordsworth, on the other hand, was more interested in the effects of the imagination and fancy as they were manifested in poetry, and his account in the Preface of 1815 was primarily illustrative. The creative activity of the imagination in both cases sets off the theory against the imagists and associationists.

Post-romantic theories of imagination and fancy are almost entirely derivative, and have little or nothing to add to the discoveries of Wordsworth and Coleridge. Carlyle pours scorn on the distinction between faculties of the mind, but his "insight" by which the poet intuits the spiritual reality embodied in the forms of nature is roughly equivalent to Coleridge's imagination. G. H. Lewes in *The Principles of Success in Literature* (1865) reduced the imagination to the mere image-making faculty, and E. S. Dallas in the *Poetics* makes an abortive attempt to define imagination in terms of the unconscious activity of the mind. For the rest, criticism merely elaborates on the earlier formulations, introducing minor variations of which the contention that fancy is

19

only a lower degree of imagination is perhaps the most worthy of record.

The single contribution of value to the theory of imagination was made by John Ruskin in the second volume of *Modern Painters*. Taking a hint from Leigh Hunt's analysis of the manifestations of imagination, Ruskin developed a theory of a penetrative function by which the imagination seizes the object in its very core of reality and meaning. Here imagination is a quality of perception itself, a theory in keeping with Ruskin's "naturalist ideal" and his theory of imitation in art. One further point should be mentioned in connection with post-romantic theories of imagination: the quality of imaginative perception or creation depends upon the poet's moral nature. In Ruskin's words,

> He who habituates himself, in his daily life, to seek for the stern facts in whatever he hears or sees, will have these facts again brought before him by the involuntary imaginative power in their noblest associations; and he who seeks for frivolities and fallacies, will have frivolities and fallacies again presented to him in his dreams.[26]

The End of Poetry

No matter how carefully or in what terms post-romantic theorists distinguished the immediate end of poetry, as pleasure, beauty, or truth, they seem to have been far more concerned with its ultimate end, in particular its relation to morals and society. It was still possible in the general cultural situation of the Early Victorian period, at least in theory, to conceive of poetry as an effective social and moral force, and so far in England it had occurred to no one to claim autonomy for the aesthetic experience. True enough, Kant, in the *Critique of Judgment*, had succeeded in delimiting an area of "pure" judgment, but this area was confined to certain natural objects such as flowers, and certain abstract designs such as architectural borders and wallpaper; in dealing with beauty, directly or even indirectly (horses or houses, for example) related to human beings, he conceded that

[26] *Op. cit.*, p. 124.

moral values necessarily condition the ideal of beauty, and that therefore judgment in these cases must be "impure." Quite simply, after ruling out the moral criterion in the judgment of taste, Kant brings it squarely in again. Thus, in England, while De Quincey is at some pains in his essay on "The Poetry of Pope" to prove that the element of instruction enters not at all even into didactic poetry, on the other hand he distinguishes a literature of power from a literature of knowledge on the ground that the former engages the "great *moral* capacities of man"; and while he defines power as the "exercise and expansion to your own latent capacity of sympathy with the infinite,"[27] he is at the same time prepared to admit a zealous public censorship. The antitheses here are by no means exclusive, but that is precisely the point. Another element of the general problem is the eminent practicality (in the Arnoldian sense) of the Early Victorians, or to put it differently, they had no real respect for contemplation. In any case one finds in their criticism, often in the criticism of a single man, a curiously ambivalent attitude towards art: a certain impatience and hostility towards the works of imagination because they are less than "reality," and an equally one-sided faith in art as a revelation of reality itself. This attitude is especially characteristic of Carlyle, Browning, and Ruskin.

All these points could be profusely illustrated. E. S. Dallas, for instance, in his *Poetics* professes to give a pleasure theory of poetry, but pulls the teeth of his argument with the statement that the poet lays "in ambush other ends as mighty and as earnest as any that rule mankind."[28] Carlyle attacks the pleasure theory head on: "On all hands, there is no truce given to the hypothesis, that the ultimate object of the poet is to please. Sensation, even of the finest and most rapturous sort, is not the end, but the means."[29] All literature

[27] *The Collected Writings of Thomas De Quincey*, edited by D. Masson, 14 vols., Edinburgh, 1890, xi, 56.
[28] E. S. Dallas, *Poetics*, London, 1852, p. 273.
[29] *The Works of Thomas Carlyle*, Centenary Edition, 30 vols., London, n.d., *Critical and Miscellaneous Essays*, xxvi, 56.

must have "a didactic character," and the modern poet is the man who can "instruct" us in the mysteries of life. Procter calls poetry a "moral science" and G. H. Lewes in "The Inner Life of Art," "the phasis of a religious Idea." Masson places the creative impulse in a state of "moral uneasiness" which stirs the poet to "scheme" a plan or story, a sort of allegory of his mood as a whole, as a means of objectifying his state.

The idea of poetry as the handmaid to reason, morals, and religion is pervasive in the period. Procter, Keble, Patmore in "The Ethics of Art," and William Allingham in his essay "On Poetry" (1865) all give compendious summaries of the practical values of poetry, and Matthew Arnold, after registering the lone protest against impure aesthetics in the early letters to Clough, will come finally to a view of poetry as a "magister vitae" and a substitute for religion itself.

The Poet

Criticism was agreed as to the ultimate end of poetry, and it found common ground again in a basic definition of poetry as the expression of genius. The definition of poetry as "that which is produced by the poet" rests firmly on the concept of original genius, a concept which was formulated in English criticism as early as 1759 in Edward Young's "Conjectures on Original Composition," and which played an important part in eighteenth century aesthetics. The concept is obviously subversive of all theory, but with Kant the problem is rather one of rationalizing the experience of genius than attempting to explain its nature, and in this form it was taken over by Wordsworth and Coleridge. On the other hand Shelley's much quoted "Defence" and most of Carlyle's remarks on poetry assume the inexplicable nature of the creative activity.

"Poetry is the image of man and nature," wrote Wordsworth, and post-romantic criticism echoed the thought in every manner of phrase. "Why do we love and reverence Art? Because it gives a natural scope, and lasting expression, to *Genius*."[30] "A perfect Poem is the perfect expression of a Perfect Human Mind."[31] "Great Art is precisely that which never was, nor will be taught, it is preeminently and finally the expression of the spirits of great men."[32] Even Matthew Arnold at times seems to have held some such theory, "Genius is mainly an affair of energy, and poetry is mainly an affair of genius."[33]

The critics split into two opposed camps on the subject of the poet's nature, one contending with Wordsworth that the poet is "a man speaking to men," the other contending that the genius differs not only in degree but in kind. In the nineteenth century the trend was away from the latter. "We are all poets when we *read* a poem well," writes Carlyle,[34] and he is followed by E. S. Dallas, "what it [the theory that the poet differs in kind] gives to genius it gives at the cost of humanity."[35] In this view the poet is merely one manifestation of "the grand fundamental character," the great man, and it is mainly due to circumstance that he expresses himself in art rather than science or politics.

The ideal poet, however, has certain distinguishing characteristics, and these are variously described. Above all the poet possesses "insight" or vision. "The ideal, the typical Poet has all but superhuman power of vision and speech," says William Allingham. Insight, intuition, intellect, imagination, these are the qualities that enable the poet to reach the Divine Ideas of Plato, to read men's hearts, and to illuminate the least fact of nature. Second only to insight in importance is the poet's "sincerity"; he humbles himself before his art and contents himself with an accurate report of his vision. Sincerity, says Carlyle, is "the measure of worth." Sincerity

[30] William Allingham, *Varieties in Prose*, 3 vols., London, 1893, "On Poetry," III, 259-60.

[31] Sydney Dobell, *Thoughts on Art, Philosophy, and Religion*, London, 1876, p. 7.

[32] John Ruskin, *op. cit.*, p. 69.

[33] *Essays in Criticism, First Series*, London, Macmillan and Co., 1895, "The Literary Influence of Academies," p. 50.

[34] *Op. cit., Heroes and Hero-Worship*, v, 82.

[35] *Op. cit.*, p. 226.

implies the moral health of the poet, and the Early Victorians were staunch in maintaining that the defective or diseased mind was incapable of poetry. For the rest, the powers of the poet are of all kinds. He thinks in images, he associates ideas under the influence of a dominant feeling, he produces "fictitious concretes." In all these operations the poet's mind performs unconsciously or almost unconsciously, for the great poet is always forgetful of self.

The critics of the nineteenth century conceived the function of the poet in grandiose, Shelleyan terms; and in this case, if in no other, practice followed theory, for it seems legitimate to recognize in the later Browning and Tennyson the attempt to realize the ideal of the philosopher-poet which criticism held out to them. Criticism was no doubt intrigued by the notion of "pure poetry" and the lyric cry, but it usually looked at the palace of art from the outside. In "a serious time, among serious men" the concept of the poet must have more practical bearings; the poet must be "the exemplar of his age," its teacher and guide. The poet is the mediator between the soul and the infinite, according to Browning, the revealer of "the open secret" of nature, according to Carlyle. He makes truth more "impressive," and above all he binds men together in fellowship of feeling.

The poets are classified and ranked in a number of different ways. The seers or men of genius, the originators, contrast with the men of talent, the men who reproduce, arrange, and modify the work of the seers. Another classification is based on a difference in the orientation of the poet's moral nature and a corresponding difference in the function of imagination. Here one class of poets is preoccupied with the outward world, and another with the aspiration for the ideal, and their poetry is "nationalist" or "ideal"—in Browning's terms, "objective" and "subjective." Both of these bases of rank and distinction enter into Ruskin's grouping of "creative" and "perceptive or reflective" poets, the former remarkable for their insight and accurate report, and the latter for the analysis of emotion. A more unusual variant of the common distinction between poets of "will" and poets of "impulse" is that of John Stuart Mill, in which the poets are divided according to the dominance of thought or feeling in the process of associating images into "poets of culture" and "poets of nature." Mill's ideal is needless to say a combination of the two in the philosopher-poet.

Early Victorian accounts of the poet are perhaps too Platonic, too remote to be of any value to modern criticism. Matthew Arnold alone registered a protest against the exalted notions of his contemporaries. The true poets, he says, "do not talk of their mission, nor of interpreting their age, nor of the coming Poet; all this, they know, is the mere delirium of vanity; their business is not to praise their age, but to afford to the men who live in it the highest pleasure which they are capable of feeling."[36]

Poetry and the Arts

If Arnold was almost alone in emphasizing the technical side of the poetic activity, the careful construction of the poem itself (and so seems closer to the more practical attitude of modern criticism towards the poet as a skilled craftsman), it was because the criticism of his time was ruled by the notion of poetry as an essence or utterance, and tended to ignore the claims of poetry as an art or craft. The distinction between "poetry," the spirit, and "poesy," the product, as Dallas puts it, was indeed admitted, but after the admission little was done with "poesy." The common attitude is suggested in Newman's strictures on Aristotle. "We may be allowed to suspect him of entertaining too cold and formal conceptions of the nature of poetical composition," Newman writes, "as if its beauties were less subtle and delicate than they really are."[37] Some interesting speculation was made during the period, however, by Masson, and by Sydney Dobell. The former has some good things to say about poetry as the art of producing "a fictitious concrete," and the latter

[36] *Poems*, London, 1853, p. xxviii.
[37] *Essays Critical and Historical*, 2 vols., London, 1871, I, "Poetry, with Reference to Aristotle's Poetics," p. 8.

almost arrives at a theory of the poem as an expanded meta-
phor.

The essence of poetry is common to all the arts, and post-
romantic criticism is frequently concerned with pointing out
its manifestations in painting, sculpture, architecture, and
music. "All the fine arts," Coleridge had said in "The Princi-
ples of Genial Criticism," "are different species of poetry.
The same spirit speaks to the mind through different senses
by manifestations of itself, appropriate to each."[38] Coleridge
defined three such kinds of poetry, poetry of language, poe-
try of the ear, and poetry of the eye, and these three were
linked by a common essence, "the excitement of emotion for
the immediate purpose of pleasure through the medium of
beauty." John Keble likewise found a common essence for
the various arts in his definition of poetry as the spontaneous
overflow of powerful feeling for the relief of the mind, and
the poetry of painting or sculpture is thus "the apt expres-
sion of the artist's feeling."[39] A favorite illustration of this
thesis is the contrast between Raphael and Rubens, in which
Rubens is condemned for his attention to technique and
workmanship. In the classification of the arts according to
essence, there is some difference of opinion as to which of
the arts is the most "poetical." Poetry itself perhaps receives
the majority of votes, but music, because its medium is the
most immaterial and its language the most universal, is
frequently preferred. Music and poetry are almost insepa-
rable, however, and the critics are fond of citing Milton's
lines,

> Blest pair of Sirens, pledges of Heav'ns joys,
> Sphere-born harmonious Sisters, Voice and Vers.

When poetry is considered as an art rather than an essence,
the argument takes a somewhat different form. B. W. Proc-
ter, for instance, writes that poetry is the first of the fine
arts because it combines all the best qualities of the other

[38] *Op. cit.*, II, 220-21.
[39] *Keble's Lectures on Poetry*, translated by E. K. Francis, 2 vols.,
Oxford, 1912, I, 42.

arts with a peculiar virtue of its own, the beauty of painting, the simplicity of sculpture, and the moving cadences of music, while it is more permanent than any of them; and Leigh Hunt writes to the same effect that "Poetry includes whatsoever of painting can be made visible to the mind's eye, and whatsoever of music can be conveyed by sound and proportion without singing or instrumentation." "But," he adds, "it far surpasses those divine arts in suggestiveness, range, and intellectual wealth;—the first, in expression of thought, combination of images, and the triumph over space and time; the second, in all that can be done by speech, apart from the tones and modulations of pure sound."[40]

Post-romantic criticism leans heavily on the great Germans, Lessing and Hegel in particular,[41] in its delimitation of the work of the separate arts, but it had a number of curious and specific comments of its own to make. James Montgomery, for instance, in his *Lectures on Poetry* states that poetry is superior to painting, because it is not limited to a moment of space and time, but he also contends that portrait-painting has the advantage of poetry, "because there the pencil perpetuates the very features, air, and personal appearance of the individual represented; and when that individual is one of eminence,—a hero, a patriot, a poet, an orator,—it is the vehicle of the highest pleasure which the art can communicate; and in this respect portrait painting (however disparaged) is the highest point of the art itself,—being at once the most real, intellectual, and imaginative."[42]

Some feeling for the formal element in poetry is revealed in the frequent reference to poetry in sculptural terms. Poetry, says Montgomery, is a "school of sculpture" in the more permanent medium of language, and John Stuart Mill notes that Tennyson's poems are "statuesque" in the precision and distinctness of their outline. Dallas will go so far as to argue from analogy that the object of the drama is beauty,

---

[40] *Op. cit.*, p. 2.
[41] Cf. Matthew Arnold's 'Epilogue to Lessing's Laocoon.'
[42] James Montgomery, *Lectures on Poetry*, London, 1833, p. 12.

the formal object of painting and sculpture, rather than truth, which is the proper object of the epic. This tendency to refer to the formal qualities of poetry in terms of another art was at least partially due to the lack of a critical vocabulary—one thinks of the universal use of the Dutch painters to stand for the concept of realism in both painting and poetry—and it marks the almost total absence of any interest in the problems of the medium in the Early Victorian period.

Poetry and Literature

The delimitation of poetry from other kinds of literary discourse is carried out along conventional lines with little originality of interpretation. Specific arguments take more than one form according to the definition of the poetic essence or the nature of the poetic activity; but the majority of the critics are content with rephrasing and adapting Aristotle's statement that poetry is more philosophical and more serious than history. Typical of this approach is John Henry Newman who writes,

> Poetry, according to Aristotle, is a representation of the ideal. Biography and history represent individual characters and actual facts; poetry, on the contrary, generalizing from the phenomenon of nature and life, supplies us with pictures drawn, not after an existing pattern but after a creation of the mind. Fidelity is the primary merit of biography and history; the essence of poetry is fiction.[43]

Because no one mistakes fiction for fact, says Montgomery, poetry is a better transmitter of knowledge, and it has a wider influence than history, for it tells us more about society, customs, arts, sciences, and domestic details.

Equally popular with the argument from universals is the distinction based on the definition of poetry as the expression of states of feeling or as the spontaneous overflow of emotion. In this category belong Mill's often quoted statement that eloquence is heard and poetry overheard, and Keble's notion that rhetoric is directly addressed to an audi-

[43] *Op. cit.*, p. 9.

ence, and is concerned with producing a practical effect, while poetry is self-contained and indirect in expression. Here, too, perhaps should be mentioned De Quincey's well-known distinction between the "literature of knowledge" and the "literature of power." "The function of the first," he says in the essay on "The Poetry of Pope," "is—to *teach*; the function of the second is—to move: the first is a rudder; the second, an oar or a sail." Newton's *Principia* is "a *provisional* work," the *Iliad, Hamlet, Paradise Lost*, "are not militant, but triumphant"; they "never *can* transmigrate into new incarnations."

Of the various theories offered during the period on this subject David Masson's is the most original and suggestive in that it stresses the peculiar imaginative structure of the poem. Masson's definition of poetry as an "artificial concrete" made up of imaginative elements serves to distinguish poetry from other forms of literature, from scientific prose, which tends to the abstract, from oratorical prose or the literature of moral stimulation, which directs the mind or induces a certain state of mind or feeling, and from history, which deals with actual facts which are presented to the mind by the memory.

In a critical tradition which tends to define poetry almost exclusively in terms of the expression of emotion, it often happens that no distinction is made between poetry and prose. Where, as in Wordsworth and the majority of Early Victorian critics, the formal element in poetry is slighted and the logical opposite of poetry is taken to be science, it is quite possible to say, as Keble does, that Plato is more poetical than Homer himself. B. W. Procter, who rejects the antithesis of poetry and science, holds that poetry differs from all prose because it is essentially complicated, while prose presents single and obvious ideas arranged for purposes of reasoning, instruction, and persuasion. The critics will thus fall into two main categories in relation to the problem of poetic form, according to whether they consider verse essential or nonessential to the definition of poetry as an art.

Verse

The theory of verse in post-romantic criticism is generally confused and unsatisfactory, and it is hard to trace any clear outline through the various discussions. Still, broadly speaking, there are two fundamental positions on the basis of which the critics can be classified. These are quite simply that verse is or is not essential to poetry. The critics who hold the latter position define poetry in terms of a poetic essence or spirit, such as creation, feeling, catharsis, or imagination, and for them verse is merely the conventional form, garb, or vehicle of the essence. Procter, Newman, Keble, Mill, and Moir, to mention only a few who come together in this respect, will naturally have very little to say about verse in their criticism. Keble, for instance, remarks in his first lecture that poetry is in one way or another associated with measure and a definite rhythm of sound, and he virtually ignores the subject throughout the remaining prelections. Two critics of this first group, while holding that verse is "accidental" (in the logical sense), to poetry, believe it is the concomitant of the emotion which generates poetry. Brimley says—and in this he agrees with critics who belong in class two—that all emotion which is not mere pain is impelled to rhythmical expression; but the essence of poetry is imaginative perception and not necessarily measured emotion. Masson makes the same observation; notes that verse is most characteristic of the poetry of feeling, the lyric; and suggests that verse was originally connected with oratory, lingering on in modern poetry only as an accepted convention.

The critics who hold that verse is essential to the definition of poetry offer various explanations for their theories. Generally, they refuse to separate form and substance. The metrical form of poetry distinguishes it from prose, and constitutes it one of the fine arts. "Verse is the form of poetry"; writes G. H. Lewes, "not the form as a thing *arbitrary*, but as a thing vital and essential; it is the incarnation of poetry. To call it the *dress*, and to consider it apart as a thing distinct, is folly, except in technical instruction. Rhythm is not a thing invented by man, but a thing *evolved* from him, and it is not merely the accidental form, but the only possible form of poetry; for there is a rhythm of feeling correspondent in the human soul."[44] In this second group also belong those critics who consider verse necessary to the "perfection" of poetry. Leigh Hunt and Coventry Patmore offer this theory of verse. In "English Metrical Critics"[45]—according to A. E. Housman one of the two works on prosody of any value in English literature—Patmore writes, "Perfect song is perfect speech upon high and moving subjects." Patmore is unique in insisting that meter should make itself felt in poetry at all times. The distinction between verse-poetry and mere versifying is made on the grounds of content; as Leigh Hunt says, fitness for song marks the poetical subject. Critics of both groups are also emphatic that verse is no trammel to the poet, but is resorted to freely and by choice.

William Allingham holds most of these theories at once, and a summary of his treatment will suggest the general line of argument in many of the critical documents. Meter as the form of poetry is not mere grace or ornament; on the contrary it makes poetry an art, for it has been found by experience to give words their greatest possible force and beauty, and in most cases it conveys the highest thoughts better than prose. Meter draws the mind into the mood of poetry and holds it there. It raises a succession of pleasurable expectations and in due succession fulfills them, thus showing a constant obedience to law and a boldness in mastery.[46] Allingham, somewhat in the manner of Carlyle, finds a "Beautiful Proportionality" in nature which is represented by a corresponding "Beautiful Proportionality" in the thoughts and their vehicle. "Plan, ideas, images, style, words,

[44] George Henry Lewes, *The Principles of Success in Literature*, edited by T. S. Knowlson, London, 1899, pp. 193-94.

[45] *The North British Review*, xxvii, 1857, pp. 67-86.

[46] Hunt also stresses the poet's pleasure in mastery of metrical difficulty.

are all modulated to one harmonious result."[47] Poetry, the most complete mode of human expression, is distinguished from prose by the suitableness of its subject matter for metrical treatment. Ideally it is harmonious thought and feeling in harmonious words.

There seems to be little in any of this of permanent value for the theory of poetry in general, for in spite of an original idea or two contributed by Dallas and Dobell, it is all vague and transcendental. Of the relation of verse to meaning, the most fruitful field of modern speculation, only hints are to be found here and there in Early Victorian criticism. Newman, for instance, states casually that meter is a "suitable index" to the sense of poetry, and Masson notes that meter "assists" in the creation of meaning. "Coleridge very pertinently remarks somewhere," says Carlyle, "that wherever you find a sentence musically worded, of true rhythm and melody in the words, there is something deep and good in the meaning too."[48]

Imagery

The critics who deny that verse is of the essence of poetry are likely to hold to imagery as the staple and substance of the poetic activity, while the critics who take the opposite point of view will generally consider imagery an embellishment or at most an element of secondary importance. The antithesis is not inevitable, however, for G. H. Lewes, after disparaging the function of imagery in 1842, went over to the other camp in 1865; and E. S. Dallas insists from the beginning that imagery and verse are "twinborn" products of the imagination.

The meaning of the word image itself was by no means fixed in the period. Ordinarily it is taken to mean a visual image, a picture presented either to the eye of the body or the eye of the mind. Critics of this narrow definition attack Erasmus Darwin, and point out that poetic imagery appeals to senses other than the visual. But there were wider defini-

[47] *Op. cit.*, p. 262.
[48] *Op. cit., Heroes and Hero-Worship*, v, 90.

tions embracing any sensuous concrete, in Procter's terms, any idea of character, person, or place. Certain critics and reviewers tended to oppose imagery as sensual, emotional, and luxurious, to the intellectual and "immortal" part of poetry, making a distinction between an image and a thought, between the purely visionary and the reality of experience. Sir Henry Taylor in the notorious preface to *Philip Van Artevelde* scores the romantic poets for their profusion of glowing imagery and the visionary quality of their imaginations, divorced from all sense of the rational and the real, and something of the same attitude is behind Matthew Arnold's discussion of Keats and Shakespeare in the Preface of 1853. Uncertainty of the precise nature and function of imagery is reflected in the various contexts in which the problem is discussed by the more systematic critics. George Moir, for example, states that imagery is not to be confused with "the lower department" of diction in poetry, while it is precisely in the department of diction that James Montgomery has his say on the subject.

Procter, Moir, and Brimley all hold to the theory that imagery is the staple of poetry. Imagery is conceived as a means of dealing with abstract ideas, of concentrating and dissipating them by means of the imagination and fancy, of presenting them as "concretions of diverse phenomena organized into phenomenal unity by the pervading vital influence of a subjective idea." The words of poetry, writes Brimley, must be "alive with presentative significance."[49] Where verse is addressed to the emotional faculties, imagery (or poetry proper) is addressed to the perceptive and speculative faculties. Poetry is performing its proper function when it is organizing diverse phenomena into unities, and for this words must present "real, living objects."

Other accounts of imagery are more or less individual. Sydney Dobell conceives of images as equivalents for objects and emotions: a poem is an expanded metaphor. Masson, while holding that verse is perhaps more essential, says that

[49] *Op. cit.*, pp. 195-96.

the aim of the poet is imagery, which he defines as a "secondary concrete adduced by the imagination in the expression of a prior concrete."[50] Its forms are simile, metaphor, and personification. Leigh Hunt finds the proper function of the imagination in the production, or perhaps discovery, of images, and other images brought in to illustrate them. The images vary in nature according to whether they are the result of the imagination or the fancy. These two terms are unsatisfactory to Hunt, for imagination suggests too great solidity in its imagery, and fancy is too much restricted in its meaning to the purely visual.

The idea of imagery as a structural element in poetry is probably the most fruitful contribution of post-romantic theory, but criticism was too preoccupied with content and the practical ends of poetry to push the idea to its logical conclusion. Arnold's attitude towards poetic expression in the Preface in 1853, while it contradicts the general feeling towards profuse imagery, is based on a subject-theory of poetry. It is worthy of note that the quality of the imagery in any given poet, like the quality of imagination and fancy, is made to depend upon the moral sensibility of the poet himself.

The pattern of the typical problems and solutions of Early Victorian poetic theory is, one recognizes, summary, tentative, and diffuse, but it may serve to suggest the main points of interest to the critics of the period, and something of the variety and range of speculation in their criticism. At the same time it may also serve to counterpoint the more detailed discussion of the nine extended statements on poetic theory which follows.

[50] *Op. cit.*, p. 174.

2. John Henry Newman

Poetry, with Reference to Aristotle's Poetics. 1829

JOHN HENRY NEWMAN's essay in criticism, "Poetry, with Reference to Aristotle's Poetics," is the considered statement of a man with a trained mind and poetic sensibility. The circumstances of its publication suggest that it is also a representative statement, the annunciation, implicit rather than explicit, of critical policy for a new periodical. If this interpretation is correct, the document is of some importance for the history of Early Victorian poetic theory.

The essay was printed in the first number of *The London Review*, founded in 1829 to take the place of the old *Quarterly*, which was in a period of change, and not entirely satisfactory to the political and religious party it represented. Its editor was Newman's friend, Blanco White, and others of his Oxford friends were its supporters. The magazine was launched with enthusiasm, and it would seem that the essay on poetry was intended to establish the same high standard in literary criticism which was aimed at in matters of church and state. The form of the essay, furthermore, tends to confirm this assumption. Ostensibly a review of a compendium of critical and historical information on the Greek theater, the essay begins with three paragraphs of general comment on the use and misuse of historical scholarship (its misuse as a short-cut to "academical success" is "an especial fault of the age"), then shifts abruptly to an extended discussion of the nature of poetry which has little, if anything, to do with the book under review. Finally, there is Newman's brief record of contemporary comment in the *Apologia* where he remembers that Dr. Whately was dissatisfied, and that Blanco White only referred to it good-humoredly as Platonic.[1]

Blanco White was right. Newman's "speculations" on Greek tragedy and the nature of poetry in general were

---

[1] Newman's account of the circumstances of publication is appended to his reprint of the essay in *Essays Critical and Historical*, London, 1871, I, 27-29.

3 5

hardly "founded on" the doctrine of Aristotle, as Newman himself confessed when he revised the phrase in 1871 to read, "suggested by." As a matter of fact, Newman's theory of poetry is Platonic and romantic, and is fundamentally opposed to the theory of the *Poetics*. At the outset Newman finds fault with Aristotle as a critic. He is too cold, too abstract, too formalistic: "It is one thing, however, to form the *beau ideal* of a tragedy on scientific principles; another to point out the actual beauty of a particular school of dramatic composition."[2] To point out actual beauties, this is for Newman the true function of the critic; analysis of poetic structures is "critical art." Under Newman's hand Aristotle sharply defines an antithetical position. The essence of poetry is not form but expression, not imitation or representation but creation, not composition but the effusion of original genius; the poetry of Greek drama is not in the action or plot but in the characters, sentiments, diction. Poetry appeals, not to "mere recognition" or the reasoning faculty, but to the imagination and the feelings. Even when Newman agrees that poetry is "ideal," it is not surprising to find him in his interpretation "platonizing" in the tradition of late eighteenth century neoclassicism: poetry is ideal because it is the perfection of the actual, the expression of the eternal forms of beauty which fill the mind of the poet.

The attack begins at once. Aristotle's contention that tragedy is the imitation of an action is surely nothing more than a truism, and, while his account of the economy of plot is interesting and valuable, it is plainly theoretical and unhistorical. The Greeks, says Newman, were not happy in their plots. Plot for them was "either a mere necessary condition of the drama, or a convenience for the introduction of mat-

---

[2] *Essays Critical and Historical*, London, 1871, i, 1. Quotations will be made from this edition unless otherwise specified. Three paragraphs dealing with the book under review are omitted from this reprint and a few minor revisions have been made in the text. A reprint of the essay in its original form can be found in *English Critical Essays, Nineteenth Century*, selected and edited by E. D. Jones, London, The World's Classics, 1935.

ter more important than itself." The implication of these facts is clear.

> The action then will be more justly viewed as the vehicle for introducing the personages of the drama, than as the principal object of the poet's art; it is not in the plot, but in the characters, sentiments, and diction, that the actual merit and poetry of the composition are found.

It is in the characters, sentiments, and diction that Newman finds the "charm," the "spirit and nature," the "beauties," he is looking for, and he is led on to his logical conclusion.

> A word has power to convey a world of information to the imagination, and to act as a spell upon the feelings; there is no need of sustained fiction,—often no room for it.

Newman is confronting Aristotle with a definition of poetry as in its essence lyric. He compares the Greek drama to "the music of the Italian school; in which the wonder is, how so much richness of invention in detail can be accommodated to a style so simple and uniform"; the analogy between poetry and music recurs throughout his argument.

There is a curious passage in the essay in a different context which seems to admit the possibility of an action poetic in the Aristotelian sense. Newman is discussing the idealization necessary to any representation if it is to be called poetic. There appear, however, to be some situations, characters, facts, poetic in themselves, in the representation of which the poet becomes merely an accurate reporter.

> Hence, moreover, when a deed or incident is striking in itself, a judicious writer is led to describe it in the most simple and colourless terms, his own being unnecessary; for instance, if the greatness of the action itself excites the imagination, or the depth of the suffering interests the feelings.

Wordsworth, from his position in 1802, could make a strong case for the inviolability of the poetic object,[3] and Arnold

---

[3] " . . . if the Poet's subject be judiciously chosen, it will naturally, and upon fit occasion, lead him to passions, the language of which,

will make a strong case for the poetic action in 1853; this passage in Newman is out of keeping with the general tenor of his theory.

The poetry of the Greek drama, then, does not inhere in its form but in its expression. The Greek drama was not even constructed on formal principles. Rather, according to Newman, "it was a pure recreation of the imagination, revelling without object or meaning beyond its own exhibition." Aristotle's rules are in practice perverse because they "tend to withdraw the mind of the poet from the spontaneous exhibition of pathos or imagination to a minute diligence in the formation of a plot." Here is the romantic core of Newman's theory of poetry, a core which expands naturally to include the doctrine of the creative imagination and the concept of original genius.

After demolishing Aristotle's theory of the drama, Newman concedes that his general theory of the nature of poetry —poetry is a representation of the ideal—is "most true and philosophical," and he paraphrases Aristotle's analysis of the distinction between poetry and history. The essence of poetry is fiction. But it becomes apparent at once that Newman's universals are not Aristotle's. Poetry "delineates that perfection which the imagination suggests, and to which as a limit the present system of Divine Providence actually tends." Newman's position is that of the Christian Platonist. The poet generalizes from nature and life according to his intuition of Divine Perfection, for "the poetical mind is one full of the eternal forms of beauty and perfection; these are its material of thought, its instrument and medium of observation,—these colour each object to which it directs its view." Newman thus rejects the theory of *mimesis* and in its place

---

if selected truly and judiciously, must necessarily be dignified and variegated, and alive with metaphors and figures. I forbear to speak of an incongruity which would shock the intelligent Reader, should the Poet interweave any foreign splendour of his own with that which the passion naturally suggests: it is sufficient to say that such addition is unnecessary." *Wordsworth's Literary Criticism*, edited by N. C. Smith, London, 1905, p. 22.

holds up the neoplatonic, perhaps Coleridgean, theory of poetry as creation.[4]

The creativity of the imagination in Newman's argument is inseparably linked to the concept of original genius. Poetry is imaginative or creative precisely in

> the originality and independence of its modes of thinking, compared with the commonplace and matter-of-fact conceptions of ordinary minds, which are fettered down to the particular and individual. At the same time it feels a natural sympathy with everything great and splendid in the physical and moral world; and selecting such from the mass of common phenomena, incorporates them, as it were, into the substance of its own creations.

The poet is the genius whose originality consists in his intuitions of "the archetypes of the beautiful" and the correctness of his moral perceptions, and as usual in poetic theories which invoke this concept, in the last analysis poetry itself is defined quite simply, if vaguely, as the "free and unfettered effusion of genius," or "originality energizing in the world of beauty."[5]

Newman's theory of the poetic genius is also the focal point for his account of the relation between poetry and morals. Since poetry is the "free and unfettered effusion of genius," the morality of poetry is a matter of the poet's moral nature. True poetic talent, according to Newman's distinction, differs from the more eccentric manifestations of originality in the rightness of its moral feeling. "A right moral

[4] In the Early Victorian period this position is commonly referred to Bacon, who becomes the stock antithesis to Aristotle and the theory of imitation. It is interesting to note that Newman quotes Bacon's Latin text in support of his interpretation. He is apparently not aware of the common critical distinction.

[5] Early Victorian critics in the romantic tradition, notably Carlyle and Dallas, emphasize the unconscious nature of imaginative creation. Newman is hinting at this when he writes, "Still there is surely too much stress laid by the philosopher upon the artificial part; which, after all, leads to negative, more than to positive excellence; and should rather be the natural and, so to say, unintentional result of the poet's feeling and imagination, than be separated from them as the direct object of his care."

state of heart," he states categorically, "is the formal and scientific condition of a poetical mind." Originality is the power of abstracting for one's self, of striking out new views. In poetry this power cannot be separated from good sense or taste which is one of its elements. By this definition poetry becomes "originality energizing in the world of beauty; the originality of grace, purity, refinement, and good feeling." Newman's theory is not narrow; the poet need not represent virtue and religion exclusively, for this is a matter, not of the materials, but of the sources of poetry. He need not even be a good man. But the beauty of his poetry will be in proportion to whatever virtue exists in him, to whatever "traces and shadows of holy truth still remain upon it." On the other hand, "a right moral feeling places the mind in the very centre of that circle from which all the rays have their origin and range." As examples of poets who approximate the "moral centre" Newman cites Milton, Spenser, Cowper, Wordsworth, and Southey. These centers may be of different kinds: "Walter Scott's centre is chivalrous honor;[6] Shakespeare exhibits the characteristics of an unlearned and undisciplined piety; Homer the religion of nature and conscience, at times debased by polytheism." The idea of the moral center is a common one in the poetic theories of the period, and it is frequently used to explain the Victorian "failure" of Byron. Newman so uses it: Byron lacked a moral center and thus the delicate mind "shrinks" from parts of "Manfred." Hume and Gibbon, of course, had "radically unpoetical minds."

The Christian religion, in the light of Newman's poetic principles, is found to be especially poetical. The world of revelation is original and full of symbols of perfection to delight the mind and engage the feelings. The symbolic interpretation of the universe and of human experience is enjoined. "With Christians, a poetical view of things is a duty,— we are bid to colour all things with hues of faith, to see a

[6] The moral sources of Scott's poetry are analyzed in detail in the third volume of Ruskin's *Modern Painters*.

Divine meaning in every event, and a superhuman tendency."
Newman's religious and his poetic theory are here one.

Newman is naturally led to take issue with Aristotle again
in his definition of the function of poetry. Poetry does not
appeal to any mere recognition of likeness to reality, but to
the passions and the imagination. It has a double end: by
"the superhuman loveliness of its views" it gives pleasure to
the imagination, and by the unified and perfected account
of nature and life which it presents and in which it resembles
"the abstract mathematical formulae of physics, before they
are modified by the contingencies of atmosphere and fric-
tion," it "provides a solace for the mind broken by the dis-
appointments and sufferings of actual life." In performing
this function, poetry becomes "the utterance of the inward
emotions of a right moral feeling, seeking a purity and a
truth which this world will not give." This is Newman's
version of the Aristotelian *catharsis*. One thinks immediately
of Arnold's demand for consolation from poetry. In truth the
disappointments and sufferings were real enough; Newman's
description is at once deeply personal and Victorian. His
sensibility was perhaps too refined, too feminine to take life
whole. He speaks elsewhere in the essay of hideous reality,
harsh contrasts, offensive peculiarities, and hardness of indi-
viduality. But as a Christian Newman should have known
better than to look for solace in poetry. He seems to have
realized this himself when in a note appended to his reprint
of the essay in 1871 he admitted to having confused the
function of poetry with its formal object, and he amended,
"Poetry may be considered to be the gift of moving the affec-
tions through the imagination, and its object to be the beau-
tiful."[7]

[7] "It is sometimes asked whether poets are not more commonly found
external to the Church than among her children; and it would not
surprise us to find the question answered in the affirmative. Poetry is
the refuge and repose of those who have not the Catholic Church to
flee to and repose upon [Arnold?], for the Church herself is the most
sacred and august of poets. Poetry, as Mr. Keble lays it down in his
University Lectures on the subject, is a method of relieving the over-
burdened mind; it is a channel through which emotion finds expression,

In accord with his general argument Newman distinguishes poetry as essentially a contemplative activity from communication, and poetic apperception from "the art of composition," which is "merely accessory to the poetical talent" and which is identified with rhetorical elaboration.[8] His remarks on this subject are brief and perhaps not entirely consistent. His location of the poetry of Greek drama in character, sentiments, and diction rather than in structure has already been noted. At one point he strongly emphasizes verbal expression.

> Gods, heroes, kings, and dames, enter and retire: they may have a good reason for appearing,—they may have a very poor one; whatever it is, still we have no right to ask for it; the question is impertinent. Let us listen to their harmonious and majestic language, to the voices of sorrow, joy, compassion, or religious emotion,—to the animated odes of the chorus. Why interrupt so transcendent a display of poetical genius by inquiries degrading it to the level of every-day events, and implying incompleteness in the action till a catastrophe arrives?

To the Arnold of the 1853 Preface, insisting rigorously on the subordination of "expression" to form, Newman in this passage would seem to be in the camp of the enemy. Later on Newman states boldly that "figure" is "the necessary medium of communication" for the poet because it is the only means, however poor, for expressing intense feeling, and in one of the most illuminating sentences in the essay (or, on the subject, in Early Victorian criticism) he notes that "verse, far from being a restraint on the true poet, is the suitable index of his sense, and is adopted by his free

---

and that a safe, regulated expression. Now what is the Catholic Church, viewed in her human aspect, but a discipline of the affections and passions? What are her ordinances and practices but the regulated expression of keen, or deep, or turbid feeling, and thus a 'cleansing,' as Aristotle would word it, of the sick soul?" From a review of *Lyra Innocentium* in *The Dublin Review* for 1846, reprinted in *Essays Critical and Historical*, ii, 442.

[8] Newman quotes from Cicero on the method of the orator.

and deliberate choice." But when separating poetry from eloquence, almost as if to preserve inviolate the poetic intuition in the poet's consciousness, Newman makes the act of composition an imposition and constraint. The poet is necessarily obscure, particularly in his lyric utterance, because of his contemplative habit of mind, the intensity of his feeling, the originality of his perceptions, and the carelessness of genius, even perhaps "from natural deficiency in the power of clear and eloquent expression"! The true poet in consequence is never interested in language for its own sake, and the true language of poetry is simple and concise (Newman and Arnold are in agreement). "Harmonious sentences" which are "especially intended to charm the ear" constitute eloquence, as does the voluntary use of illustration for clarity or adornment. In these distinctions Newman again and again adumbrates other Early Victorian critics, particularly Carlyle and Mill. In Milton "the harmony of the verse is but the echo of the inward music which the thoughts of the poet breathe," and Homer's style is "the style of one who rhapsodized without deference to hearer or judge, in an age prior to the temptations which more or less prevailed over succeeding writers—before the theater had degraded poetry into an exhibition, and criticism narrowed it into an art."

What might be called the body of Newman's essay is a discussion of three kinds of poetry in the light of his definition of poetry as ideal. This definition is neoplatonic and Coleridgean, but it also owes something to Reynolds and the eighteenth century doctrine of central forms and to the eighteenth century school of taste. Newman is not always consistent, however, because, while in general he claims that poetry arises from the modification of nature and experience by the poet's imagination, occasionally he will allow that the natural object is poetic in itself. One or two points in Newman's argument may be of interest here. Natural history and philosophy may constitute the materials of poetry, but only when they have been operated on by the imagination, when they are painted "with a meaning, beauty, and harmonious order not their own."

43

Thomson has sometimes been commended for the novelty and minuteness of his remarks upon nature. This is not the praise of a poet; whose office is rather to represent known phenomena in a new connection or medium. In L'Allegro and Il Penseroso the poetical magician invests the commonest scenes of a country life with the hues, first of a cheerful, then of a pensive imagination.[9]

The echo of Coleridge is clear, and perhaps there is an echo of Wordsworth, "It is the charm of the descriptive poetry of a religious mind that nature is viewed in a moral connexion." The principle of generalization also distinguishes between historical and poetical narrative; the poet will reject the individual and particular aspects of his subject. "Thus he selects, combines, refines, colours,—in fact, poetizes." In this mood Newman will have no compromise with the theory or practice which was to become, largely through the influence of Ruskin, nineteenth century realism.

If it be said, the fidelity of the imitation is often its greatest merit, we have only to reply, that in such cases the pleasure is not poetical, but consists in the mere recognition. All novels and tales which introduce real characters, are in the same degree unpoetical. Portrait-painting, to be poetical, should furnish an abstract representation of an individual; the abstraction being more rigid, inasmuch as the painting is confined to one point of time. The artist should draw independently of the accidents of attitude, dress, occasional feeling, and transient action.[10]

[9] "A landscape thus conducted, under the influence of a poetical mind, will have the same superiority over the more ordinary and common views, as Milton's *Allegro* and *Penseroso* have over a cold prosaic narration or description." *The Discourses of Sir Joshua Reynolds*, with an introduction by Austin Dobson, London, The World's Classics, 1907, p. 203.

[10] "Perhaps in portrait alone can painting claim the advantage of poetry; because there the pencil perpetuates the very features, air, and personal appearance of the individual represented; and when that individual is one of eminence,—a hero, a patriot, a poet, an orator,— it is the vehicle of the highest pleasure which the art can communicate;

Newman adds that his doctrine is not meant to destroy individuality in character-drawing, but merely to avoid "such violations of general nature, such improbabilities, wanderings, or coarsenesses, as interfere with the refined and delicate enjoyment of the imagination." This passage might have been written by Sir Joshua himself.

"Poetry, with Reference to Aristotle's Poetics," as far as one can make out, was quickly buried and forgotten; it had no influence. But it is a good sample of Early Victorian criticism. Its serious, combative, and yet persuasive tone, its point of view, independent and disrespectful of old authority, its enthusiasm for originality, imagination, emotion, its preference for these to formalism of any kind, its confusion of Aristotelian and neoplatonic theory, its tendency to assimilate all poetry to the quality of the lyric, are all representative. If there is little that is fresh or new in the essay, and if the temperament of the author is perhaps a little too delicate and refined, it nonetheless points up the perennial conflict between the belletristic and the "scientific" critic, between the idealist and the realist, and it affirms the value of poetry in a period of crisis in values. Newman, like Arnold, whose Preface of 1853 (it might well have been called "Poetry, with Reference to Aristotle's Poetics") stands in meaningful contrast to Newman's essay, looked to poetry for an experience of those perfections which the world did not give. Most interesting to the modern reader probably is Newman's account of the morality of art which might profitably be expanded to answer some twentieth century nonsense and misunderstanding on this subject.

---

and in this respect portrait painting (however disparaged) is the highest point of the art itself;—being at once the most real, intellectual, and imaginative." James Montgomery, *Lectures on Poetry*, London, 1833, p. 12.

3. John Keble

Praelectiones Academicae. 1844

As PROFESSOR of Poetry at Oxford over a period of ten years from 1831 to 1841, John Keble, priest, poet, and Tractarian, delivered a remarkable series of Latin lectures on the nature of poetry and the poetic practice of the major Greek and Roman poets. Collected and printed in 1844 under the general heading, *Praelectiones Academicae Oxonii Habitae, Annis MDCCCXXXII . . . MDCCCXLI*, with the subtitle, *De Poeticae Vi Medica*, the lectures were praised at the time by Newman and others of Keble's Oxford friends; George Saintsbury in 1904 noticed them briefly but appreciatively—had literary criticism been more than a pastime with Keble, "he would, I think, twenty years before Arnold, have given us the results of a more thorough scholarship, a reading certainly not less wide, a taste nearly as delicate and catholic, a broader theory, and a much greater freedom from mere crochet and caprice";[1] and in 1912 the lectures were made available in English in a translation by Edward Kershaw Francis.[2]

The *Praelectiones* are really essays in Christian criticism. Open war is declared on secularism, materialism, utilitarianism, and liberalism. God, the sacramental universe, analogy, are working concepts; order, tradition, and decorum are pervasive ideals. Poetry is prayer, contemplation, a means of grace, the predisposition to piety. Unhappily, and in spite of many good things by the way, Keble's position is defensive and radically conservative. Not only is orthodoxy, especially in the matter of morals, the ultimate standard of literary value, but in politics and in the social and economic order orthodoxy is interpreted to mean conformity to Tory and High Church principles. The humanistic studies

[1] George Saintsbury, *A History of English Criticism*, New York, n.d., p. 535.

[2] *Keble's Lectures on Poetry 1832-1841*, translated by E. K. Francis, 2 vols., Oxford, 1912. Quotations are from this text.

are defended against both pietist and utilitarian rather as effective conditioning of the feelings than of the intellect; and of the Christian virtues exemplified in the creative act and the artistic product, it is to the shyer, the more senti-mental, the less virile, that Keble seems to be temperamen-tally committed.

Plato is perhaps the strongest single influence on Keble's poetic theory. The epigraph to the printed lectures is the figure of the rhapsode and the ring from the *Ion*, "Through them God moves men's souls in the way he pleases, and sus-pends one man from another." The intimate correspondence of the visible universe with the human mind, the symbolic nature of objects and events, divine inspiration in a literal sense, possession, the profound and disturbing emotional power of poetry, the necessity of moral censorship, are all Platonic ideas central to Keble's argument. Keble's "seminal principle" of poetry from which he deduces all the rest owes much to Aristotle's concept of *catharsis*, but in general, like Newman, Keble finds Aristotle too narrow, too intellectual, too formalistic. Among other predecessors Longinus and Cicero are quoted with approval, and Reynolds supplies the point of departure for more than one discussion. Modern poetry, and with it modern criticism, are in a period of de-cadence, irresponsible and pretentious in their straining for original effect, lacking in clarity and repose. Exception is made, however, for Scott and Southey, and particularly for Wordsworth, to whom the lectures are dedicated, "true philosopher and inspired poet who by the special gift and calling of Almighty God whether he sang of man or of nature failed not to lift up men's hearts to holy things nor ever ceased to champion the cause of the poor and simple and so in perilous times was raised up to be a chief minister not only of sweetest poetry but also of high and sacred truth." Wordsworth's characteristic ideas and beliefs turn up everywhere in the text with little modification. Coleridge, on the other hand, probably for theological reasons, is never mentioned by name, although Keble had certainly read him, and in some important respects Keble's theory is closer to

Coleridge than it is to the Wordsworth of the early preface
with its prevailing tendency towards "realism."

Keble's definition of poetry is by confession unsystematic,
the elaboration of a single root metaphor: poetry is "a kind
of medicine divinely bestowed upon men: which gives
healing relief to secret mental emotion, yet without detri-
ment to modest reserve: and, while giving scope to enthusi-
asm, yet rules it with order and due control."[3] In terms of
the metaphor the poetic sensibility is "diseased," and there
is evidence that at times Keble so considered it in fact.
Poets are "sufferers" and their condition often approaches
insanity. Poetry, then, is the release, the expression of emo-
tion—as Keble calls it, a safety-valve; but it is the expression of
emotion under peculiar and characteristic conditions, "with-
out detriment to modest reserve." Poetic expression is never
open or direct, but consists, as it were, of "certain veils and
disguises" which yet "reveal the fervent emotions of the
mind."[4] Aristotle's *catharsis*, romantic expressionism, and the
Christian virtue of modesty come together here in an odd
simulacrum of the Freudian theory of art as the means by
which the neurotic introvert sublimates his libido.

The basic function of poetry is *catharsis*. All men, accord-
ing to Keble's psychology, naturally find relief for strong
emotion in expression. In primitive and uncultivated socie-
ties the expression of emotion is direct and uninhibited,
but generally and almost invariably an innate reticence, a
sense of "shame," enforces the repression of personal feeling.
To the sensitive, tortured by emotion and yet restrained by
this "noble and natural" shame, and to some obsessed with
vague aspirations to greatness or with "the vicissitudes of
human affairs," with "the marvellous ordered symmetry of
the universe," or with "the holy vision of true and divine
goodness," and for whom therefore the language of daily
life as well is utterly inadequate, to these "sufferers," un-
willing, or unwilling and unable, to declare openly their
inmost feelings, God in the gift of poetry has furnished the

[3] *Ibid.*, i, 22.   [4] *Ibid.*, i, 47.

comfort which tears give to the harassed body. "It is the function of Poetry to facilitate, yet without prejudice to modest reserve, the expression of glowing emotion."[5]

By this account there is in some sense a poetry of life in those characters and incidents which carry with them "evidence of some hidden emotion," some refined consolation which appeases a yearning desire for the moment denied satisfaction. The play-acting of children and the inarticulate expression of the rural classes of their affection for particular places, their regard for the dead and for religion, are "incipient poetry." In Wordsworthian vein Keble maintains that countryfolk have more in common with poetry than townspeople, but his reasons are his own:

> Townsmen have less becoming reserve; they are more habituated to daily avocations in the full light of publicity: and so waste no time in search for expedients and indirect methods, but give full vent to their feeling.[6]

The idea of "publicity," it should be apparent, is always painful to Keble; so much so, in fact, that in its extreme statement his theory rejects the element of communication in art altogether, and approaches Crocean expressionism. He speaks, for instance, of "those who are made poets by Nature and true feeling before they occupy themselves with literary style and metrical form";[7] and in another place he is quite explicit, "For in the present discussion we do not give the title of poet to him who publishes his verse with great popular acclaim, but rather to the man who meditates the Muse at home for his own delectation and solace."[8] Again in the extreme statement of the theory, and as the natural corollary, there is a sharp break between "nature" and "art," expression and technique, content and form. In general the second term of each pair is a pejorative. The entire process of externalization is, at best, suspect and strictly secondary. It also follows that the essential characteristic of poetic expression according to this theory

[5] *Ibid.*, I, 19-24, 36.   [6] *Ibid.*, I, 24-37.
[7] *Ibid.*, II, 218.   [8] *Ibid.*, I, 317.

is spontaneity (Wordsworth?). That is "not poetry at all" which is not "obviously the spontaneous outburst of the poet's inmost feeling."[9] The concept of spontaneity brings up at once the familiar romantic difficulty with determinism, a difficulty of particular danger to Keble as a Christian critic, and a difficulty which he does not always succeed in avoiding. "Indeed," he writes, "there is nothing for which this human lot of ours is more wont to be deplored than the fact that we cannot ourselves command our feelings or solace them by expression."[10] And he frequently uses the words blind impulse, instinctive, unconscious, unintentional, necessity, inevitable fate, in connection with the poetic process in a sense which can only be interpreted as deterministic. In all fairness, however, it must be said that, when he is aware of the issue, he is unequivocal, "It has indeed always been God's method not to override the free-will of men, even of His prophets when most strongly moved by the fervour of inspiration."[11] He emphatically rejects historical literary determinism, the "too clever speculation of certain contemporary would-be critics, whose constant theme is that the age, not the writer, is the real author of all that is written: and that results both of talent and of literary achievement are produced by a kind of fatalistic destiny."[12]

Keble takes notice of the classical doctrine of *mimesis* only to bend it to his own theory. He points out that Plato, who considered imitation the very essence of poetry, applied the term to all the arts, treating them under the general heading of music. This suggests that "each several one of the so-called liberal arts contains a certain poetic quality of its own, and that this lies in its power to heal and relieve the human mind when agitated by care, passion, or ambition," and that poetry, of all the arts, is best fitted for this office because it makes use of rhythmical language.[13] Keble, like Newman, is pursuing "the poetical," an essence or spirit of

[9] *Ibid.*, II, 37.   [10] *Ibid.*, II, 276.   [11] *Ibid.*, I, 61.
[12] *Ibid.*, I, 99. Does Keble mean Carlyle?
[13] *Ibid.*, I, 53.

poetry which can be expressed in terms of feeling. He clinches his argument by observing that poets have always been considered a little mad, but that artistic imitation is hardly characteristic of the mentally deranged; therefore it is obvious that imitation "does not carry the whole power" of poetry. It is the man who can use imitation to give relief who is the true poet. This, says Keble, is essentially Aristotle's position in his remarks on poetic enthusiasm and versatility.

"We share," he says, "the agitation of those who appear to be truly agitated—the anger of those who appear to be truly angry. Hence it is that Poetry demands, either great natural quickness of parts, or an enthusiasm allied to madness. By the first of these we mould ourselves with facility to the imitation of every form; by the other, transported out of ourselves we become what we imagine." For what else do these phrases, "enthusiasm allied to madness," "transported out of ourselves," imply, but that images of distant objects have sunk deeply into the poet's mind and that he fixes his gaze upon, or reaches out towards them with an almost morbid longing, utterly oblivious of present realities.[14]

Keble here seems to be somewhat closer to Freud than to Aristotle.

What is expressed, the matter of poetry, is emotion, "some hidden emotion," some "yearning desire which for the present is denied satisfaction."[15] The richest of these emotions for poetry is "the unquenchable longing for some object which is absent."[16] We may "infer," for instance, that Homer "betook himself to composition in order to appease in some measure his restless, burning passion for bygone days and departed heroes."[17] If the matter of poetry is powerful emo-

[14] *Ibid.*, I, 56.　　　　　　　　[15] *Ibid.*, I, 25-26.

[16] *Ibid.*, II, 262. One of the characteristics of Wordsworth's Poet is "a disposition to be affected more than other men by absent things as if they were present." *Wordsworth's Literary Criticism*, edited by N. C. Smith, London, 1905, p. 23.

[17] *Ibid.*, I, 100.

tion, however, and its mode of expression spontaneous, the form of poetry would necessarily seem to be confined to the lyric. To meet this objection Keble goes to Quintilian for a classification of the emotions into *pathos* and *ethos*, feeling and character, or more broadly, passionate feelings and mild and gentle feelings. The longer forms are produced by *ethos*.

> Now, strong passion visits us but rarely: we ordinarily follow the natural bent of our temperament and character; no wonder, then, that far the greater number of poetic productions strike the gentler note. Indeed, except some lyrics and elegies, and a few satires, I hardly recall one famous poem which is a pure and simple outcome of passion. All other poems reflect the character of a lifetime, and tastes which have become familiar to the mind by long association. Yet none the less, they must be acknowledged to spring from the inmost heart: you might indeed say that really and truly they are framed after and accord with the man's secret nature even more faithfully. Other remedies are at hand to allay or distract sudden access of anger or grief. Swift emotion both dies away spontaneously, and, moreover, is wont to arouse and stimulate genuine and stable strength of spirit. But what remedy is to be found for troubles which have clearly grown up with the character, silent and unnoticed, interpenetrating a man's whole life? Certainly, it will be a most effective solace if a man can, in some sort, enshrine in verse something of the form and feature of that which is closest to his heart.[18]

At this point Keble reinforces his theory by introducing his version of the eighteenth century concept of "the ruling passion": "I am inclined to believe that no poet, indeed no human being, is without some master feeling which focuses and binds together into somewhat of a unity the fluctuating and many varying distractions of the mind."[19] It is the presence and especially the quality of the master passion

[18] *Ibid.*, I, 86-91.   [19] *Ibid.*, II, 96.

that distinguishes the "Primary" poet, and it is the critic's
task (which, by the way, is mainly instinctive)[20] precisely
to discover and lay bare this central feeling. It is also char-
acteristic that the poet is "for the most part unaware"[21] of
his obsession. Virgil's master passion, for instance, is the
desire for the joy and beauty of natural objects; his interest
in the epic machinery of the *Aeneid* is purely accidental
and perfunctory; and Sophocles is denied Primary rank
altogether largely because Keble can find no single emotional
source for all of the plays. In the end Keble's theory puts
a premium (a clear index of his moralistic bias) on the self-
consistency of the poet's emotion with the result, curious
in the light of his basic principles, that he has to defend the
lyric poet against charges of "inconstancy," and therefore
of insincerity. There is a strong resemblance, it will be noted,
between Keble's *ethos* and Newman's "moral centers."

The definition of poetry as "the index to men's cares and
the interpreter of their fancies"[22] leads to a preoccupation
with the poet's biography, real or imagined. "Indeed, the
special hope which stimulates us to devote ourselves to these
studies is the hope that we may in time become familiarly
acquainted with great men and penetrate into their most
intimate counsels: whence it follows that there is always
something for us to learn."[23] Interestingly enough, in the
case of Homer this preoccupation suggests an analysis in
some detail of Homeric imagery along lines rather similar
to those developed later by Miss Caroline Spurgeon. Keble
observes that his theory runs counter to the critical temper
of the times; readers "will be repelled completely by this
view, and will not, without reluctance, suffer themselves to
be drawn away from the charms of language and imagery,
and the outward show and ornament of Poetry, in order to
pry into the secrets of the poet's mind. How, they demand,
does it concern us, in what spirit and with what disposition

[20] *Ibid.*, I, 67-68.   [21] *Ibid.*, II, 397.   [22] *Ibid.*, I, 44.
[23] *Ibid.*, II, 225. Sophocles' interest in stagecraft is scored against
him: "All such things have to do with the stage effect, not with the
author." *Ibid.*, II, 221.

the poet wrote, so long as his writings are such as delight and stimulate men's thought and feelings?" Allegory is rejected by modern taste on the same grounds; but in any case, whether the effect of poetry is achieved "by allegorical symbolism or by the transference of the poet's own passion and disposition to actual characters," the reader "who once surrenders himself heartily to the poet's real meaning, will have little leisure for mere ornament and prettiness." Keble is here insisting on the primacy of theme and subordination of artistic means, and at the same time he attempts to reconcile the rival claims of representation and expression:

> Whether, therefore, throughout the whole course of a poem one story is really told in fact and substance, another outwardly in words—which is the characteristic of Allegory: or whether we make the true tenor of a poem to depend not so much upon the things described as upon the spirit and temper of the poet, in either case it is clear that the force and beauty of true poetry is twofold. For not only are the direct themes of the poem themselves expressed with lucidity and beauty, but the whole work is tinctured with the character and leanings of the poet as by some mysterious aroma: and in such wise, indeed, that all recognize that he burst forth into such expression naturally, and not for artistic effect. Should either of these two qualities be lacking, the poetry will be maimed and defective, or absolutely not poetry at all: maimed, unless the subject be faithfully and finely treated; not poetry at all, should it not be obviously the spontaneous outburst of the poet's inmost feeling.[24]

This is a balanced statement, reminiscent of Wordsworth and pointing towards Arnold, but it does not excuse Keble from the "intentional fallacy." For the most part, his attempts at biographical reconstruction and ventriloquism (like those of other nineteenth century critics) are practically worthless and almost invariably diversionary. Often, as with Sophocles,[25] one has the uncomfortable suspicion

[24] *Ibid.*, II, 35-37. [25] *Ibid.*, II, 222.

that moral prejudice against known or imputed biographical detail prevents Keble from really looking at the poetry. The "poetry" of Milton, Burns, Byron, and Shelley, seems to be vitiated in this way.

Although he uses both of the terms original and genius, and although he undoubtedly admired great men, Keble was too much of a traditionalist to come under the influence of the concept of original genius. His understanding of originality is rather classical or neoclassical than romantic. The Primary poet will be indifferent to novelty and untouched by ambition; he will repeat the old familiar themes; he will even plagiarize when he pleases.[26] By the same token, and in keeping with the moral reticence of his basic theory, self-expression is summarily ruled out. He will allow that "it is the prerogative of Homer, and of such as stand forth commandingly like Homer, to impress their own personality and standpoint upon their contemporaries";[27] but he says that Byron, "one who should have been a minister and interpreter of the mysteries that lie hid in Nature, has, in spite of all the vehement passion and variety of his poetry, in the main given us nothing but the picture of his own mind and personality, excited now by an almost savage bitterness, and now by voluptuous exaltation."[28]

Keble's "seminal principle" acts to separate all poets into two classes: "on the one hand, we have those who, spontaneously moved by impulse, resort to composition for relief and solace of a burdened or over-wrought mind; on the other, those who, for one reason or another, imitate the ideas, the expression, and the measures of the former." The first he calls "Primary Poets"; the second are poets only by courtesy title. The classification has old roots as Keble points out, the inspired rhapsodes of Plato and Democritus, Aristotle's versatile poet, the poet born-not-made of Horace.[29] In another form the distinction is that between "poets by Nature and necessity" and poets of "consummate skill and culture." The Primary poets are again subdivided into poets

[26] *Ibid.*, i, 71-72. [27] *Ibid.*, i, 167.
[28] *Ibid.*, ii, 339 and 398. [29] *Ibid.*, i, 53ff.

of *pathos* and *ethos* (lyric and elegiac, and tragic, epic, and didactic); and poets who derive their basic impulse from *ethos* are further distinguished by their temperamental pre-occupation with human action or with nature into active and contemplative. Homer and Virgil represent these two great types. Keble finds in the historical order of the appearance of active and contemplative poetry an index of Divine Benevolence revealing the two great sources of hidden solace to suffering mortals.[30]

The characteristic marks of Primary poets are four, all of them, incidentally, moral. First, consistency; this is the evidence of truth of character and sincerity which can be observed in the poet's tastes and particularly in his choice of themes. Shakespeare, for instance, was always "heartily on the side of virtue" (his looser scenes are mere concessions to the spirit of the times). Second, the genuine poet will be indifferent to the desire for originality, and third, he will always show a modest reserve in expressing his profound emotions. The last of these has interesting consequences for the poet's technique. The parallel of the *arcana disciplinae* in the Early Christian Church will justify a certain obscurity in his poetry. Generally, fear of ridicule imposes the principle of indirection: the poet will avoid the real object of his enthusiasm; he will rather hint and suggest by subtlety of detail than describe fully or flatly; and he will frequently resort to understatement and "innocent" irony.[31] These devices, it will be noted, prefigure the early Eliotine theory of the impersonality of art. One passage is particularly clear: according to the theory the poet's intimate feelings do not lie "wholly hidden," but take "refuge as it were in a kind of sanctuary."

[30] *Ibid.*, I, 86ff.; II, 202-3 (Mill, Browning, Ruskin, and Arnold were all interested in the classification of poets); II, 274ff.

[31] *Ibid.*, I, 82-83. Spenser "betrays to us what was really ever in his thought, even when writing his *Faerie Queene*. Being, as he was, the most loyal and devoted of lovers, he has in many passages cleverly worked in allusions to his own love amid the praises of his Queen, and thus, without alienating the sympathy of his readers, or betraying his secret passion, he could ease his own love troubles through poetic expression."

Now, in the case of those who set themselves to weave a regular plot, I mean dramatic and epic poets, it is obvious that the composer's personality naturally holds itself apart and retires into the background. Opinions are expressed, judgments passed, praise and blame are meted out, not however as the utterances of Homer or Aeschylus, but as those of an Achilles or a Prometheus.[32]

It is also characteristic "that those suffering most keenly through real, perhaps irreparable affliction, are the very men who most lightly trifle and play with words"[33] (George Herbert hid "the deep love of God which consumed him behind a cloud of precious conceits," and Shakespeare jested in his scenes of grief).[34] Keble does not develop any of these points, but the mere recognition of the poetic function of irony and word-play is surprising in the theory of the period.

The critic who is primarily interested in emotion and moral ideas is unlikely to spend much time over questions of the medium or of form. Keble's attitude towards the medium is Hegelian with perhaps a suggestion of early Christian iconoclasm. Sensuous and material, the medium is conceived as an impediment to the expression of the artist's spiritual intuition. An art is more "poetical" as it succeeds in effecting expression by subordinating the medium. "Conception" (in eighteenth century terms) is all important; "execution," particularly when it calls attention to itself, is the clear sign of artificiality. "The poetry of painting simply consists in the apt expression of the artist's own feeling." Raphael, who embodies "in beautiful form the inner conception of the mind," is poetical in contrast to Rubens, who "seizes those unlooked-for combinations of colour, light, and form which endlessly present themselves to the artist's mind and eye at the very moment of painting." Raphael's weakness is really his strength, for

it is said that Raffaelle, while possessing a noble and lofty though perhaps somewhat unelastic genius, was

[32] *Ibid.*, II, 97.   [33] *Ibid.*, I, 82-83.   [34] *Ibid.*, II, 99; I, 83.

somewhat careless and has left some works too crudely executed: as one who would indeed far rather violate the rules of art than not satisfy the inner vision, which he had conceived with marvellous beauty.[35]

Sir Joshua Reynolds, by the way, is cited as the authority for Keble's argument. Sculpture, architecture, and music, in rising scale of perfection according to the transparency of the medium, approach poetry "on that side of its effect which is concerned in piercing into, and drawing out to the light, the secrets of the soul."[36] By the same standard of expressiveness applied to the distinction between poetical prose and rhetoric, Plato is more poetical than Homer himself, while Cicero never rises to poetry. This is because Cicero always has his audience in mind; he is interested in producing a moving effect. Plato on the other hand, "seems absorbed in his own delightful themes; he writes to please himself, not to win over others; he generally hints at rather than speaks out his deeper truths; rich as he is in most beautiful thoughts, he seems to leave even more unsaid."[37]

There is no general discussion of the problems of form in the lectures. The weight of the theory bears heavily on "Nature," expression, inner spirit, away from art (by which Keble usually means artifice), form or formalism, structure, framework, plot, "machinery." If it is true that "a poet's fine frenzy is subject to law or control,"[38] according to Keble's principles the law or form ought to be organic. He seems to recognize this, but at the same time he also thinks of form in eighteenth century terms, even when, in keeping with the basic metaphor of the theory, he ascribes to it a medicinal function. The use of "those indirect methods best known to poets" already mentioned is part of this function.[39] At its best, Keble's argument calls for the due artistic subordination of all the formal elements of poetry to the presentation of theme. His position is roughly that of Newman, but there are anticipations of Arnold's Preface of 1853.

[35] *Ibid.*, I, 39-42.   [36] *Ibid.*, I, 48.   [37] *Ibid.*, I, 49.
[38] *Ibid.*, I, 91.   [39] *Ibid.*, I, 22.

The attack on Aristotle follows the lines laid down by Newman and is plainest perhaps in the lectures on Sophocles. Sophocles is generally praised by Aristotelian critics for the finish and subtlety of his diction and for his skill in plot construction. But it is a question whether either of these grounds "necessarily touch the real art and poetic gift, or may not merely be viewed as their formal part and machinery."[40] Words and meters, however, are "mere instruments" of "the heavenly flame," and praise for these qualities raises the suspicion that the poet has nothing in common with "those who are made poets by Nature and true feeling before they occupy themselves with literary style and metrical form."[41] In the matter of plot construction, Keble finds Aristotle and the critics pandering to popular taste for exciting incident. There is, indeed, a legitimate use of plot by the poet, "not with intent that his books may be devoured by boys and girls for mere amusement, but that he himself may enjoy a profounder sense of the laws which silently control and govern all things."[42]

The "seminal principle" carries with it the implication "that there are plainly as many kinds of Poetry as of opinions and of men (for Poetry, native and true Poetry, is nothing else than each poet's innermost feeling issuing in rhythmic language."[43] But if the "seminal principle" can give rise to expressionistic form, it also gives rise, apparently, to its opposite. In the case of the sonnet with all of its formal difficulties as practiced by genuine poets Keble is persuaded that "it was by no mere chance, but by a deeply-rooted instinct, that such men as these adopted this form, because the fact that it is unusually stringent enabled it to soothe and compose their deepest emotions and longings without violating a true reserve."[44] Lyric poets in the same way deliberately choose to work with elaborate meters, so that

[40] *Ibid.*, II, 217. Aristotle "nowhere even hints at his feeling any delight in the charms of Nature and all the beauty of earth and sky." *Ibid.*, II, 264.

[41] *Ibid.*, II, 218. [42] *Ibid.*, II, 219. [43] *Ibid.*, II, 35.

[44] *Ibid.*, II, 102.

with "marvellous skill, art of the most exquisite kind is made to minister its healing touch to disordered Nature."[45] Keble's conclusion seems to be that, rightly understood, form is the principle of indirection in poetry, cleanly separable from its essence, which is emotion, and strictly subordinate to expression.

Indeed, on the same principle on which we have before declared that verse has more power to soothe than prose, we may, I think, plainly perceive why it is, that in composing a poem too, it is better to have some story or settled plan before us, than to utter the changing impulse of the moment. The very fact of orderly and methodized progress may not a little conduce to settlement of mind. . .[46]

Poets, particularly young poets, are wrong in condemning skill and plan. "They think they have indeed written something great if by lucky chance they have stitched in, here and there, some striking and clever patches; caring nothing whether they are appropriate or inappropriate, since they deny that a poet's fine frenzy is subject to law or control."[47] The subject must be faithfully treated *and* the poem must show evidence of spontaneous emotion. Keble would force classical and romantic elements together into an organic unity of which the integrating principle is theme. Of Aeschylus he writes,

All these descriptions are so splendid, if we only judge them by the test of poetic "vividness," that it should surprise no one if most men, while duly honouring the philosophy of Aeschylus, yet at the same time contend that he was not seriously concerned about anything, except those artistic beauties which, as they insist, are the peculiar glory of Poetry. But if they once read with more kindly eyes even the *Eumenides* alone, willing to credit the poem with an aim a little more sacred and the possession of an under-meaning, it is almost impossible to say how greatly their delight would be increased even in that one pleasure,

45 *Ibid.*, ii, 100.   46 *Ibid.*, i, 90-91.   47 *Ibid.*, i, 91.

which they praise at the expense of all others; and how much more deeply skilful narration, or smooth sweetness of the verse, or charm of the imagery, would penetrate and permeate the inmost recesses of their hearts, when bathed and illuminated in a kind of heavenly light, glorifying a picture already beautiful in itself.[48]

Matters of style, diction, imagery, and versification are all subordinate to expression. Keble disposes of the general problems of meter and imagery quite simply by making it axiomatic "that Poetry, of whatever kind, is in one way or another, closely associated with measure and a definite rhythm of sound," and "that its chief aim is to recall, to renew, and bring vividly before us pictures of absent objects"; "it is the handmaid to Imagination and Fancy." Meter and imagery both subserve the remedial function of poetry "in soothing men's emotions and steadying the balance of their mind."[49] Like Newman the Platonist, however, Keble will call attention to the power of single words, "Truly, it is past belief how powerfully single words or phrases, even perhaps the cadences of syllables falling on the ear in a happy hour, call forth the hidden fire."[50] This sort of statement surely holds the seeds of a theory of "pure poetry."

Keble has little to say about the imagination. At least once in the course of the lectures it is given Coleridgean function along with Keble's own psychotherapeutic one.

Forthwith the fevered anxieties and ponderings which were spreading hither and thither like a flood, are now controlled and confined to a single channel: thither are directed or naturally flow all that crowds into the mind from all sides: and as Imagination strives to draw them together, while consciously or unconsciously she gives them outline and ornament, men gradually become their own physicians and do not resent the change that comes over them.[51]

At other times, however, Keble thinks of it in eighteenth

48 *Ibid.*, ii, 41-42.   49 *Ibid.*, i, 21.   50 *Ibid.*, i, 322.
51 *Ibid.*, i, 59.

century terms as a mode of memory, the image-making faculty, an associative power of the mind. When he says of it that "it paints all things in the hues which the mind itself desires," he seems to place himself with Newman squarely in the category of the Baconian idealist. But in his analysis of the two-fold nature of poetry he claims that it is immaterial whether the imagination projects its own values into nature or whether it finds them already there.[52] There is, in fact, some evidence in the lectures, especially in the passages dealing with nature poetry, that Keble also recognized the "naturalism" of Wordsworth and Ruskin. Homer, for instance, is praised for his "realistic power, and simple, direct clearness," and Virgil is "the most delightful priest and interpreter of Nature."[53]

Keble's psychological analysis of Homer's imagery has been mentioned earlier. The view of imagery as the key to the poet's subconscious interests is a basic principle of Keble's theory, and his application of it is an interesting pointer towards modern critical method. Compare, he says, the lines, "in which Virgil treats, as I said, of his own favorite delights, with such lines as his description of Fame, or the picture of Mount Etna, or of the night vision of the fury Alecto. We shall infallibly find that these, which it is more than likely he introduced through poetic convention, not through any feeling of his own, are elaborated with a wealth of language and an ordered sequence of metaphor, whereas those springing from his own feeling are merely touched by the way, as it were, and incidentally."[54] Keble goes on to define the emotional and moral centers, and the dominant and subordinate themes of his subjects very largely through examination of dominant and recurrent imagery.

On meter Keble has very little to add to what has already been said. By definition poetry is "nothing else than each poet's innermost feeling issuing in rhythmic language." Verse

[52] *Ibid.*, II, 36.
[53] *Ibid.*, I, 168; II, 375; also I, 163, 173; II, 229, 244, 429.
[54] *Ibid.*, I, 78.

has more "power to soothe" than prose; as a means of control, a principle of indirection, of escape from personality into form, poets, particularly lyric poets, voluntarily commit themselves to elaborate verse forms in the working out of which "art of the most exquisite kind is made to minister its healing touch to disordered Nature."

The end of poetry in its psychological aspect is *catharsis*, which means relief and delight, perhaps delight in relief, at any rate delight. But poetry also has its moral aspect in which the end of poetry is truth, and especially Christian truth:

> . . . in reading the Scriptures, we assuredly know that we are in presence of truth itself, and that not even the smallest detail need be withdrawn from their full story. Consequently it is by their standard, when we have once ascertained and tested it, that Homer and his fellows must be judged.[55]

Ultimately, then, the function of poetry is moral and religious, "to lift to a higher plane all the emotions of our minds, and to make them take their part in a diviner philosophy,"[56] and Keble is on the horns of the familiar dilemma. He is not unaware of his problem, however, and while there is at times a crude moralistic bias in both the theory and the individual critical judgments, he does to some extent attempt to escape his own limitations. He recognizes the validity of "natural truths";[57] he leans heavily on symbolic interpretation which he calls analogy or platonizing:

> In fact, in modern times, good and pious men take pleasure in the study of the ancient poets largely for this simple reason, that they can tacitly transfer to the Great and Good God that which is said in Homer (it may be) or in Pindar, in honour of the fabled Jove, regarding them as dimly feeling after Him and foreshadowing the true Revelation and Sacrifice.[58]

[55] *Ibid.*, I, 174.
[56] *Ibid.*, II, 157; also II, 272-73.
[57] *Ibid.*, II, 471; also II, 464.
[58] *Ibid.*, II, 314; also II, 199.

Surprisingly enough, he fights stubbornly through a whole series of ingenious and sometimes amusing manoeuvres for Lucretius' right to rank as a Primary poet in spite of his atheism. He was probably afflicted with insanity (which "for a time, holds us like a tragedy, rapt with a kind of pleasing horror" !); he may have been suffering from possession by evil spirits; in any case, we must not suppose "that nothing but what is base and impious could issue from such a source: for it seems with the Great and Good Ruler of us all to have been almost a law, to emphasize and declare his own decrees by the testimony, willing or unwilling, of his enemies, whether men or evil spirits."[59] Finally, one can resort to "parody" in dealing with the parts of his poem.

> And, in truth, you will not easily find any one among the poets who lacked the enlightenment of revealed Truth, who affords so many splendid lines which, as it were spontaneously, cast their testimony in favour of sound and sincere piety. Not one of them has left more numerous passages which any one, perhaps changing here and there a word or two, but yet maintaining the general tenor of the whole, can quote on the side of goodness and righteousness. Such a method of quotation is technically called a "parody" ($\pi\alpha\rho\omega\delta\iota\alpha$).[60]

Keble does not really develop an adequate answer to his problem, however, unless it is implicit in the idea of "the unwilling witness," and his own judgments often seem to be arbitrary.

The final lecture in the long series stresses the interrelationship between poetry and religion, the true remedy for human ills. They are alike in their powers of healing. Both approach "each stage of beauty by a quiet and well-ordered movement." Truth for both is difficult and will yield only to devotion. Poetry and religion are equally subject to "the vision of something more beautiful, greater and more lovable, than all that mortal eye can see";[61] and they make common

[59] *Ibid.*, II, 331ff.; also II, 442.   [60] *Ibid.*, II, 350.
[61] *Ibid.*, II, 480.

use of the external world: poetry leads men "to the secret sources of Nature" for images and symbols which it lends to religion; religion clothes them with its splendor and returns them to poetry as sacraments.[62] Poetry is the prelude to piety. All the great religious revivals of history have been prepared for by great poets, Plato and Virgil in antiquity, Spenser and Shakespeare in the Renaissance. Acknowledging the decline of religion and poetry in modern times, Keble sees no reason why men should not be raised gradually to a better life, "by a new order of Poetry."[63]

Keble's theory of poetry is strongest in its statement of value, weakest in its handling of form, and most interesting in its psychological basis. The *malaise* of the nineteenth century discovered in poetry a consolation, and consolation was justified times over in theory, by Keble, by Newman, by Mill and Arnold. Keble stands with Wordsworth and the romantics in their emphasis on the emotions and faithful expression (not self-expression, for there are always the methods of indirection), with Arnold and the neoclassics in their recognition of the importance of subject and the subordination of parts to whole. Although he tends to think of imagery and verse in theoretical contexts as decorative, he gives a psychological function to both, and in the case of imagery develops a strikingly modern technique of analysis. The theory is confused and often mistaken, but it offers its anticipations, it insists on the human values of poetry, and it tries to reconcile the best of old and new.

[62] *Ibid.*, II, 481.   [63] *Ibid.*, II, 478.

4. John Stuart Mill

Thoughts on Poetry and its Varieties. 1833

JOHN STUART MILL came to poetry late and then only after a nervous breakdown caused by an egregious flaw in the educational theory of his incredible father. At the age of twenty, Mill's mind was a precision instrument for logical analysis, but he was emotionally bankrupt. The measure of his emotional immaturity can be taken in the sentimental incident from Marmontel's *Mémoires* which moved him to tears and started him on the way to recovery. In Wordsworth, however, whom he began to read in 1828, he discovered his real medicine (the word is Mill's).[1] If the habits of analysis are "a perpetual worm at the root" of the passions and desires, the antidote must be the cultivation of feeling. For the first time Mill began to see the use of poetry. "I had now learnt by experience that the passive susceptibilities needed to be cultivated as well as the active capacities."[2] And thus eventually the cultivation of the feelings became a cardinal point in his ethical and philosophical creed. It is rather ironic that John Stuart Mill, the great liberal, should find himself at the outset in the same critical boat with the forces of reaction, two High Anglican divines. The situation, of course, can be largely attributed to the pervasive influence of Wordsworth and Coleridge, and to something which is conveniently called the spirit of the age.

Mill's theory is grounded in his unique experience of poetry, but it is also conditioned more abstractly by Jeremy Bentham's (and presumably James Mill's) attitude towards the arts. In the popular opinion of the early decades of the nineteenth century the Benthamites were notorious enemies of poetry. There was certainly some reason for the belief. Bentham could see no "utilitarian" values in the arts, which he classified as "anergastic; (no work producing) or say aplopathoscopic (mere-sensation-regarding)" in contrast to

[1] John Stuart Mill, *Autobiography*, The World's Classics, 1935, p. 125.

[2] *Ibid.*, p. 121.

ethics, which is "ergastic (work producing) or say thele-
matoscopic (volition regarding)";[3] and in the *Chrestomathia*
he excludes the fine arts and belles-lettres from his course
of instruction as a waste of time because their utility was
"not sufficiently general." His famous remark, "the game of
push-pin is of equal value with the arts and sciences of music
and poetry," might be paired with another of his character-
istic remarks to the effect that the most useful function of
the arts is to provide pleasure for the idle who might other-
wise have no amusement but "in the hazardous and bloody
game of war."[4] Even the more cultivated Benthamites such
as John Arthur Roebuck, with whom Mill shortly after his
conversion debated the relative merits of Wordsworth and
Byron, could not be made to see that poetry had any value
as an aid in the formation of character. Poetry to them was
matter of illusion. It was thus in an atmosphere of hostile
debate that Mill worked out his theory of poetry with its
special emphases, on the use of poetry, the truth of poetry,
the nature of poetic discourse, and the psychology of the
poet.

Mill seems to have had some help from Wordsworth him-
self. He spent some time with Wordsworth during a visit to
the Lake Country in 1831 and was much impressed with the
extensive range of his thought and the largeness and expan-
siveness of his feelings. He was particularly interested in
Wordsworth's concern with "real life and the active pursuits
of men." At least one conversation had to do with poetry:

> Then when you get Wordsworth on the subjects which
> are peculiarly his, such as the theory of his own art, if it
> be proper to call poetry an art (that is, if art is to be de-
> fined as the expression or embodying in words or forms
> of the highest and most refined parts of nature), no one
> can converse with him without feeling that he has ad-
> vanced that great subject beyond any other man, being
> probably the first person who ever combined, with such

[3] *The Works of Jeremy Bentham*, edited by J. Bowring, 11 vols.,
Edinburgh, 1843, viii, Table v.
[4] *Ibid.*, ii, 253-54.

eminent success in the practice of the art, such high powers
of generalisation and habits of meditation on its princi-
ples.[5]

Although Mill's own theory of poetry is radically idealist
and thus closer to Coleridge than to Wordsworth, Mill was
strongly influenced by Wordsworth at a number of points,
and Wordsworth is his example *par excellence* of the poet of
culture in "Thoughts on Poetry."

Another acquaintance of this period who was to be an
effective force in Mill's thinking about poetry was Thomas
Carlyle. Quite naturally up to this time, Mill had considered
Carlyle's articles "consummate nonsense," but Carlyle im-
proved with knowing. He seemed to Mill "a man who has had
his eyes unsealed."[6] After a few months Carlyle calls Mill
one of his teachers, and Mill replies that if he is, "it is as yet
only in the sense in which a schoolmaster might speak of
his teachers, meaning those who teach under him." He has
been reading the essay on Johnson and has found it edifying.
His own vocation, he says, lies in a humbler sphere,

> I am rather fitted to be a logical expounder than an
> artist. You I look upon as an artist, and perhaps the only
> genuine one now living in this country: the highest destiny
> of all lies in that direction; for it is the artist alone in whose
> hands Truth becomes impressive and a living principle
> of action.[7]

Mill will meditate between artist and public to show the
public, first, the logical side of the artist's truth, and then,
that this is identical with its poetic truth. His concern is
notable if his theory confused. Carlyle also seems to have
brought out Mill's early tendency towards hero-worship and
towards Carlyle's own theory of poetry as the word of gen-
ius; Mill almost sounds like Carlyle in an article in the
Monthly Repository for 1833:

> Let the word be what it may, so it be but spoken with

[5] *The Letters of John Stuart Mill*, edited, with an introduction, by
H. S. R. Elliot, 2 vols., London, 1910, i, 11-12.
[6] *Ibid.*, p. 16.   [7] *Ibid.*, p. 35.

a truthful intent, this one thing must be interesting in it, that it has been spoken by a man—that it is the authentic record of something which has actually been thought and felt by a human being. . . . What is there in the writings of Plato or Milton so eternally valuable to us as the assurance they give that a Plato or a Milton might have been? been in this very world of ours, which, therefore, we also, according to the measure of our opportunities may, if we like, be the like.[8]

It was to Carlyle that Mill submitted for criticism his first attempts as a mediator, some "thoughts on poetry." These were contained in two essays, "What is Poetry?" and "The Two Kinds of Poetry" (later reprinted together under the title "Thoughts on Poetry and its Varieties"), published in the *Monthly Repository* in January and October 1833.[9] Both are essays in definition. The first sets out to distinguish the essence poetry from other modes of discourse, scientific, narrative, dramatic, and descriptive, and from other elements in the fine arts, touching by the way on the nature of poetic truth; and the second deals with the nature of the poet, his psychological processes and their manifestations. Bentham had said that poetry, because it was the language of the emotions, was misrepresentation. The essays embody the conviction of which Mill wrote to Carlyle in the summer of 1833, that it is the artist, not the man of science, who is most familiar with some of "the highest truths," and who has the ability "to declare them and make them impressive."[10]

[8] "Junius Redivivus," *The Monthly Repository*, 1833, VII, 263.

[9] "What is Poetry?", *The Monthly Repository*, 1833, VII; "The Two Kinds of Poetry," *The Monthly Repository*, 1833, VII; reprinted as "Thoughts on Poetry and its Varieties" in Mill's *Dissertations and Discussions*, 2 vols., London, 1859, I. Quotations are from this text.

[10] *The Letters*, I, 54. "It was in vain I urged on him [Roebuck] that the imaginative emotion which an idea, when vividly conceived, excites in us, is not an illusion but a fact, as real as any of the other qualities of objects; and far from implying anything erroneous and delusive in our mental apprehension of the object, is quite consistent with the most accurate knowledge and most perfect practical recognition of all its physical and intellectual laws and relations. The intensest feeling of the beauty of a cloud lighted by the setting sun, is no hin-

Against the charge that poetry is of no use in bettering the lot of mankind, Mill is now preparing the way for the statement, "the noblest end of poetry as an intellectual pursuit" is "that of acting upon the desires and characters of mankind through their emotions, to raise them towards the perfection of their nature."[11]

What is poetry? Mill agrees with Wordsworth (and with Newman and Keble) that it is not metrical composition, for it may be a quality of prose; it is not necessarily verbal, for it can also be a quality of music and the visual arts. As a starting point, it is universally agreed that the object of poetry is to act on the emotions. It is thus distinguished from its logical opposite which, as Wordsworth had already said, is not prose but science.

> The one addresses itself to the belief, the other to the feelings. The one does its work by convincing or persuading, the other by moving. The one acts by presenting a proposition to the understanding, the other by offering interesting objects of contemplation to the sensibilities.

There is rather a nice ambiguity in Mill's use of the word moving here which exposes what is perhaps the basic weakness of his theory as a whole. In context it seems to mean simply "engaging the feelings" and is not incompatible with "offering interesting objects of contemplation to the sensibilities." But the word is also susceptible of a Ciceronian and Renaissance interpretation, "moving to action," and there are other indications in the essays that this meaning is latent here. The best evidence, however, is from a later statement; Mill is speaking of science and art.

> These two ideas differ from one another as the understanding differs from the will, or as the indicative mood

---

drance to my knowing that the cloud is vapour of water, subject to all the laws of vapours in a state of suspension; and I am just as likely to allow for, and act on, these physical laws whenever there is occasion to do so, as if I had been incapable of perceiving any distinction between beauty and ugliness." *Autobiography*, pp. 128-29.

[11] "Tennyson's Poems," *The London Review*, 1835, i, 419.

in grammar differs from the imperative. The one deals in facts, the other in precepts. Science is a collection of *truths*; art, a body of *rules*, or directions for conduct. The language of science is, This is, or This is not: This does, or does not, happen. The language of art is, Do this; Avoid that. Science takes cognizance of a *phenomenon*, and endeavours to discover its *law*; art proposes to itself an *end*, and looks out for means to effect it.[12]

Thus Mill will have poetry at once in its essence a mode of contemplation, disinterested in its activity, and a kind of moral propaganda which will change the world. A guess would be that Mill experienced poetry as contemplation, and that Carlyle was responsible for the rules of conduct.

To "bring thoughts or images before the mind for the purpose of acting upon the emotions," however, is also the function of the novelist and the dramatist, so a further distinction must be made. This distinction is the familiar romantic one between imitation and creation, between the Aristotelians and the neoplatonists. The interest of poetry derives from the representation of states of human feeling, the interest of story from "a series of states of mere outward circumstances." Furthermore, the two sources of interest can be traced to two distinct and mutually exclusive characters of mind: story interests the immature, children, and primitive peoples; the shallowest adults make up the contemporary novel-reading public (Mill echoes Wordsworth's "gross and violent stimulants"). Poetry has to do with "the world within," "the deeper and more secret workings of human emotion." Similarly, the truth of poetry differs from the truth of fiction. "The truth of poetry is to paint the human soul truly: the truth of fiction is to give a true picture of life." The two kinds of knowledge are different, the poet's drawn mainly from self-observation, the novelist's from his observation of other men. Poetry and narrative may and do combine, in the drama for instance, but the two elements

[12] "On the Definition of Political Economy," *The London and Westminster Review*, 1836, IV, 3.

are always distinct. The reductive tendency of Mill's basic definition here is reminiscent of both Newman and Keble and is probably characteristic of romantic theory in general.

The idealism of Mill's position comes out even more clearly in his discussion of descriptive poetry where he leaves Wordsworth and the later "naturalists" such as Ruskin. Poetry is the delineation of states of feeling; the description of external objects is not poetry; but an object or "a truth which may fill a place in a scientific treatise" may "generate" poetry to which we give the name descriptive or didactic. "The poetry is not in the object itself, nor in the scientific truth itself, but in the state of mind in which the one and the other may be contemplated." Poetry describes things not as they are but as they appear; it paints them "not in their bare and natural lineaments, but seen through the medium and arrayed in the colours of the imagination set in action by the feelings." In a poem about a lion the poet will select the details which excite his emotions.

> Now this is describing the lion professedly, but the state of excitement of the spectator really. The lion may be described falsely or with exaggeration, and the poetry be all the better; but if the human emotion be not painted with scrupulous truth, the poetry is bad poetry, *i.e.* is not poetry at all, but a failure.

There is no respect for the sanctity of God's lion in John Stuart Mill.

Facts, ideas, impressions, which can be absorbed into the human consciousness may become poetry when seen through any impassioned medium, when invested with emotion. Poetry is "impassioned truth." But in this sense eloquence is also "impassioned truth," and a further distinction must be made. Quite simply, Mill narrows his definition of poetry to self-communion. In his well-known phrase, "eloquence is *heard*, poetry is *overheard*." Eloquence supposes an audience, where

> the peculiarity of poetry appears . . . to lie in the poet's

utter unconsciousness of a listener. Poetry is feeling con-
fessing itself to itself, in moments of solitude.

Eloquence is feeling pouring itself out to other minds: all
poetry is of the nature of soliloquy. The similarity between
the theories of Mill and Keble in this particular matter is
marked.

The problem is, of course, that of communication. In
poetry, according to Mill, the act of utterance is an end in
itself, not a means. "If the feeling declares itself by such
signs as escape from us when we are unconscious of being
seen," it is poetry; "if the signs are those we use for the
purpose of voluntary communication," it is oratory. But in
other contexts the theory of involuntary communication (Mill
does not deny that poetry does communicate) is unsatis-
factory to him. The great poet makes truth "impressive." It
is through his thoughts and images that

> the feeling speaks, and through their impressiveness
> that it impresses itself, and finds response in other hearts;
> and from these media of transmitting it (contrary to the
> laws of physical nature) increase of intensity is reflected
> back upon the feeling itself.

Mill's final statement on the subject in the essay is an attempt
to reconcile both elements. He is discussing the point at
which the orator ceases to be an orator and becomes the poet;

> when (for example) either his words, or the mode of
> their arrangement, are such as we spontaneously use only
> when in a state of excitement, proving that the mind is at
> least as much occupied by a passive state of its own feel-
> ings, as by the desire of attaining the premeditated end
> which the discourse has in view.

Illuminating in this connection is Mill's test of genuine
poetry. If the unintelligent and unfeeling critic says "not
'this is prose,' but 'this is exaggeration,' 'this is mysticism,' or
'this is nonsense,'" he is probably talking about poetry. While
Mill's stand is not unusual in this general matter, one cannot
help feeling that Carlyle's doctrine of the "unconscious poet"
had something to do with it.

Mill supports his distinction between poetry and elo-
quence by tracking it through the various arts. In music, for
instance, Rossini and the Italian School (whom Newman
had used as an illustration of the poetic) represent "garru-
lous passion," passion "calculated for dramatic effect," in
contrast to much of the music of Mozart and Beethoven.
In painting Raphael is poetic and Rubens is "without the
slightest tincture" of poetry (as, in fact, Keble had re-
marked). The standard in every case is the typically roman-
tic standard of lyricism. Mill is explicit in dealing with liter-
ary forms,

> Lyric poetry, as it was the earliest kind, is also, if the
> view we are now taking of poetry be correct, more emi-
> nently and peculiarly poetry than any other: it is the poetry
> most natural to a really poetic temperament, and least
> capable of being successfully imitated by one not so en-
> dowed by nature.[13]

The epic, which, in so far as it is narrative is not poetry at
all, is "esteemed" the greatest of the literary forms because
it includes the other kinds; and the drama, which would
always be prose except when a poet is one of the characters,
is poetry only because all men speak poetry in moments of
strong emotion!

In the most reduced form of Mill's definition, then,
poetry is simply "feeling itself," "human feeling," and all
men are at moments poets. "The poet" is a "man speaking
to men"; he differs from other men only in degree, not in
kind. Mill exorcises all magic from the formula *poeta nas-
citur* with the mental science of his century, rejecting at the
same time the exaggerations of the idea of original genius.

> The days are gone by, when every raw youth whose
> borrowed phantasies have set themselves to a borrowed
> tune, mistaking, as Coleridge says, an ardent desire of
> poetic reputation for poetic genius, while unable to dis-

[13] The nature of lyric poetry is discussed in some detail in Mill's
alert review of Alfred De Vigny's poems and prose in *The London and
Westminster Review*, 1838, vii, 42-43.

guise from himself that he had taken no means whereby he might *become* a poet, could fancy himself born one.

Such people are now born novelists. No, poetic excellence "is subject to the same necessary conditions with any other mental endowment," and the poet has need of "a high and assiduous intellectual culture." There is, however, such a thing as a poetic nature. Mill turns and approaches a definition of poetry through the psychology of the poet. Poets are those "who are so constituted, that emotions are the links of association by which their ideas, both sensuous and spiritual, are connected together," and who usually owe this peculiarity to "intense sensibility." All others are poets in an extended sense of the word. "In the one, feeling waits upon thought; in the other, thought upon feeling." Or put in another way, the "poet of culture sees his object in prose, and describes it in poetry; the poet of nature actually sees it in poetry."

Mill's associationism derives from David Hartley through his father. It seems to be a purely mechanical activity and at points in the argument poetry seems to be a kind of automatic writing: the "thoughts and imagery are suggested by the feeling, and are such as it finds unsought"; "feeling, when excited and not voluntarily resisted, seizes the helm of their thoughts, and the succession of ideas and images becomes the mere utterance of an emotion." It is the element of passivity, possession, spontaneity, that Mill praises in the poetry of Shelley, his example of the poet of nature. Mill's one significant use of the word imagination in the essay, however, is susceptible of a Coleridgean interpretation, although his psychology as a whole seems to run counter to Coleridge.

The combinations which the mind puts together; the pictures which it paints, the wholes which Imagination constructs out of the materials supplied by the Fancy, will be indebted to some dominant *feeling*, not as in other natures to a dominant *thought*, for their unity and consist-

ency of character, for what distinguishes them from in-
coherencies.

Mill's use of the concept of "the ruling passion" in this con-
nection is notable; it suggests another relation to the theories
of Newman and Keble.

Shelley is the ideal poet of nature. His poetry is the poetry
of exquisite sensation and emotion, not of ideas. When it
deals with ideas, they are not developed, but are clothed
in three or four brilliant, suggestive images, which in turn
evoke other associations and images. His poetry is unified
in terms of feeling, for it was written to "relieve" states of
feeling "oppressive" from their vividness! His poetry, the
"poet's" poetry, "is little else than a pouring forth of the
thoughts and images that pass across the mind while some
permanent state of feeling is occupying it." "Exuberance"
of imagery is the identifying mark of this kind of poetry.

But Shelley was a natural poet precisely because he lacked
culture, because he had escaped the stultifying effects of a
conventional education, because "voluntary mental disci-
pline" had done little for him. In the end, for Mill (rather
before Arnold) Shelley did not know enough. It is the poet
of culture (who is not really a poet at all) Mill prefers; it
is Wordsworth, calm and deliberate, unebullient, unpos-
sessed, unlyrical even, whose poetry is merely the setting
for his thought; it is Wordsworth the great teacher, whom
Mill prefers. Mill is, of course, attempting to describe the
polarity of the poetic temperament, but it is interesting that
in common with other Early Victorian critics who distinguish
the poet of impulse from the poet of will he wants, not his
own poet's poet, but the poet of ideas. Mill's last word is
to insist that the poet is not incompatible with the philoso-
pher. Passion can be calm, and from the capacity for strong
feeling come the motives which lead human beings to the
search for truth (a parallel to Keble's poetry of *ethos*?).
Given the peculiar nervous organization of the poet, what
he makes of his materials will depend on culture; "the
achievements of any poet in his own art will be in propor-

tion to the growth and perfection of his thinking faculty.[14] If the most impassioned natures do not ripen into powerful intellects, the defect is a sign of the times. Ironically, Mill thinks the state of education in his own times so bad that there is a question whether the poet of acquired ideas has any advantage over the poet who learns from his feelings alone.

The disillusion of the end of the essay must have been momentary, however, because soon after he wrote to Carlyle of his conviction that "most of the highest truths" are intuitive, that "the poet or artist is conversant with *such* truths, and that his office in respect to truth is to declare them and to make them impressive."[15] Poetry for Mill and Carlyle, and for the other critics of the period, was not a disinterested activity of the mind, definitions and protestations to the contrary: its issue was really action. When the public has accepted the poet's truths, Mill says, it "may build on them and act on them, or at least act nothing contradictory to them."[16] Mill, however, and in this he differs from Carlyle,

[14] "Every great poet, every poet who has extensively or permanently influenced mankind, has been a great thinker;—has had a philosophy, though perhaps he did not call it by that name;—has had his mind full of thoughts, derived not merely from passive sensibility, but from trains of reflection, from observation, analysis, and generalization; however remote the sphere of his observation and meditation may have lain from the studies of the schools. Where the poetic temperament exists in its greatest degree, while the systematic culture of the intellect has been neglected, we may expect to find, what we do find in the best poems of Shelley—vivid representations of states of passive and dreamy emotion, fitted to give extreme pleasure to persons of similar organization to the poet, but not likely to be sympathized in, because not understood, by any other persons; and scarcely conducing at all to the noblest end of poetry as an intellectual pursuit, that of acting upon the desires and characters of mankind through their emotions, to raise them towards the perfection of their nature. This, like every other adaptation of means to ends, is the work of cultivated reason; and the poet's success in it will be in proportion to the intrinsic value of his thoughts, and to the command which he has acquired over the materials of his imagination, for placing those thoughts in a strong light before the intellect, and impressing them on the feelings." "Tennyson's Poems," *The London Review*, 1835, I, 418-19.

[15] *The Letters*, I, 54.

[16] *Ibid.*, p. 55.

77

never completely surrendered the truth of logic to the truth of imagination. The ideal poet is indeed the philosopher-poet, but it is the philosopher who supplies the materials upon which the poet works. It is worth remarking that towards the end of his life Mill completely lost faith in the ability of the artist to contribute anything to the progress of mankind. Perhaps the nineteenth century demanded too much of its poets.

Mill's theory of poetry is that of a gifted amateur, a witness of the power of Wordsworth's and Coleridge's poetry and of their ideas, and of the strong hand of Carlyle. "Thoughts on Poetry and its Varieties" is full of half-truths. Mill's statement of the part which poetry can play in the cultivation of the feelings is still valuable as is his clear and accurate description of the "idealist" or "subjectivist" aesthetic; but his theory reduces poetry to the expression of emotion on the one hand, and expands it to a *magister vitae* in the concept of the philosopher-poet on the other. His arguments on the subject of communication in poetry still draw fire in contemporary theorizing; his account of the poet's psychology perhaps retains a certain historical interest; and his phrase, "eloquence is heard, poetry is overheard," frequently turns up when poetry is being talked about in academic circles. On the whole, however, the theory is most useful for those elements which it holds in common with other theories of the early nineteenth century as this body of ideas can be brought to bear on a fresh study of Victorian poetry.

5. Thomas Carlyle

The Hero as Poet. Dante: Shakespeare. 1840

THOMAS CARLYLE was by profession a critic and man of letters, by vocation (or was it self-election?) the moral conscience of Early Victorian England. He was a man with a gospel, the gospel according to Goethe and Immanuel Kant, and, more important perhaps, a man with a style, a strange, furious, infuriating way of saying things that commanded attention. As a literary critic primarily a popularizer, he took directly from the great German romantics, largely bypassing their great English contemporaries, the general metaphysics of transcendental idealism and a theory of art as revelation, and appeared before the public with his version of the "new criticism." In a series of notable essays, ranging in subject from Goethe, Schiller, Heine, and Jean Paul Richter, to Voltaire and Diderot, and Boswell, Burns, Scott, and Ebenezer Elliott, Carlyle expounds a theory of poetry as the utterance of the gifted man, who finally takes his rightful place within the larger concept of the hero in that part of *Heroes, Hero-Worship and the Heroic in History* given to Dante and Shakespeare.

In *The State of German Literature* (1827) Carlyle announces the word. Criticism is no longer, as it was in the eighteenth century, "a question concerning the qualities of diction, the coherence of metaphors, the fitness of sentiments, the general logical truth, in a work of art," nor is it, and this time Carlyle is addressing the English romantics, "a question mainly of a psychological sort, to be answered by discovering and delineating the peculiar nature of the poet from his poetry." The real matter of criticism is inclusive of, and transcends, these: "the essence and peculiar life of the poetry itself." The basic problem of criticism is to determine in what sense poetry is true—whether the plays of Shakespeare are "not veri-similar only, but true; nay, truer than reality itself, since the essence of unmixed reality is bodied forth in them under more expressive symbols."

And again, in what does the unity of the great work of art consist. These are the questions for the new critic. "Not only who was the poet, and how did he compose; but what and how was the poem, and why was it a poem and not rhymed eloquence, creation and not figured passion?"[1]

The answers are given in terms of the idealistic philosophy and aesthetic variously presented by Kant, Fichte, Schelling, and Goethe. Two or three general propositions of this philosophy will set Carlyle's poetic. The external world is a world of appearance. Behind the world of appearance is the world of reality, a spiritual reality, which exists in the mind of God. The mind of man is also spirit and therefore real, but even man is hardly more than a flicker in the eye of God. Man's intellectual tools are reason and understanding: understanding is the pedestrian, discursive faculty of the mind; reason or insight (roughly equivalent to the creative imagination of the English romantics), its supreme power of intuition. It is the reason which intuits the real, fact, the true, the good, the beautiful (Carlyle often uses the terms synonymously), behind the world of appearance. Intuition itself is ultimately a moral activity. The interchangeability of terms allows Carlyle to quote Goethe, "The Beautiful is higher than the Good; the Beautiful includes in it the Good"; but he quickly notes that he means "the *true* Beautiful."[2]

All art, then, in Carlyle's adaptation of transcendentalism, is revelation, revelation of "Fact," the "Soul of Fact," behind the world of sensuous appearance. The end of art is "Truth," absolute, unitary, universal. Poetry is an inclusive term for any medium which reveals truth; religion, philosophy, art, even action, can be poetry when they are truthful. In the same way any man who reveals truth, regardless of the medium in which he works, is a poet. The poet proper is not a poet in virtue of the form his utterance takes, but be-

[1] *The Works of Thomas Carlyle*, Centenary Edition, 30 vols., London, 1896-99, *Critical and Miscellaneous Essays*, xxvi, "The State of German Literature," pp. 51-52. Quotations are from this edition.
[2] *Heroes and Hero-Worship*, v, 81.

cause he is a "seer," a man who reveals the ideal in the actual, the spirit of beauty in the world which is also its truth. The concept of the seer is filled with significance for Carlyle.

> The true Poet is ever, as of old, the Seer; whose eye has been gifted to discern the godlike Mystery of God's Universe, and decipher some new lines of its celestial writing; we can still call him a *Vates* and Seer; for he *sees* into this greatest of secrets, "the open secret"; hidden things become clear; how the Future (both resting on Eternity) is but another phasis of the Present: thereby are his words in very truth prophetic; what he has spoken shall be done.[3]

Poetry is what the poet "sees" with his extraordinary powers of intellection and passion. He "sees" or creates (these two words are also the same in Carlyle's thinking) meaning, structure, harmony, in short, artistic wholes. In the poet the intellect works as a unifying force and poetry is thus creation expressing itself in organic form. The creative activity itself springs unconsciously from the depths of the poet's moral being; it is the voice of his whole harmonious manhood: the Poet's art is his morality, and his word is the man.

The unconscious nature of all significant activity is a key concept in Carlyle's theory. "The uttered part of a man's life, let us always repeat, bears to the unuttered unconscious part a small unknown proportion; he himself never knows it, much less do others."[4] It is the element of the unconscious in its very mysteriousness that distinguishes artistic creation from the conscious manufacture of the mere "demonstrator," art from artifice, form from formalism. The form of the work of art is organic to the insight which constitutes the work of art; it is determined from within by the nature of the intuition, not from without by convention and rule. In practice, Carlyle's stress on the unconscious often seduced him into the familiar romantic determinism, psychological and historical, and, more fatal, into the denial of discursive

[3] *Essays*, XXVII, "Death of Goethe," p. 377.
[4] *Ibid.*, XXIX, "Sir Walter Scott," p. 49.

reason, theory, and ultimately, criticism. If the creative proc-
ess is unconscious, the artistic experience unanalyzable,
there is obviously no excuse either for criticism or theory.
A number of nineteenth century critics, when pushed, seem
to wind up with the subversion of the critical act, and Car-
lyle, with his enormous influence, seems to have been to
blame.

Carlyle took common ground with the English romantics
in rejecting the poetic standards of the eighteenth century.
Literature was then in a state of decline; all was "polish and
languor, external glitter and internal vacuity." It had for-
saken its true vocation:

> . . . it no longer held the mirror up to Nature; no longer
> reflected in many-coloured expressive symbols, the actual
> passions, the hopes, sorrows, joys of living men; but dwelt
> in a remote conventional world, in *Castles of Otranto*, in
> *Epigoniads* and *Leonidases*, among clear, metallic heroes,
> and white, high, stainless beauties, in whom drapery and
> elocution were nowise the least important qualities.

For this situation the sensational psychology of John Locke
was ultimately responsible. The mind was reduced from
"its immaterial, mysterious, divine though invisible charac-
ter" to "some composite, divisible and reunitable substance,
some finer chemical salt, or curious piece of logical joinery,"
and as a result, religion, poetry, and all "high and heroic
feeling" became merely useful amusements, mere stimu-
lants like opium and Scotch whiskey.[5] This invasion of the
realm of poetry by materialistic science is the burden of a
dozen passages in the early essays. One from "Signs of the
Times" will make the point.

> We enjoy, we see nothing by direct vision; but only by
> reflection, and in anatomical dismemberment. Like Sir
> Hudibras, for every Why we must have a Wherefore. We
> have our little *theory* on all human and divine things.
> Poetry, the workings of genius itself, which in all times,

[5] *Ibid.*, xxvi, "Goethe," pp. 213-15.

with one or another meaning, has been called Inspiration, and held to be mysterious and inscrutable, is no longer without its scientific exposition. The building of the lofty rhyme is like any other masonry or bricklaying: we have theories of its rise, height, decline and fall,—which latter, it would seem, is now near, among all peoples. Of our "Theories of Taste," as they are called, wherein the deep, infinite, unspeakable Love of Wisdom and Beauty, which dwells in all men, is "explained," made mechanically visible, from "Association" and the like, why should we say anything.[6]

If poetry is to be explained at all, it is not in these terms. It comes and goes "with little or no regard to any the most cunning theory that has yet been devised of it." Carlyle may have been right, but in opposing "scientific criticism" he was swimming against flood tide.

Carlyle gives "no truce" to the theory of poetry as pleasure; it is to be loved because it is "the highest in man, and the soul of all beauty." The poetry of the great masters aims, not at "furnishing a languid mind with fantastic shows and indolent emotions," but at "incorporating the everlasting Reason of man in forms visible to his Sense, and suitable to it."[7] He was impatient with any book which did not give him some kind of edification, and in his theory of poetry the end was always didactic. The poet is the man who by poetical methods instructs other men, evolves for them "the mystery of our Life." But even literature tends to disappear out the window when the "Didactic Spirit" enters.

> At the era of the Reformation, it reaches its acme; and, in singular shape, steps forth on the high places of Public Business, and amid storms and thunder, not without brightness and true fire from Heaven, convulsively renovates the world. This is, as it were, the apotheosis of the Didactic Spirit, where it first attains a really poetical concentration, and stimulates mankind into heroism of

[6] *Ibid.*, xxvii, "Signs of the Times," p. 76.
[7] *Ibid.*, xxvi, "Goethe," p. 255. Cf. *supra* Mill's statement on p. 77, n.14.

word, and of action also. Of the latter, indeed, still more
than of the former; for not till a much more recent time,
almost till our own time, has Inquiry in some measure
again reconciled itself to Belief; and Poetry, though in
detached tones, arisen on us as a true musical Wisdom.
Thus is the deed, in certain circumstances, readier and
greater than the word: Action strikes fiery light from the
rocks it has to hew through; Poetry reposes in the skyey
splendour which that rough passage has led to.[8]

Eventually, for Carlyle, as for his contemporaries, action is
greater than contemplation, and he will leave literature
for sociology and cultural history.

By the time Carlyle came to write his lectures on *Heroes
and Hero-Worship*, the concept of the hero, the original
genius, had already been worked out in the early essays. This
concept accounts for his biographical approach to literature;
it is the ultimate standard of value by which Goethe and
Burns are exalted, Scott and Byron cast down; "true and
genial" as Burns' poetry is, "it is not chiefly as a poet, but
as a man, that he interests and affects us."[9] Goethe is the
"clear and universal man," the "Teacher and exemplar of his
age." Two such universal men, Dante and Shakespeare, are
the subject of "The Hero as Poet," the third of the striking
series of six lectures on heroism which Carlyle delivered in
London in May 1840.

Within the general framework of the lectures the poet
appears as only one manifestation of "the grand fundamental
character," the "Great Man" with his great heart and clear,
deep-seeing eye. The Great Man is potentially all kinds of
men, and it is only as the quality of his native genius is
modified by personality and circumstance, especially by cir-
cumstance, that he appears in society as politician, legislator,
warrior, or poet. "Napoleon has words in him which are like

[8] *Ibid.*, xxvii, "Early German Literature," p. 284. "At bottom, it
is the Poet's first gift, as it is all men's, that he have intellect enough.
He will be a poet if he have: a Poet in word; or failing that, perhaps
still better, a Poet in act." *Heroes and Hero-Worship*, v, 105.
[9] *Ibid.*, xxvi, "Burns," p. 264.

Austerlitz Battles";[10] or again, "I cannot understand how a Mirabeau, with that great glowing heart, with the fire that was in it, with the bursting tears that were in it, could not have written verses, tragedies, poems, and touched all hearts in that way, had his course of life and education led him thitherward."[11] The hero as poet, however, has this characteristic which distinguishes him from the hero as deity and the hero as prophet: he is a figure of all ages, a more or less constant exemplar of the genius.

In the last analysis Carlyle's theory of poetry is merely an elaboration of the implications in his theory of original genius. The discussion of the poet begins with the classical *vates*, at once poet and prophet. These two are alike in that they both penetrate the sacred mystery of the universe—the realized thought of God, and the function of both is to make the mystery more impressively known. Like the prophet, the poet "reveals"; he intuits directly in virtue of his insight and belief; he lives in the very "Fact" of things and is "in earnest" with the universe. He is the *vates* precisely in the strength of his sincerity. If there is a distinction between poet and prophet, it is that the prophet seizes the secret of Nature in its moral aspect, as good and evil, the poet in its aesthetic, as the beautiful.[12] "The one we may call a revealer of what we are to do, the other of what we are to love." But beauty and goodness are ultimately one, and the two functions are inextricable; the poet is singer *and* teacher.

The poet does not differ from other men in kind. Some poets have been called "perfect," but strictly this is an illusion, for no poet is of poetic imagination all compact; there

[10] *Heroes and Hero-Worship*, "The Hero as Poet." Quotations not marked are from this essay.

[11] "The subject, then, of his poem a writer should fix upon with whatever care and insight he can command: but it will not greatly matter, I think, whether the form is dramatic or narrative, whether you give it to the world with the help of actors or of a rhapsodist; for surely no one would suggest that Homer would have failed in Tragedy or Shakespeare in an Epic." *Keble's Lectures on Poetry*, i, 92.

[12] Poetry is "originality energizing in the world of beauty." J. H. Newman, "Poetry, with Reference to Aristotle's Poetics," p. 21.

is always the alloy of the man. And at the same time, no man is wholly without a touch of poetry, even a touch of "the Universal." "We are all poets when we *read* a poem well." The difference is merely a matter of degree. "A man that has *so* much more of the poetic element developed in him as to have become noticeable, will be called Poet by his neighbors." In the same way the universal or world-poets are those who rise so far above their fellows that they are judged perfect.

But there must also be a difference between "true poetry" and "true speech." There is perhaps a difference in essence, a certain *Unendlichkeit* which poetry communicates, but simpler and more meaningful for Carlyle is "the old vulgar distinction": poetry is metrical, has music in it, is song. It should be noted quickly that Carlyle is not saying poetry is metrical composition. The logical opposite of poetry in this theory is the prosaic, not prose, and the distinction is grounded in disparate functions of the mind. The prosaic is produced by the "understanding," poetry by the "reason." Metrical composition for Carlyle, as for many of the Early Victorian critics, is purely external to the creative process. Poetry is "musical not in word only, but in heart and substance," "in the whole conception of it." The music of poetry is a matter of the structure of reality, or perhaps more accurately, of the harmonizing power of the mind which perceives or creates meaning through a kind of rhythmical organization like that of music.[13] "A *musical* thought," Carlyle says, "is one spoken by a mind that has penetrated into the inmost heart of the thing; detected the inmost mystery of it, namely the *melody* that lies hidden in it; the inward harmony of coherence which is its soul."[14] Furthermore, all

[13] "Coleridge remarks very pertinently somewhere, that wherever you find a sentence musically worded, of true rhythm and melody in the words, there is something deep and good in the meaning too. For body and soul, word and idea, go strangely together here as everywhere." "The Hero as Poet."

[14] "The Greeks fabled of Sphere-Harmonies: it was the feeling they had of the inner structure of Nature; that the soul of all her voices and utterances was perfect music." "The Hero as Poet."

speech, particularly popular speech, has its accent and tune, has something of music in it; and all passionate language tends to generate musical expression. Thus, "Song" is the "primal element of us; of us, and of all things"; and poetry becomes by definition *musical Thought.* " The poet is the man who thinks musically. "At bottom," however, "it is a man's sincerity and depth of vision that makes him a Poet." These are the qualities which are still worshiped in great men, even if the modern age refuses to call them divine or prophetic. In witness Carlyle offers the "canonization" of Dante and Shakespeare.

It is precisely the element of song that characterizes Dante's great poem. It is rhythmical in its material and substance. "A true inward symmetry, what one calls an architectural harmony, reigns in it, proportionates it all: architectural; which also partakes of the character of music." The inward symmetry is reflected in the outward form. "The three kingdoms, *Inferno, Purgatorio, Paradiso*, look-out on one another like compartments of a great edifice; a great supernatural world-cathedral." The poem is rhymed by inward necessity, and in "the very sound of it there is a *canto fermo*; it proceeds as by a chant." It is "the sincerest of all Poems," born of struggle and pain, worked out in whole and elaborate parts "with intense earnestness" into truth and clear visuality. "It is the soul of Dante, and in this the soul of the middle ages, rendered for ever rhythmically visible there."

The prevailing quality of Dante's mind is its intensity. If he is world great, it is "not because he is world-wide, but because he is world-deep." His vision pierces through all objects "down into the heart of Being." His images, the outward body of his vision, present essential types, stripped, precise, condensed. His ability to strike a likeness is evidence of the value of the man, his sympathy and his sincerity; "a man without worth cannot give you the likeness of any object; he dwells in vague outwardness, fallacy, and trivial hearsay, about all objects. And indeed may we not say that intellect altogether expresses itself in this power of discerning what an object is [Wordsworth! Ruskin!]?" Dante's painting is not only graphic, it is noble; therefore, "morally great, above all, we must call him; it is the beginning of all."

The *Divine Comedy* is a vision of "the true Unseen World" in terms of the Christianity of the Middle Ages, a symbol of Dante's belief that "the real world, as it is called, and its facts, was but the threshold to an infinitely higher Fact of a World," of his belief that, at bottom, "the one was as *preter*natural as the other." The critic mistakes who thinks the poem a mere allegorical construct; it is true symbol, valid in its essence for all men and all time; an unconscious (!) emblem, to be sure, but the "indubitable awful facts" were there, "the whole heart of man taking them for practically true, all Nature everywhere confirming them." In Dante ten silent centuries "found a voice" (the century is the agent).

> The *Divina Commedia* is of Dante's writing; yet in truth *it* belongs to ten Christian centuries, only the finishing of it is Dante's. So always. The craftsman there, the smith with that metal of his, with these tools, with these cunning methods,—how little of all he does is properly *his* work! All past inventive men work there with him;—as indeed with all of us, in all things.

In Dante, Christianism, the "noblest *idea* made *real* hitherto among men, is sung, and emblemed-forth abidingly, by one of the noblest men." And what is the "use of this Dante" (addressed to utilitarians with big and little 'u's'?)? Utility cannot measure the "human soul who has once got into that primal element of *Song*, and sung-forth fitly somewhat therefrom, has worked in the *depths* of our existence; feeding through long times the life-*roots* of all excellent human things whatsoever." But this much can be said, "Dante speaks to the noble, the pure and great, in all times and places."

As Dante was sent to embody musically the inner life, the faith or soul of Modern Europe, Shakespeare was sent to do the same for its outer life, the practice or body.[15] He, too, had the singing voice and the seeing eye, but where Dante was deep and fierce, he was wide, placid, far-seeing. His powers of vision and thought have no equal, and in the "construction" of his plays there is an understanding comparable to that of Bacon in the *Novum Organum.*

> The built house seems all so fit,—everyway as it should be, as if it came there by its own law and the nature of things,—we forget the rude disorderly quarry it was shaped from. The very perfection of the house, as if Nature herself had made it, hides the builder's merit. Perfect, more perfect than any other man, we may call Shakespeare in this: he discerns, knows as by instinct, what condition he works under, what his materials are, what his own force and its relation to them is.[16]

This is not a matter of transitory insight; "it is deliberate illumination of the whole matter; it is a calmly *seeing* eye; a great intellect, in short." Shakespeare creates a world out of chaos. Creation of this sort (as medieval and renaissance poetic theorists had pointed out, and neoclassical ones discarded) is a prototype of the divine. "Can the man say, *Fiat Lux*, Let there be light; and out of chaos make a world? Precisely as there is *light* in himself, will he accomplish this."

Like Dante, Shakespeare is great in his "painting," especially portrait-painting. His creative insight—"poetic creation, what is this too but *seeing* the thing sufficiently"—reveals, not surfaces, but the "inmost heart, and generic secret" of the object; and once more the quality of the insight is the index of the poet's morality, Shakespeare's "valour, candour, tolerance, truthfulness." Shakespeare is no "*twisted*, poor convex-concave mirror, reflecting all objects with its own convexities and concavities; a perfectly *level* mirror," which is to say, a man justly related to all men and all things,

[15] Cf. Browning's "subjective and objective" poets.
[16] Carlyle is referring to the organic unity of Shakespeare's plays, which Coleridge in England had already pointed out.

a good man.[17] In his characters Shakespeare gives us all kinds of men in all their dimensions, inner and outer, himself "loving, just, the equal brother of all."

Degree of vision measures the man. When Carlyle has said that Shakespeare's distinction is "superiority of Intellect," he has said everything, for what are the attempts to break the mind into intellect, imagination, fancy, and so on, but juggling with words; all of these are but names for the "Power of Insight."[18] Shakespeare's intellect, however, was an unconscious intellect; "there is more virtue in it than he himself is aware of." His art is not artifice; its noblest worth is not there "by plan or precontrivance"; his plays are rather "Products of Nature," and Shakespeare himself is a "voice" of Nature. "It is Nature's highest reward to a true simple great soul, that he get thus to be *a part of herself*." In the end Shakespeare and Carlyle are one "with rocks, and stones, and trees."

Carlyle notes in Shakespeare the joyful tranquillity which Arnold was to single out in Wordsworth. In Shakespeare it is meaningful as the result of his victory over sorrow and suffering. But the works give us only a poor picture of the man; they are "windows, through which we see a glimpse of the world that was in him"; they are "cursory, imperfect, written under cramping circumstances." Passages gleam with eternal radiance, but we "feel that the surrounding matter" is heavy, temporary, conventional. Carlyle is describing the losing struggle of the Hegelian artist with his medium.

Shakespeare was also a prophet in his way. He was a priest of the religion of Nature, but he sang, and did not preach, except musically. He was not "indifferent," a sceptic, as some have thought; it is merely that "his whole heart was in his own grand sphere of worship." Because his eye was so clear, he is an eye to us all, "a blessed heaven-sent

[17] There is a comparison to be made here with the Wordsworthians and Ruskinians, a contrast with Mill and the "distortionists."

[18] Cf. G. H. Lewes, who must have learned much from Carlyle, on "the faculties" in *The Principles of Success in Literature*, edited by T. S. Knowlson, London, 1899, "The Principle of Vision" and "Of Vision in Art," pp. 22ff.

Bringer of Light." And the "use" of him? "apart from spiritualities; and considering him merely as a real, marketable, tangibly-useful possession"? Soon the Island of England will hold only a small fraction of the English; soon "there will be a Saxondom covering great spaces of the Globe."

> And now, what is it that can keep all these together into virtually one Nation, so that they do not fall-out and fight, but live at peace, in brotherlike intercourse, helping one another? This is justly regarded as the greatest practical problem, the thing all manner of sovereignties and governments are here to accomplish: what is it that will accomplish this?

Not Acts of Parliament, not prime ministers, but Shakespeare, the articulate voice of a nation.[19]

Carlyle is an odd figure, hard to judge dispassionately. His influence on Early and Mid-Victorian criticism was wide and effective, even on the camp of the enemy; now, his method and his meaning both seem somehow remote. Perhaps in some quarters of the twentieth century there is need to be reminded that life is more than literature, man more than mechanism, and in man, particularly man as artist, a *je ne sais quoi* that cannot be compassed by the manuals of science. And there is a sense in which art and poetry are revelation, and in which great art and great poetry do provide patterns for living. There is also a sense in which the successful work of art must have "organic" unity and "organic" form. But in the end Carlyle's poetic is quite simply too transcendental. He has the general romantic tendency to dissolve and blur distinctions into indefinable absolutes, and he ignores the whole problem of the medium of art. His rejection of the insights which science was even then offering the critic marked the quality of his reaction. The status of the poet in modern society, which looks to Einstein, not Eliot, for "truth," hardly allows, and with reason, the attributions of hero and prophet, and modern criticism has

[19] Cf. Aubrey De Vere's remarks on "national" poets in "Two Schools of Poetry," *Essays*, London, 1887, ii, 100-43.

rightly distinguished man from poem and the morality of the poem from the morality of the man (Carlyle's statement, once more, lacks the logical distinction which forbids abuse). There is more to be said about poetry than that it is "rhythmical thought."

6. Leigh Hunt

Essay in Answer to the Question
"What is Poetry?" 1844

LEIGH HUNT, like Carlyle, was a professional critic and man of letters, and, in addition, something of a poet in his own right. In his literary criticism he is best characterized, perhaps, as a conservative romantic in the English tradition: conservative, in the sense that he started from mid-eighteenth century ideals and to the end retained a lively interest in the formal effects of poetry; romantic, in the sense that he was primarily a man of feeling, who moved from antagonism to admiration for the achievement of Wordsworth and Coleridge. It is probably accurate to say that Hunt worked out his own theory of poetry in conscious opposition on the one hand to the "artificial school" of Pope and the eighteenth century, and on the other to the "transcendental school" of Coleridge and Wordsworth. "I offended all the critics of the old or French school," in *The Feast of the Poets* (1811), "by objecting to the monotony of Pope's versification, and all the critics of the new or German school, by laughing at Wordsworth, with whose writings I was then unacquainted, except through the medium of his deriders. On reading him for myself, I became such an admirer, that Lord Byron accused me of making him popular upon town."[1] Hunt's retrospect of 1850 is a little misleading, as, in fact, even after he had read Wordsworth with attention, he disagreed with both theory and practice, and it was only with the gradual modifications in Wordsworth's own position that Hunt was able to give a wider assent. The assimilation was never complete, although Wordsworth became the "prince of the bards of his time." A sensibility and not an intellect, Hunt was always impatient with Coleridge's speculative side. "I dislike his tergiversation and his subtleties," he wrote to Jeffrey shortly after the publication of the *Biographia Lit-*

[1] Leigh Hunt, *Autobiography*, The World's Classics, 1928, p. 271.

eraria.[2] But there is much in Coleridge accessible to the lesser mind, and his final verdict on the *Biographia* was "the most masterly criticism of poetry in the language."[3] Hunt knew these men, and he also knew and learned from Hazlitt, Shelley, Keats, and Carlyle. It is not surprising that, in spite of certain weaknesses, a tendency towards dilettantism effeminacy of taste, discontinuity of energy, he should be a critic of merit.

Wordsworth and Coleridge are roughly handled in the first version of *The Feast of the Poets* which appeared in *The Reflector* for 1811. Wordsworth in the poem has reverted to childhood, and Apollo, the god of the feast, complains of poets who look for subjects in the commonplace feelings of everyday life. The poem was revised for separate publication in 1814, and now Wordsworth has exchanged his harp for a whistle. The god chides him; he might have become the first poet of the age and led poetry back to the great tradition. Of greater interest, however, is the "inordinate note" in which Hunt attacks Wordsworth's theory. He begins by saying that Wordsworth is the greatest English poet since Spenser and Milton, and he protests against the critics who simply regard his poems as childish; nevertheless, Wordsworth has abused his genius. In the abstract Hunt declares himself in fundamental agreement with "the curious and, in many respects, very masterly preface to the Lyrical Ballads." For one thing, the taste of modern society, crowded together in the towns, requires "the counteraction of some simpler and more primitive food." The poet of the present age "should chuse subjects as far removed as possible from artificial excitements," and these subjects "should be clothed in language equally artless." Wordsworth is wrong in the matter of verse, but the principal charge is that he has not lived up to his own theory. He protests against gross and violent stimulants in his preface while his poems are full of idiot boys, mad mothers, and frantic mariners. These are

[2] *The Correspondence of Leigh Hunt*, edited by his eldest son, 2 vols., London, 1862, I, 102.

[3] *The Poetical Works of Leigh Hunt*, New York, 1860, p. 441.

diseased stimulants; the theory carried to excess. The craving after intelligence in poetry is healthy in comparison to these "morbid abstractions." Wordsworth is in fact anti-social; he encourages "making a business of reverie." His principle of giving importance to actions and situations by the feelings can be utterly subversive, as to a certain extent it has been, in the hands of irresponsible imitators; and in the matter of language his theory is much too exclusive. "He would have all poetry to be one and the same in point of style." Surely the poet can legitimately appeal to more particular associations, those of classical literature, for instance, than Wordsworth will allow. Artifice is on occasion as delightful as simplicity. Wordsworth's theory of language "would take away from the poetical profession something that answers to good breeding in manners, and that keeps it clear from rusticity and the want of universal reception."[4] Before the second edition of *The Feast of the Poets* was ready in 1815, Wordsworth's *Poems* with their preface had appeared. Hunt notes that Wordsworth seemed to have retracted the idea that poetry can exist apart from verse. Wordsworth's beauties outweigh his faults, but Hunt still does not agree with his theory. It is the theory, in fact, which has hindered the development of Wordsworth's genius.

So far, Hunt's analytical criticism has been almost entirely destructive; but it is not hard to determine the broad base of his judgment. It is still very largely that of the eighteenth century man of sensibility. Poetry is a social activity of at least some sophistication and refinement with a wide appeal. Its subjects are the beauties of nature, happy and youthful feelings, hopes, everything that rejoices and calms mankind; and its end is to delight and instruct. It may draw on books and tradition as well as external nature. Verse is of its essence, and in versification the ideal is "that proper mixture of sweetness and strength, of modern finish and ancient variety,—from which Pope and his rhyming facilities have so long withheld us."[5] Poetry makes use of artifice, but

[4] *The Feast of the Poets*, London, 1814, pp. 90-103.
[5] *Ibid.*, p. 38.

rejects the artificial, of formality without formalism; in other words, it commands a variety of artistic effects (including certain valid ones in Dryden and Pope) to be recognized and pointed out as such by the critic of taste and shared with the reader. From this position Hunt moves towards the romantic theory of Wordsworth and Coleridge. The catchword is imagination.

The preface to *Foliage*, a volume of poems printed in 1818, opens with a flourish. "The downfall of the French school of poetry has of late been encreasing in rapidity; its cold and artificial compositions have given way, like so many fantastic figures of snow; and imagination breathes again in a more green and genial time."[6] Pope and his followers are reconsidered in the new light: modern criticism "justly appreciates their wit, terseness, and acuteness," but does not recognize "the real spirit of poetry in their town habits, their narrow sphere of imagination, their knowledge of manners rather than natures," and repudiates their classicism, based on Horace and the Latins rather than "the elementary inspiration of Greece."[7] Poetry, in Hunt's first attempt at a definition, is "a sensativeness [sic] to the beauty of the external world, to the unsophisticated impulses of our nature, and above all, imagination, or the power to see, with verisimilitude, what others do not."[8] The preface to the *Poems* of 1832 contains a fuller description, one part Wordsworth and one part Coleridge.

Poetry, in the most comprehensive application of the term, I take to be the flower of any kind of experience,

---

[6] *Foliage*, London, 1818, p. 9.

[7] *Ibid.*, pp. 11-12. Hunt returns to "the elementary inspiration" of Greece in "What is Poetry?" He is writing of "the natural" in connection with mythological figures. "The Grecian tendency in this respect is safer than the Gothic; nay, more imaginative; for it enables us to imagine *beyond* imagination, and to bring all things healthily round to their only present final ground of sympathy—the human." *Imagination and Fancy*, New York, 1845, p. 14. Hunt's remark is interesting in the light of Ruskin's chapter on true and false griffins in the third volume of *Modern Painters*.

[8] *Ibid.*, p. 13.

rooted in truth, and issuing forth into beauty. All that the critic has a right to demand of it, according to its degree, is, that it should spring out of a real impulse, be consistent in its parts, and shaped into some characteristic harmony of verse.[9]

And in the same preface there is a closer, but still summary, description of the imagination, which has now become "the first quality" of the poet.

> The first quality of a poet is imagination, or that faculty by which the subtlest idea is given us of the nature or condition of any one thing, by illustration from another, or by the inclusion of remote affinities: as when Shakespeare speaks of moonlight *sleeping* on a bank; or of nice customs *curtseying* to great kings (though the reader may, if he pleases, put this under the head of wit, or imagination in miniature).[10]

Hunt, it will be noted, describes the imagination in terms of its modifying power as this had been analyzed by Wordsworth; and the use of "wit" instead of "fancy" in the second example seems to be a conscious attempt to avoid Wordsworth's classification.

Hunt's remarks on poetry up to this time have been more or less casual and illustrative. In 1844, however, he published *Imagination and Fancy*, a volume of selections from a dozen English poets, in which he took occasion to present, along with a considerable amount of practical criticism, his own account of the theory of poetry in the form of "An Essay in Answer to the Question 'What is Poetry?'" The book as a whole is late, mature, and eminently representative of Hunt's critical method at its best. Hunt states in his preface that *Imagination and Fancy* is the first of a projected series to include *Action and Passion, Contemplation, Wit and Humor* (only this last was completed), and intended to illustrate the elements of poetry in distillation. The sections from the poets in *Imagination and Fancy* point "those First Requisites of

[9] *The Poetical Works of Leigh Hunt*, London, 1832, p. viii.
[10] *Ibid.*, p. ix.

their Art" and show "what sort of poetry is to be considered *as poetry of the most poetical kind.*"[11] Hunt's argument accurately betrays the concept of "pure" poetry in his theory, just as the fragments expose his disinterest in "structure" and total effect. In printing the selections Hunt italicizes words, phrases, and passages to which he wants to call attention, marks accent and pause in the versification, and annotates generously from dictionary, editor, commentator, and critic, other poets, French and Italian as well as English, and from his own catholic appreciation. There is precedent for all of this: in the volumes of "Beauties" and "Elegant Extracts" of the eighteenth century; the work of the eighteenth century critics and editors of Spenser, Shakespeare, and Milton; the lectures of Coleridge and Hazlitt; but this relaxed, urbane version of the modern "close reading" is Hunt's peculiar forte, and in its constant awareness of specific poetic effects, particularly formal effects, sets Hunt off sharply from most of the Early Victorian critics.

The essay opens with a full dress definition of poetry.

> Poetry, strictly and artistically so called, that is to say, considered not merely as poetic feeling, which is more or less shared by all the world, but as the operation of that feeling, such as we see it in the poet's book, is the utterance of a passion for truth, beauty and power, embodying and illustrating its conceptions by imagination and fancy, and modulating its language on the principle of variety in uniformity. Its means are whatever the universe contains; and its ends, pleasure and exaltation. Poetry stands between nature and convention, keeping alive among us the enjoyment of the external and spiritual world.

Characteristically, Hunt distinguishes at once between "poetry" and "poem" (Coleridge's terms), and wastes no time on "the poetical." The medium, imagery and rhythm, is inte-

[11] *Imagination and Fancy; or Selections from the English Poets, Illustrative of those First Requisites of their Art; with Markings of the Best Passages, Critical Notices of the Writers, and an Essay in Answer to the Question "What is Poetry?,"* New York, 1845. All quotations are from this edition.

gral. "Fancy" replaces "wit," which is demoted to pair with "humor," and "exaltation" is introduced (a good substitute, weighted towards delight), for the more usual, flatly moral, end of contemporary theory. Passion, "an ardent subjection of one's self to emotion," is the element of personal experience; truth (Hunt means "truth of feeling"), the moral element;[12] beauty, "the loveliest form of pleasure," the element of delight in poetry. Parallels for all of these can be found in Wordsworth; the notion of power, however, seems to have come from Hazlitt.[13] Power is "impression triumphant, whether over the poet, as desired by himself [Hunt is no disciple of the Great Unconscious], or over the reader, as affected by the poet." Is this the element of effective expression?

The content of poetry is thus the poet's impressions as determined by consideration of truth, beauty, and power, and its form is determined by the imagination and fancy, as they embody and illustrate impressions, and by the principle of perfection, as it requires "modulation" to "make difficulty itself become part of its facility and joy," and to exploit fully the possibilities of both unity and variety. Hunt states at once that the "quickest and subtlest test" of the essence of poetry is in expression, and he adds a list, apparently modeled on Wordsworth's list in the Preface of 1815, of the qualities necessary for the poet: thought, feeling, expression, imagination, action, character, and continuity.

[12] Taste, according to Hunt, is a better criterion of truth than "the abstract figment called judgment," which "does but throw you into guesses and doubts." "Hence the conceits that astonish us in the gravest, and even subtlest thinkers, whose taste is not proportionate to their mental perceptions; men like Donne, for instance; who, apart from accidental personal impressions, seem to look at nothing as it really is, but only as to what may be thought of it. Hence, on the other hand, the delightfulness of those poets who never violate truth of feeling, whether in things real or imaginary; who are always consistent with their object and its requirements; and who run the great round of nature, not to perplex and be perplexed, but to make themselves and us happy."

[13] "The poetical impression of any object is that uneasy, exquisite sense of beauty or power that cannot be contained within itself." *Selected Essays of William Hazlitt*, edited by G. Keynes, London, 1934, "On Poetry in General," p. 389.

Whoever has all of these in the highest degree is the greatest poet. It will be noticed that there is no pair for the characteristically Wordsworthian "observation" and "description," which Hunt, skeptical of the ability to perceive objects apart from feeling,[14] shifts to the faculty of imagination (he also disagreed with Wordsworth in insisting that the mere presentation of images of external objects to the mind was a form, the lowest form, of imagination). There is no pair again for Wordsworth's "judgment," possibly another implied criticism of the Preface. In any event, elsewhere in the essay Hunt writes,

> An idle distinction has been made between taste and judgment. Taste is the very maker of judgment. Put an artificial fruit in your mouth, or only handle it, and you will soon perceive the difference between judging from taste or tact, and judging from the abstract figment called judgment. The latter does but throw you into guesses and doubts.

Here (and in other places) Hunt reveals himself as a sensationalist, and it is assumed that feeling performs the functions of Wordsworth's judgment.[15] Expression and continuity are the two free terms in Hunt's catalogue, and it is notable that both have something to do with form.

In one paragraph Hunt disposes of the customary discussion of painting and music. "Poetry includes whatsoever of painting can be made visible to the mind's eye, and whatsoever of music can be conveyed by sound and proportion without singing or instrumentation." But poetry is more effective than painting and music in "suggestiveness, range,

[14] "What is meant by facts totally divested of the feelings with which they are regarded, or lights in which they are seen?" Hunt wrote in the margin of *Modern Painters*. Quoted in an unpublished thesis on *Leigh Hunt's Theory of Poetry* by V. E. Lichtenstein, University of Iowa, 1939, p. 16. Here is evidence that Hunt read Ruskin; Ruskin in the second volume of *Modern Painters* quotes from Hunt.

[15] "But in poetry, feeling and imagination are necessary to the perception and presentation even of matters of fact. They, and they only, see what is proper to be told, and what to be kept back; what is pertinent, affecting, and essential." "What is Poetry?"

and intellectual wealth," while, on the other hand, painting and music include all those elements of poetry which can be "expressed and heightened by the visible and melodious." Hunt elaborates somewhat on painting and poetry in a brief introduction to a set of "portraits" from Spenser in the body of the book. Each portrait is fancifully provided with a suitable painter.

It has been a whim of late years with some transcendental critics, in the excess of the reaction of what may be called spiritual poetry against material, to deny utterly the old family relationship between poetry and painting.

Erasmus Darwin's "absurd" pronouncement that nothing is poetry which cannot be painted has been taken as license for the contrary extreme. The method of poetry is not the method of painting.

The finest idea the poet gives you of anything is by what may be called sleight of mind, striking it without particular description on the mind of the reader, feeling and all, moral as well as physical, as a face is struck on a mirror.

To exclude the visible in poetry is to reject half the poems in existence.[16]

Hunt goes directly to Wordsworth for his argument on poetry and science.

Poetry begins where matter of fact or of science ceases to be merely such, and to exhibit a further truth; that is to say, the connexion it has with the world of emotion; and its power to produce imaginative pleasure. Inquiring of a gardener, for instance, what flower it is that we see yonder, he answers, "a lily." This is matter of fact. The botanist pronounces it to be of the order of "Hexandria Monogynia." This is matter of science. It is the "lady" of the garden, says Spenser; and here we begin to have a poetical sense of its fairness and grace. It is

[16] *Op. cit.*, p. 72.

1 0 1

The plant and flower of *light*,

says Ben Jonson; and poetry then shows us the beauty of the flower in all its mystery and splendour.

For Hunt, the sensationalist, feeling or perception is "the only final proof" of truth, even the truth of science, and therefore the mere existence of such imaginative perceptions as Jonson's, the "consent and delight of poetic readers," is evidence enough of their truth. Furthermore, and now Hunt is using the imagination as an instrument of perception itself, the "remotest imaginations" of the poet may have the "closest connexion" with matter of fact, might always have, "if the subtlety of our perceptions were a match for the causes of them."

> Consider this image of Ben Jonson's—of a lily being the flower of light. Light, undecomposed, is white; and as the lily is white, and light is white, and whiteness itself is nothing *but* light, the two things, so far, are not merely similar, but identical.

Hunt quotes Bacon, "the same feet of Nature" tread "in different paths," and comes to the conclusion that there may be poetry in the plainest fact. He will straddle both the "realist" and "projectionist" positions. "Nay, the simplest truth is often so beautiful and impressive of itself" that the greatest art can do no more than present it without comment. Homer, Chaucer, the ballads, Shakespeare in *Lear*, are full of such "sufficing passages of nature."[17]

Leigh Hunt's analysis of imagination and fancy is chiefly distinguished by the choice of examples with which it is illustrated. In framing it he had in mind rather a set of touchstones to direct the reader's appreciation than "a torch of

[17] "Even the exquisite pathos of Lear, at the end of that mighty play, when his frenzy quits him, under the influence of Cordelia's care ('Pray do not mock me,' &c.), cannot be called essentially poetical, though they are to us more touching than the grandest poetry. They are simple and unimaginative, and purely pathetic, as the situation of Lear then required that they should be." B. W. Procter, *Essays and Tales in Prose by Barry Cornwall*, Boston, 1853, "On English Poetry" (1825), p. 142.

guidance to the philosophical critic"; and his method, "from the different effects to conclude their diversity in kind," is closer to that of Wordsworth than to the "tergiversations" of Coleridge. Imagination and fancy are the means by which the poet embodies and illustrates his conceptions and impressions. Imagination operates in "images of the objects of which [poetry] treats, and other images brought in to throw light on those objects, in order that it may enjoy and impart the feeling of their truth in its utmost conviction and affluence." Fancy is "a lighter play of imagination, or the feeling of analogy coming short of seriousness, in order that [poetry] may laugh with what it loves, and show us how it can decorate it with fairy ornament." Imagination

> is all feeling; the feeling of the subtlest and most affecting analogies; the perception of sympathies in the natures of things, or in their popular attributes. Fancy is sporting with their resemblance, real or supposed, and with airy and fantastical resemblances.

Hunt complains that the terms imagination and fancy are not completely adequate; imagination is loaded with suggestions of the solid, material "image," and while fancy means "spiritual image," it is rarely free from "visibility which is one of the highest privileges of imagination."

Although Hunt's language lacks something of philosophical precision, it is possible to distinguish at least two functions of the imagination. It presents images to the mind, single or in combination (a function rejected by both Wordsworth and Coleridge), and as a kind of intuition, it discovers subtle analogies and sympathies between objects, analogies which are either real or assumed to be real. Into one or the other of these categories all seven of the "kinds and degrees" of imagination which Hunt describes can be put. It will be noted that he does not use the words creative or modifying, key terms for both Coleridge and Wordsworth, in connection with either imagination or fancy, but rather borrows or invents a vocabulary of his own.

The first two "kinds" of imagination are the product of the

image-making faculty; the one presents to the mind "any object or circumstance in every-day life," the other, "real, but not every-day circumstances" (King Alfred tending the loaves); both seem to be simple memory-images. The fourth kind of imagination is the neoclassical "invention" of non-existent creatures such as the hippogriff, and the third is a composite of two and four, by which "character and events directly imitated from real life" are combined with "imitative realities of its own invention" to make "natural fiction," such as the probable parts of the histories of Priam and Macbeth. Classes five, six, and seven, roughly correspond to Wordsworth's two classes of modifying and creative imagination; they are all classes of comparison illustrating different uses of metaphor. The imagination of class five gives variety to the single image by crossing it with another (Byron's "*starry* Galileo"; Milton's "*sultry* horn"). The imagination of class six does just the reverse; it gives unity to variety, "makes a variety of circumstances take color from one, like nature seen with jaundiced or glad eyes, or under the influence of storm or sunshine."[18] Hunt's examples are "pathetic fallacies" (the term is Ruskin's, not Hunt's), and "the witch element" in Macbeth. Class seven, in which the imagination, "by a single expression, apparently of the vaguest kind, not only meets but surpasses in its effect the extremest force of the most particular description," is perhaps a sub-variety of class six, for it seems to have been suggested by a comment of Wordsworth on a passage illustrating the unifying force of imagination in which variety of impression is "merged" in the splendor of an "indefinite abstraction."[19] It is distinguished from class six in that the analogies and affinities which it perceives are more "spiritual" (Coleridge's "*And lay down in her loveliness*": that "most lovely inclusion of physical beauty in moral").

[18] Coleridge had written of "the sudden charm, which accidents of light and shade, which moonlight or sunset diffused over a known and familiar landscape." *Biographia Literaria*, edited by J. Shawcross, Oxford, 1917, ii, 3.

[19] *Wordsworth's Literary Criticism*, edited by N. C. Smith, London, 1905, "Preface to Poems," p. 161.

Hunt follows Wordsworth at a distance again in his ac-
count of fancy. He recognizes no such metaphysical distinc-
tion from imagination as that of Coleridge, and, again, the
fancy has no creative power. Fancy is "the younger sister of
Imagination," without imagination's weight of thought and
feeling. It "sports with resemblances," real or supposed, be-
tween objects and situations, and it indulges in "airy and
fanciful creations" (creations *usage de couturier*). More tech-
nically, it is "a combination of images not in their nature
connected, or brought together by the feeling, but by the
will and pleasure," and it has just enough "hold of analogy
to betray it into the hands of its smiling subjector." Fancy
is marked by caprice, one image "capriciously suggested by
another, and but half connected with the subject of dis-
course"; it is toying, childlike, sportive, quaint, light, showy,
"the poetical part of wit" (which brings "antipathies together"
and makes them "strike light on absurdity"). Thus, by Hunt's
definition, fancy belongs to comedy, while imagination be-
longs to the serious or tragic muse. But fancy can coexist
with imagination, and is found with it in all the greatest
poets. Spenser, for instance, has great imagination, but his
poetry is prevailingly fanciful; Milton, who has both, is pre-
dominantly imaginative. Shakespeare alone combines the
two in equal measure of greatness.

Imagination, then, for Hunt, is a kind of cognitive feeling.
As sense perception on the lowest level it presents images
to the mind; in its middle ranges it functions as a kind of
intuition, discovering analogical relationships between ob-
jects; and in its highest power it functions as a kind of judg-
ment: feeling and imagination, "they only, see what is proper
to be told, and what to be kept back; what is pertinent,
affecting, and essential." Hunt is by no means clear on any
of these points, and hard and fast distinctions should be made
only with caution. He does say plainly that metaphor is "the
common coin of discourse." Furthermore, it is perhaps signif-
icant that he makes no use of his seven types of imagination
in his practical criticism, which usually takes this form:

"The owl, for all his feathers, was a-cold."—Could he have selected an image more warm and comfortable in itself, and, therefore, better contradicted by the season? We feel the plump, feathery bird, in his nook, shivering in spite of his natural household warmth, and staring out at the strange weather. The hare cringing through the chill grass is very piteous, and the "silent flock" very patient; and how quiet and gentle, as well as wintry, are all these circumstances, and fit to open a quiet and gentle poem! The breath of the pilgrim, likened to "pious incense," completes them, and is a simile in admirable "keeping," as the painters call it; that is to say, is thoroughly harmonious with itself and all that is going on. The breath of the pilgrim is visible, so is that of a censer; the censer, after its fashion, may be said to pray; and its breath, like the pilgrim's, ascends to heaven.[20]

In *Wit and Humour*, where there is a comparable classification, Hunt states that the "mode, or form, is comparatively of no consequence, provided it give no trouble to the apprehension."[21] In the same way, the seven types are probably window dressing. One incidental point is worth noting. The perceptive or intuitive function of the imagination in Hunt's description seems to have furnished Ruskin with the clue for his own "penetrative" imagination.

Behind a loose and often vague vocabulary Hunt's observations on verse are keen and to the point. He had Coleridge in front of him, of course, and by implication at least, Wordsworth as a whipping boy. What Hunt takes to be an organic relationship between verse and poetry is defended in terms both of aesthetic principle and poetic effect, and once again he salts his argument liberally with analysis of particular effects. He begins with "the principle of Variety in Uniformity," according to which, contrary to Wordsworth, fitness or unfitness for "metrical excitement" distinguishes the poetic from the prosaic "subject," and according to which,

[20] *Imagination and Fancy*, p. 244.
[21] *Wit and Humour*, London, 1846, p. 10.

as the principle of "perfection," in the matter of form, the poetic impulse must express itself through technical mastery of the medium. Metrical organization, "the answer of form" to the poet's "spirit," is necessarily conditioned by the inner laws of proportion which are the laws of beauty itself, in their striving towards perfection of expression. Furthermore, metrical organization represents the conscious acceptance by the poet of the conditions of his medium in all their difficulty.

> Verse is no dominator over the poet, except inasmuch as the bond is reciprocal, and the poet dominates over the verse. They are lovers playfully challenging each other's rule, and delighted equally to rule and to obey. Verse is the final proof to the poet that his mastery over his art is complete.

Hunt notes that Hazlitt, in advocating the prose poetry of *Ossian*, "judiciously abstained from saying anything about the form," and one might add that, in general, the exponents of the "unconscious" rarely, if ever, tackle the problem of meter. Hunt concludes quite flatly that every poet "is a versifier; every fine poet an excellent one."

For his description of the effects of versification, Hunt uses the terms "strength, sweetness, straightforwardness, unsuperfluousness, variety, and oneness." Most of these are obvious enough. Strength is the "muscle" of verse, and is a matter of "the number and force" of accents; sweetness, of "smooth progression between variety and sameness, and a voluptuous sense of the continuous,—'linked sweetness long drawn out'" (it also has something to do with vowel and consonant harmony). Straightforwardness is the arrangement of words in their natural order (Dryden provides a successful example); but Hunt is careful to point out that there is a legitimate use of inversion: when the poet "is superior to it." Hunt is good on the subject of unsuperfluousness, which is really, as he says, a matter of style. Every word not justified by sheer "animal spirits" or the "genius of luxury" (Spenser) which can be taken out of a poem is

107

"a damage; and many such are death." Here is a concern with the poem, as poem, rare in Early Victorian criticism. He warns the neophyte:

> Young writers should bear in mind, that even some of the very best materials for poetry are not poetry built, and that the smallest marble shrine, of exquisite workmanship, outvalues all that architect ever chipped away. Whatever can be dispensed with is rubbish.

The remark is set in a context which shows that it is aimed against the more formless of the romantic "excogitations" in verse. Variety is simply the exploitation of all the possibilities of tone and rhythm, and is ultimately a matter of sensibility, imagination, genius, as they assimilate sound to sense, music to feeling. It is under this head that Hunt suggests a "time" theory as the true answer to the problem of English metrics.

> The same time and quantity which are occasioned by the spiritual part of this secret, thus become its formal ones,—not feet and syllables, long and short, iambics or trochees; which are the reduction of it to its *less* than dry bones. You might get, for instance, not only ten and eleven, but thirteen or fourteen syllables into a rhyming, as well as blank, heroical verse, if time and the feeling permitted; and in irregular measure this is often done; just as musicians put twenty notes in a bar instead of two, quavers instead of minims, according as the feeling they are expressing impels them to fill up the time with short and hurried notes, or with long.

English versification would be more "numerous" if the theorists had not presented the poet with an either-or choice between syllabic and quantitative metrics. Coleridge's "Christabel" is, of course, behind Hunt's argument; Hunt quotes several stanzas, and is generous in his praise. The poem exemplifies not only variety at its subtlest and most winning but "oneness" as well. Oneness is "consistency, in general impression, metrical and moral," or as Hunt puts it in his comment on "Christabel," the feeling that *the whole is one and of the same character*, the single and sweet unconsciousness of the heroine making all the rest seem more conscious, and ghastly, and expectant. It is thus that *versification itself becomes part of the sentiment of a poem*, and vindicates the pains that have been taken to show its importance." Hunt closes his remarks on versification with a defense of rhyme as "a sustainment for the enthusiasm, and a demand to enjoy."

The last few paragraphs of the essay are a plea for a catholic enjoyment of poetry. He tells the young reader to read attentively, and to love truth and beauty (after having brought them virtually together in his analysis of versification, Hunt separates them again) in which the greatness of poets is grounded. The reader will also love all things in nature, large and small, which interest the poet, even "the steam-engine itself, thundering and fuming along like a magic horse." Hunt ranks "the kinds" for his beginners, the epic first, then the dramatic, lyric, contemplative, satirical, didactic, epigrammatic; but he warns them that "the first poet of an inferior class may be superior to followers in the train of a higher one."[22] He returns to the qualities of the poet; repeats once more that "thought by itself makes no poet at all"; and encourages the reader to rely on his own response in feeling to poetry, a response that must be as wide as the multifold truths of poetry themselves, if he is not to be wanting in "complexional fitness" for the enjoyment of literature.

> Exclusiveness of liking for this or that mode of truth, only shows, either that a reader's perceptions are limited, or that he would sacrifice truth itself to his favorite form of it.

Hunt routs the theory of poetry as make-believe; the poet "will get no good by proposing to be 'in earnest at the

[22] Unlike Keble and Carlyle (and the proponents of original genius in general), Hunt is not so sure Homer and Shakespeare could have exchanged roles: "it is to be doubted whether even Shakespeare could have told a story like Homer, owing to that incessant activity and superfoetation of thought, a little less of which might be occasionally desired even in his plays."

moment'."" His earnestness must be innate and habitual (Carlyle!). Poetry is its own reward, as both Coleridge and Shelley had witnessed; and Hunt quotes with approval Shelley's brilliant observation on the morality of poetry:

A man, to be greatly good, must imagine intensely and comprehensively; he must put himself in the place of another, and of many others: the pains and pleasures of his species must become his own. The great instrument of moral good is imagination; and poetry administers to the effect by acting upon the cause.

The proponents of "useful knowledge" should be instructed that the superiority of the poet is in the very power of imagination which undervalues no one and no thing.

Leigh Hunt must suffer from comparison with Wordsworth and Coleridge; he lacked Coleridge's intellectual powers and Wordsworth's psychological ones; but in comparison with his Early Victorian peers his theory of poetry is quietly satisfying. The theory in its philosophical aspect is weak in its imprecision of key terms, although it makes a certain lay sense, and is one of the few in the period to insist on the claims of the medium. The tendency towards a concept of "pure poetry," however, leads Hunt into concern for isolated formal effects to the neglect of the larger structure of the poem as a whole. He has little to add to the popular romantic discussion of imagination and fancy, but his brief remarks on a "time" theory of English metrics stand out in a dreary waste of muddled thinking on that subject. Hunt is at his best in reconfirming the conscious artistry of the poet, and in pointing out particular technical successes in the poets whom he takes in hand. As a careful and sensitive reader of poetry who never sacrificed delight in its many shapes to high seriousness, Hunt deserves not the least place in Victoria's critics' row.

7. Robert Browning

Introductory Essay. 1852

ROBERT BROWNING's unique venture into prose criticism was his introduction to the spurious Shelley letters published by Edward Moxon in 1852. "I have just done the little thing I told you of—" he wrote to Carlyle from Paris in October 1851, "a mere Preface to some new letters of Shelley: not admitting of much workmanship of any kind, if I have it to give. But I have put down a few thoughts that presented themselves—one or two, in respect of opinions of your own (I mean, that I was thinking of those opinions while I wrote)."[1] Carlyle liked the essay "extremely well" in a letter of the following March, "a solid, well-wrought, massive, manful bit of discourse." He admired its "grave expressiveness of style" in spite of its being "a *little* too elaborate here and there";[2] and he asked for more of the same kind. The letters, naturally (and fortunately for Browning), contained nothing new, and were quickly exposed and suppressed; but the very lack of biographical interest pushed Browning, willing or unwilling, into a general discussion of the relation of biography to the poet and his work, and into a general defense of Shelley's character and writing. The introductory essay, as it happened, not only escaped the discredit which covered the letters, but acquired the significance of broad critical statement.

One of Carlyle's ideas which Browning certainly had in mind while writing his essay was the idea of the original genius as philosopher-poet; as a matter of fact, however, Browning's aesthetic as a whole differs only slightly, if at all, from Carlyle's: a version of the transcendental or idealistic theory of Kant and the post-Kantians in Germany. The artist is a leader in the search for divine knowledge. The arts are so many mediators between the soul and the infinite. The materials of art are intuitions, and its methods, for Browning

---

[1] *Letters of Robert Browning Collected by Thomas J. Wise*, edited by T. L. Hood, London, 1933, p. 36.
[2] *Ibid.*, p. 367.

in any case, probation, aspiration, and progress. Since the end of art is Truth (with a capital T), and since this Truth must be communicated through the relatively distorting medium of human nature, the theory, as has already been pointed out in Carlyle, attracts unusual interest to the personality, and especially to the morality, of the artist. The artist's morality witnesses the truth of his intuitions, is the condition and the content of his intuitions, and therefore his art is nothing more than a reflection, a poor reflection because refracted through material media, words, paint, stone, of his personality. Poems and paintings become part of the man, and biography, which is fascinating enough, becomes the Queen of the Sciences.[3] Browning stops a little short of this position; after all, he was a poet, albeit the philosopher-poet himself at the end, and there was always Shakespeare. Thus, in elaborating the relation between poetry and biography Browning distinguishes between two types of the original genius as poet, the "objective" and "subjective."

A similiar distinction had already been made in German criticism by Schiller. In his essay "On Naive and Sentimental Poetry" Schiller divided poets into two classes in accord with their attitude towards nature: the "naive" poet ap-

---

[3] F. J. Furnivall, in his preface to a reprint of the "Introductory Essay," *Browning Society Papers, No. 1*, London, 1881, writes of his interest in the Essay, "The interest lay in the fact, that Browning's 'utterances' here are *his*, and not those of any one of the 'so many imaginary persons' behind whom he insists on so often hiding himself, and whose necks I, for one, should continually like to wring, whose bodies I would fain kick out of the way, in order to get face to face with the poet himself, and hear his own voice speaking his own thoughts, man to man, soul to soul. Straight speaking, straight hitting, suit me best." There is a note to these remarks. "The end of *The Ring and the Book* gives the defence of maskt advances and flank movements:

> Art may tell a truth
> Obliquely, so the thing shall breed the thought,
> Nor wrong the thought, missing the mediate word.

But if the reader is thick-headed, or can't spare time to study and think a poem out, should not a poet give him a helping hand by a 'mediate word'?"

proaches nature directly, the "sentimental" poet, at second hand. The classification was primarily a historical one since classical poetry was predominantly naive, and modern romantic poetry sentimental; but certain of the moderns, notably Shakespeare and Goethe, were naive. Schiller makes his point in an account of his early difficulties in appreciating Shakespeare.

> Misled by my acquaintance with recent poetry so as in every work to look first for *the poet*, to meet him heart to heart, and to reflect with him upon his object, in short to look at the object only as it is reflected in the subject, I found it intolerable that here the poet never showed himself and would never let me question him.[4]

The naive poet is Browning's objective (or realistic) poet, and the sentimental poet is his subjective or idealistic poet, a contrast admirably exampled in Shakespeare and Shelley; but in Browning's estimation the function of the subjective poet, the original genius *par excellence*, if it does not completely transcend that of the objective poet, is far higher than anything suggested by Schiller's notion of the sentimental.

The terms objective and subjective had also been used in literary criticism before 1852. Browning implies that they are current, referring to the "objective poet, as the phrase now goes," and "the subjective poet of modern classification." If Coleridge's use in the *Biographia Literaria* was somewhat remote, there is closer evidence in two articles by Aubrey De Vere in the *Edinburgh Review* for 1849, which Browning may very well have seen. In the first of these articles, "Taylor's *Eve of the Conquest*," De Vere anticipates Browning's distinction strikingly.

> The highest poetry rests upon a right adjustment of contending claims. Some persons are advocates of the sensuous, and others of what has latterly been called the subjective; but poetry of the first order reconciles both demands,—being of all things the most intellectual in its

[4] Bernard Bosanquet, *A History of Aesthetic*, London, 1934, p. 299.

method and scope, while in its form and imagery it is the largest representation of visible things.[5]

This argument is developed in the second article on "Tennyson's *Princess*" by a split of the English poets into two classes, "national" and "ideal"; Shakespeare on the one hand, and Keats and Shelley on the other, represent the two schools.

It does not depend on the circumstances of the age alone whether the poet find his materials in the circle of surrounding things, or seek them elsewhere: this will in the main be determined by the constitution of his own moral nature, and the preponderance in it of a vivid sympathy with reality on the one hand, or, on the other, of an ardent aspiration after the ideal. In either case the imagination will lend to him its high mediating powers; in the former interpreting the outer world to him, in the latter interpreting him to his fellow men.[6]

If it is impossible to know whether Browning read these articles in the *Edinburgh*, it is quite certain that he saw an appreciation of his own poetry, written by his friend Milsand, and published in the *Revue des Deux Mondes* in August 1851, just before he began work on the Shelley essay. Some of Milsand's remarks are to the point. The ancients, he says, saw objects in isolation as forms and appearances. Browning's poetry is a new human genre which can distinguish not only forms and facts but relations and processes. This faculty of seizing relations is at the service of his imagination; this is Browning's originality.

M. Browning, au contraire, est de la famille de Milton plutôt que des Shakespeares. Ses excursions sont des voyages d'esprit; ses facultés semblent se dépenser en

[5] *The Edinburgh Review*, LXXXIX, 1849, p. 380.
[6] *Ibid.*, XC. 1849, p. 409. The moral personality is related to poetical genius in such a way that it gives rise to two classes of poets, "that class whose poetry exhibits an evident connexion with the personal character and history of the poet; and that class whose poetry exhibits no such connexion. Dante and Byron are examples of the former; Shakespeare and Goethe of the latter." *The British Quarterly Review*, I, 1845, p. 574.

dedans, au fond de son intelligence . . . Chez lui, en un mot, il y a deux êtres: il y a un penseur qui descend sur la terre pour connaître . . . puis il y a un poète qui regarde le caractère déjà conçu.[7]

Browning has not made his mark as a poet by continuing and perfecting traditional materials, but by unveiling a corner of the unknown.

The basic elements of Browning's theory of the poet objective and subjective are contained in essence in De Vere and Milsand. It would be a mistake, however, to infer that Browning owed anything to either of them beyond, perhaps, a suggestion here and there, for he himself had already made the fundamental distinction in verse at least as far back as *Paracelsus* and *Sordello*. In *Sordello* two kinds of poet are described. The first, in the search for ordered beauty, invest nature with the motion of their own minds, and eventually come to find God in the beautiful combinations of "earthly forms" (the later objective poets). The second, on the other hand, believe that every revelation of beauty "is born a twin With a distinctest consciousness within." The Soul of these poets reaches out to the divine "Idea."

> Laugh thou at envious fate,
> Who, from earth's simplest combination stampt
> With individuality—uncrampt
> By living its faint elemental life,
> Dost soar to heaven's complexest essence . . .[8]

With it in its ascent the soul carries the "more bounded wills" of all men. These are the subjective poets, whose function, further developed in the essay on Shelley, is to lift men to the knowledge of divine truth. The distinction in aim

[7] *Revue des Deux Mondes*, XI, Parte 2, 1851, p. 676. "Chacun son rôle: aux uns de centraliser toutes les émotions humaines, aux autres de centraliser toutes nos conceptions." p. 688. Milsand accuses Browning of an excess of "spiritualisme."

[8] *The Complete Poetic and Dramatic Works of Robert Browning*, Cambridge Edition, New York, 1895, p. 79. Cf. also, *Paracelsus*, pp. 23-24; *Sordello*, pp. 115ff.; *Pippa Passes*, p. 142; *Transcendentalism*, pp. 335-36; and *Fra Lippo Lippi, Andrea del Sarto*, and *Abt Vogler*.

between the two kinds of poet is the cause of a correspond-
ing distinction in the kind of art each class will produce.
The poetry of the objective poet takes the form of represen-
tation, and its literary medium, the drama or the epic; that
of the subjective poet, of expression, and its medium, the
lyric. Browning's "invention" of the dramatic lyric was, in
fact, the result of his effort to unite representation and ex-
pression, to incorporate both the real and the ideal in a
single poetic form.

> So write a book shall mean beyond the facts,
> Suffice the eye and save the soul beside.[9]

The substantive ideas of the essay on Shelley can thus be
found in Carlyle, in the periodical criticism of the time, and
in certain speculative passages in Browning's own poetry.
These can be summed up briefly as the philosophy of "real-
idealism," and an aesthetic in which the chief part is played
by the original genius, and in which the formal aspects of
art are subordinated to the expression of ultimate truths.
A dual potentiality in the original genius is the basis for a
distinction between objective and subjective poets, and a
historical theory of their alternation and rise in terms of
the concept of progress. The simplicity of the elements of
Browning's theory is somewhat obscured by the involuted,
highly metaphorical style of the essay, which wraps them
in an implausibly gorgeous quilt. The structure of the essay
is clear enough; there are three sections: one on the rela-
tion of biography and poetry; one on the aims and functions
of the artist, with particular reference to the use of biogra-
phy in evaluating the subjective poet; and a final section
which attempts to habilitate Shelley's moral reputation. The
argument here will confine itself largely to the first two
sections of the essay as Browning's contribution to Early
Victorian poetic theory.

Browning distinguishes two aims of the poetic genius,
which in turn imply two types of the poetic mind. As the
poet endeavors to reproduce the external world of natural

[9] *Ibid., The Ring and the Book,* p. 601.

phenomena and human thought and action, with immediate reference to "the common eye and apprehension of his fellow men," he may be called an "objective poet." On the other hand, as the poet utters the intuitions of his own soul, not in reference to men, but to the absolute truth which is God, he may be called a "subjective poet."[10] There is a distinction in the matter, a latent distinction in the manner, and a very important distinction in proximate end (for the objective poet, effective communication).[11]

The objective poet has a double gift, an insight (Carlyle!) into nature keener than that of the average man, and a sympathy with the limitations of the average mind. He also has a double function, to point out the value of external objects and actions to the imperceptive, and to provide the perceptive with maps for their own exploration of the "reality" which lies behind objects and events, spiritual Baedekers of fresh country, and points of reference for the familiar. This man is the ποιητης, "the fashioner." He shapes his insights to conform to the understanding of the limited intelligence, "careful to supply it with no other materials than it can combine into an intelligible whole" (a suggestion of arrogance, of "writing-down," here?); and the works of art he produces, his poetry, will be "substantive, projected from himself and distinct." The poet himself, in other words, gives no explanation of the origin, development, or meaning to him of his insight; the reader is presented with the work, to make of it (a little impatiently) what he can.

The biography of such a poet—of Shakespeare, for instance—is coveted. Browning wants to know a great many things about him, the process by which he gathered and arranged his materials, his possible difficulties, the origin of his impulse, the furnishings of all the rooms, light and

[10] *Letters of Percy Bysshe Shelley. With an Introductory Essay, by Robert Browning*, London, 1852. Quotations are from this edition.

[11] G. H. Lewes reviewed the Shelley letters in *The Westminster Review*, LVII, 1852. He interprets objective and subjective (or, as he would prefer, impersonal and personal) to mean that in one case the poet has contrived to express himself, in the other he has only expressed a mood. p. 506.

dark, of his psyche; but in the end, the biography of the objective poet can be dispensed with. "The man passes, the work remains." The work he has made is complete in itself; it is distinct from the personality of the poet, and can be interpreted apart from the facts of the poet's life.[12]

In contrast, the subjective poet is a "seer" rather than a fashioner. Both poets see, but whereas the objective poet looks at, the subjective poet, perhaps, looks around or looks through; and, more important, he is less interested than the objective poet in adapting his visions to a limited human understanding. He is striving to apprehend and to express absolute truth.

> Not what man sees, but what God sees—the *Ideas* of Plato, seeds of creation lying burningly on the Divine Hand—it is toward these that he struggles. Not with the combination of humanity in action, but with the primal elements of humanity he has to do; and he digs where he stands,—preferring to seek them in his own soul as the nearest reflex of that absolute Mind, according to the intuitions of which he desires to perceive and speak.

This man is less interested in the sensuous patterns of things than in their essence and laws, and what he produces is "less a work than an effluence," an effluence which it is hard to apprehend apart from the personality of the poet, since it is "the very radiance and aroma of his personality, projected from it but not separated." At its best Browning's statement justifies the precarious position of the genuine mystic and his partial speech; at its worst, of course, it rationalizes imperfected communication. In any case, if the statement is taken as true, it is plain that we can only know the poetry as it is studied in close connection with the poet's biography, and thus the biographical method becomes integral to the criticism of any subjective poet.

[12] "Shakespeare, in like manner, in whose works we can detect no subjective influence produced by his own mind, and who seems to range like the universal sun over the provinces of emotion, enlightening all alike, produces the same deep impression on the learned and the unlearned." George Moir, *Treatises on Poetry, Modern Romance, and Rhetoric*, Edinburgh, 1839, p. 21.

The basis of distinction between his two types of poet, Browning repeats, is not so much in any essential difference in their faculties or in their materials, as it is in the adaptability of their materials to their purposes. Thus the objective poet, whose aim it is to appeal to "the aggregate human mind," will choose for his subject matter human actions, and his poetry will naturally take dramatic form; while the subjective poet, whose aim is to express the intuitions of the absolute which he finds more or less developed in his own personality, will choose as his subject matter "those external scenic appearances which strike out most abundantly and uninterruptedly his inner light and power" (as Wordsworth did, for example?).[13] Presumably this subject matter will find its proper art form in lyric and reflective poetry. The two modes of the poetic activity, Browning insists, are equally valid. "If the subjective might seem to be the ultimate requirement of every age, the objective, in the strictest state, must still retain its original value." We must always start from the real world and come back to it as the raw material of our perceptions no matter how many and how refined the individual insights of it we have. As a matter of fact, in most poets both objective and subjective elements exist side by side; occasionally one or the other will predominate in a man, but there is no poet purely objective or subjective. There is no reason, however, why a single poet should not produce perfect works of both kinds in succession. Undoubtedly, here, Browning had in mind his own efforts in the substantive drama and in the spiritual epic.

The appearance of these two kinds of poets alternately in the history of civilization Browning interprets in the light of his concept of progress.

[13] For illustration of the defects of either poet Browning draws on painting. They are plain "when subsidiarily to the human interest of his work his occasional illustrations from scenic nature are introduced as in the earlier works of the originative painters—men and women filling the foreground with consummate mastery, while mountain, grove and rivulet show like an anticipatory revenge on that succeeding race of landscape-painters whose 'figures' disturb the perfection of their earth and sky." This passage should be read in connection with the chapters on classical, medieval, and modern landscape in the third volume of *Modern Painters.*

There is a time when the general eye has, so to speak, absorbed its fill of the phenomena around it, whether spiritual or material, and desires rather to learn the exacter significance of what it possesses, than to receive any augmentation of what is possessed. Then is the opportunity for the poet of loftier vision, to lift up his fellows, with their half-apprehensions, up to his own sphere, by intensifying the import of details and rounding the universal meaning.

Such was Homer, the subjective poet (!); his work lasts a long time. It is imitated and enlarged upon, until one day, "unawares," the world realizes that the substance and meaning of the vision are gone, and it is subsisting on shadow, sentiment, tradition, and convention.

Then is the imperative call for the appearance of another sort of poet, who shall at once replace this intellectual rumination of food swallowed long ago, by a supply of the fresh and living swathe; getting at new substance by breaking up the assumed wholes into parts of independent and unclassed value, careless of the unknown laws for recombining them (it will be the business of yet another poet to suggest those hereafter), prodigal of objects for men's outer and not inner sight, shaping for their uses a new and different creation from the last, which it displaces by the right of life over death. . .

One wonders if this is Shakespeare; Browning does not say. The movement is not a cyclical one, however, for each new vision raises men one degree higher on "the mighty ladder" (a neoplatonic ladder?) toward the eternal and absolute. In this theory, has "the poet," in good transcendental fashion, assimilated the religious leader, the philosopher, and the scientist? And is Browning covertly trying to point to the so-called "breakdown of the Graeco-Christian synthesis"? Again there is silence.

Since the poetry of the subjective poet is for critical purposes virtually inseparable from his personality, it is for the study of his poetry that biography assumes the first importance. Biography will participate in judgment of the work itself.

Apart from his recorded life altogether, we might fail to determine with satisfactory precision to what class his productions belong, and what amount of praise is assignable to the producer.

Furthermore, on *a posteriori* grounds, greatness in a work of art implies greatness in the instrument; Browning thus gets around to the subject of the poet's moral nature. But, the difficulty at this point for Browning (and Early Victorian criticism in general), with his deliberate theoretical confusion of man and work, is that the unsuspecting critic may be deceived in his evaluation, which is of necessity a moral evaluation, of the work.

We are not sufficiently supplied with instances of genius of his order [the subjective poet's], to be able to pronounce certainly how many of its constituent parts have been tasked and strained to the production of a given lie, and how high and pure a mood of the creative mind may be dramatically simulated as the poet's habitual and exclusive one.

Something of this difficulty may be felt by all theories of poetry as knowledge. In any case, Browning brings biography to the rescue; it will reveal the various states of the poet's moral aim, his moral capabilities and defections.

All the bad poetry in the world (accounted poetry, that is, by its affinities) will be found to result from some one of the infinite degrees of discrepancy between the attributes of the poet's soul, occasioning a want of correspondency between his work and the verities of nature,— issuing in poetry, false under whatever form, which shows a thing not as it is to mankind generally, nor as it is to the particular describer, but as it is supposed to be for some unreal neutral mood, midway between both and of value to neither, and living its brief minute simply through

121

the indolence of whoever accepts it or his incapacity to denounce a cheat.

Shades of Wordsworth, Carlyle, Ruskin, and Arnold! Biography will answer the critic's questions, including the question, "Did he know more than he spoke of?"

Now, in the case of Shelley, to whose defense as the subjective man-poet half of the introduction is devoted, a false and uncharitable biography has subvented true criticism. Disbelief in the man came before, and brought about, disbelief in the artist; "certain charges" are made against "his private character and life, which, if substantiated to their whole breadth, would materially disturb, I do not attempt to deny, our reception and enjoyment of his works, however wonderful the artistic qualities of these"(!). In truth, the verse alone, "under usual circumstances," would be a sufficient index of the moral and intellectual qualities that produced it. It would show that Shelley was equipped with "the complete enginery of a poet"; on the one hand, the transcendental virtue of seeing in a particular good or beauty a new and higher potential one, and of attempting to realize that higher potentiality in himself, in order, step by step, to transcend "the eventual Human" in "the actual Divine"; and on the other, the "subordinate" power of expressing himself in verse

> more closely answering to and indicative of the process of the informing spirit, (failing as it occasionally does, in art, only to succeed in highest art [!]),—with a diction more adequate to the task in its natural and acquired richness, its material colour and spiritual transparency,—the whole being moved by and suffused with a music at once of the soul and the sense, expressive both of an external might of sincere passion and an internal fitness and consonancy,—than can be attributed to any other writer whose record is among us.[14]

[14] This is, of course, a version of the Hegelian aesthetic. The contrast between the poet and the musician a few pages later is informative in this light. "The musician speaks on the note he sings with; there is no change in the scale, as he diminishes the volume into familiar intercourse. There is nothing of that jarring between the man and the

The verdict on Shelley, the poet, has not been accepted by the public; and while the earlier "Remains" and correspondence witnessed the essential purity and beauty of Shelley's life and aspirations, the present letters are further welcome evidence of his "sincerity" and "sympathy" (Carlyle!).

> Letters and poems are obviously an act of the same mind, produced by the same law, only differing in the application to the individual or collective understanding. Letters and poems may be used indifferently as the basement of our opinion upon the writer's character; the finished expression of a sentiment in the poems, giving light and significance to the rudiments of the same in the letters, and these, again, in their incipiency and unripeness, authenticating the exalted mood and reattaching it to the personality of the writer.[15]

After the worst has been laid bare, Shelley is still the original genius, who, Browning emphatically declares, differs in kind, not degree, in the hierarchy of creative minds, spinning his swift and subtle "films" between the concrete and the absolute. Browning will not haggle over his literary merits.

> I would rather consider Shelley's poetry as a sublime fragmentary essay towards a presentment of the correspondency of the universe to Deity, of the natural to the spiritual, and of the actual to the ideal, than I would isolate and separately appraise the worth of many detachable portions which might be acknowledged as utterly perfect in a lower moral point of view, under the mere conditions of art.[16]

---

author, which has been found so amusing or so melancholy; no dropping of the tragic mask, as the crowd melts away; no mean discovery of the real motives of a life's achievement, often, in other lives, laid bare as pitifully as when, at the close of a holiday, we catch sight of the internal lead-pipes and wood-valves, to which, and not to the ostensible conch and dominant Triton of the fountain, we have owed our admired waterwork."

[15] G. H. Lewes in the article quoted from above notes that the publication of Keats's letters in 1848 damaged his reputation.

[16] "But I will say, of Shakespeare's works generally, that we have no full impress of him there; even as full as we have of many men. His works are so many windows, through which we see a glimpse of

In the end,

> There is surely enough of the work "Shelley" to be known enduringly among men, and, I believe, to be accepted of God, as human work may; and around the imperfect proportions of such, the most elaborated productions of ordinary art must arrange themselves as inferior illustrations.

The poet is his own most successful poem.

In summary, Browning's poetic has the virtues and vices of the transcendental theory on which it is based; its chief virtue, the recognition of the moral and spiritual value of art, its chief vice, an inadequate account of form and medium. Browning's particular formulation (perhaps this is as much a matter of style as anything else) is ingenuously successful in exposing the critical weaknesses of the theory, notably the confusion of man and poem, but at the same time the *exposé* is of considerable value as an accurate record of the ambient in which the Early Victorian poets actually wrote. Goethe was only the first of the romantic philosopher-poets; there were also Hugo, and, in England, Wordsworth, Tennyson, and, of course, Browning himself. Distinctions between kinds of poets were the delight and preoccupation of period critics, and the "Introductory Essay" is a good representative of both. Browning's distinction makes a certain amount of sense, but at best such transcendental categories are hard to use meaningfully—harder in general than distinctions made in techniques. For his argument in favor of the biographical approach to the "subjective poet," there will be warm disagreement: the strict formalist will reject it out of hand (together with the notion itself of such a poet); the moderate formalist will admit with due reservation; and the naive moralist (there are still a few about) is likely to follow in the train. Browning's usage, in any event,

---

the world that was in him. All his works seem, comparatively speaking, cursory, imperfect, written under cramping circumstances; giving only here and there a note of the full utterance of the man." Carlyle, *Works*, v, 110.

is extreme and clear; the ground is laid open in which was to grow that fine flower of nineteenth century evil, *Historismus Omniformis*. It is a little ironic that the importance of the "Essay" now is almost wholly biographical and historic.

8. Eneas Sweetland Dallas

Poetics: An Essay on Poetry. 1852

ENEAS SWEETLAND DALLAS is a critic without reputation—a
fact doubly curious. To begin with, his equipment was un-
usually good for the job: an academic ground of philosophy
and psychology, wide literature, far and away the most
comprehensive knowledge of the history of criticism in the
period, a lively play of mind, and a readable style. Further-
more, the equipment was turned to good account: he wrote
a book on poetics; completed two of four volumes on aesthet-
ics, and as a professional journalist he covered the major
poems and novels of some thirty years in a remarkable suc-
cession of highly responsible reviews. Unhappily, the re-
views seem to have gone into the wastebaskets, and the
books (theory is always dry stuff except to the *aficionado*)
to have remained on the publisher's shelves. Biographical
notices say he was best known to his contemporaries as the
author of a cook book; more recently he has lacked even
this distinction.[1] Nor is the meagre detail of Dallas' personal
history very helpful. He was born in Jamaica in 1828 of Scot-
tish parents, and was educated at the University of Edin-
burgh, where he studied under Sir William Hamilton, and
where he picked up his interest in criticism. From Edinburgh
he went to London, joining the literary staff of *The London
Times*, apparently doing free-lance reviewing and reporting
in various fields, and stepping out, once at least, as an editor
on his own. *Poetics: An Essay on Poetry* was published in

[1] George Saintsbury, of course, knew about the good things to be
found in Dallas (*A History of English Criticism*, New York, n.d., pp.
464-66); John Drinkwater quoted extensively from *The Gay Science*
in a chapter devoted to Dallas in *The Eighteen Sixties*, London, 1932,
pp. 201-23; Michael Roberts presented the most original aspects of
his criticism in "The Dream and the Poet, A Victorian Psycho-
Analyst" in *The Times' Literary Supplement*, January 1936, p. 42; and
Francis X. Roellinger, in an exceptionally perceptive and well-written
doctoral dissertation, *E. S. Dallas, A Study in Victorian Criticism*, Uni-
versity of Michigan, 1938, put together what is known of Dallas'
biography, reviewed and analyzed the principles of Dallas' aesthetic,
and brought together an important body of periodical criticism.

1852, two volumes of *The Gay Science* in 1866, and in 1877, two years before he died, *Kettner's Book of the Table* under an assumed name. Since the reviews have never been re-printed, Dallas has been left to stand or fall on his two books, which, fascinating as they may be to the historian, are by the best standards only partially successful.

The setting for both the *Poetics* and *The Gay Science* is Dallas' sense of the disorder in modern criticism and of a chronic want of systematization.

> We have critical opinions in great abundance, and often of great value, but we have no critical system. The critics feel their way, do not see it; we walk by faith, not by sight; our judgments too often show instinct without under-standing.[2]

The founding question, then, is, Is a science of criticism possible? History reveals some interesting facts. Aristotle's doctrine of *mimesis*, based on "a too small induction of facts," and, in any case, strictly applicable only to the drama, has given all subsequent criticism a "hereditary squint." Fur-ther, since the Renaissance, criticism has been assimilated to grammar, the analysis of figures and meters, and system, in so far as there has been system, has been understood in vastly simplified grammatical terms (Scaliger, Johnson, and Ruskin are offered in evidence). The Germans, who escape this censure, sin by excess in the opposite direction; their criticism is all "aboriginal" idea, the irrelevant working out of hypothesis. Underlying the actual universal condition, Dallas detects a crisis of culture which he calls "the despair of a science": first, in the discredit of metaphysics; second, in the exaltation of the physical or exact sciences; last, in the despair, altogether, of the human sciences (Wordsworth had something to do with the split), psychology and moral philosophy. "In point of fact, the great fault of criticism is its ignorance—at least its disregard of psychology."[3] But all sciences are not exact, and there is no reason to suppose that

[2] *Poetics: An Essay on Poetry*, London, 1852, p. 3.
[3] *The Gay Science*, London, 1866, i, 57.

a true science of art is not within reach. What is needed is not "editorial," biographical, or historical criticism—each of these tends to take the part for the whole; what is needed is "comparative" criticism.

> The comparison required is threefold; the first, which most persons would regard as in a peculiar sense critical, a comparison of all the arts one with another, as they appear together and in succession; the next, psychological, a comparison of these in their different phases with the nature of the mind, its intellectual bias and its ethical needs as revealed in the latest analysis; the third, historical, a comparison of the results thus obtained with the facts of history, the influence of race, of religion, of climate, in one word, with the story of human development.[4]

The *Poetics* and *The Gay Science* are Dallas' "plea" for a science of poetry and a science of fine art.

The two books are really unique in Early Victorian Criticism; no others are so extensive in treatment, so single in purpose, so purely speculative in method. And they are perhaps unique, again, in their insistence that art and poetry are in essence a form of pleasure, specifically imaginative pleasure, and in their persistence in analysis of the nature of pleasure and imagination. The books are by no means critical "sports," however, for Dallas was full of the spirit of German metaphysics and criticism, as it came to him, purged of its flightiness, from his Scottish masters, and he had read his Coleridge, even if he did not always understand him. Something too he seems to have learned from the second volume of *Modern Painters*; but then Dallas' method is always at the outset to bring together relevant opinion, dissect, analyze, and move forward to his own statement. The point is, that the books belong to what could already by 1852 be called the metaphysical tradition of criticism. In fact, Dallas' weaknesses, his ultimate failure to establish a workable theory, are the weaknesses of that tradition, infatuation with *a priori* laws and schemata, inadequate in-

[4] *Ibid.*, p. 41. Dallas does not mention Taine, whose *Histoire de la Littérature anglaise* had appeared in 1863.

duction, consequent forcing, and final inability to show a necessary relation between principle and poem. One is further inclined to suspect that, to begin with, Dallas did not have a first class philosophical mind; his misunderstandings, notably of the classical theory of *mimesis*, his arbitrary dealings with absolutes, the true, the beautiful, and the good, and his fantastic classifications, can hardly lead to another conclusion. Dallas' extraordinary command of the history of criticism also on occasion plays him false here; he balks his argument, smothering, or trying to smother, his reader under what he names his "cloud of witnesses," Greek, Latin, Italian, Spanish, French, German, and English. It is a measure of the Procrustean nature of Dallas' laws and principles that such knowledge, superficial as it may be in spots, should have produced no better issue. Still, the effort was a worthy one, and there are plenty of telling points and interesting discussions along the way, enough to rank Dallas prominently among Victorian critics.

The *Poetics*, an investigation of "the laws of operative power" in poetry, is an essay towards a science of criticism. It begins, appropriately, with the problem of definition. A definition is wanted, broad enough to take in all kinds of poet, and deep enough to account for all kinds and schools of poetry. Dallas engages at once Coleridge's contention that the original genius differs from the man of talent not only in degree but in kind. This theory puts the poet beyond criticism by all except his peers, and in any case it is unfounded; the testimony of men of genius themselves, Johnson, Reynolds, Wordsworth, Carlyle, is conclusive against it: the genius is simply the man of enlarged growth and power. On behalf of his second clause Dallas tackles two more giants, Aristotle and Bacon.

It is remarkable that two of the world's greatest thinkers, Aristotle and Bacon, have defined poetry not in itself, but by its accidents; the former laying stress on the fact that it is imitative and truthful, the latter on the fact that it is creative or feigned.[5]

[5] *Poetics*, pp. 6-7.

That this is so, Dallas says, cutting through the familiar Early Victorian antithesis, is proved by Plato, who, in different places, held both theories. Unsatisfactory, too, are the definitions (romantic ones?) which account for the glowing colors of a Shakespeare, but not the "unadorned works" of "such a stern painter as Crabbe"; or which fail to make room for poems of wit and humor. A scientific definition, then, will have extension and intention, and (as Coleridge had already indicated), it will recognize two objects, a state of mind in which, whatever the incitement, poetry is felt, and a state of mind in which the feeling is expressed. The feeling Dallas will call "poetry," the expression in words, "poesy"; investigation of the former is a matter of general psychology, of the latter, a matter of the whole art of composition. Now the consensus of opinion among poets and philosophers has always been that the immediate aim of poesy is pleasure; they differ in their interpretations of the nature of this pleasure; but pleasure of one kind or another is undoubtedly the object of poesy. Poesy,

> on the one hand, is the record of pleasure, and, on the other, is intended to produce pleasure in the reader's mind.[6]

The nature of pleasure is thus the subject of investigation in Book First of the *Poetics*.

Pleasure is "the harmonious and unconscious activity of the soul." This definition brings together three great "laws," the Law of Activity, the Law of Harmony, and the Law of Unconsciousness. Intense mental or spiritual activity, as in contemplation, approximates a state of rest, which is harmony: a simple and immediate satisfaction of the appetite in its object, and at the same time a more general, more sustained agreement between the whole being and its proper end. Finally, pleasure is "unconscious," by which Dallas means "forgetting Self, and looking chiefly to the Unself"; pleasure throws the mind out of itself, into the objective, into ecstasy. Self-consciousness is painful and constrained;

[6] *Ibid.*, p. 12.

in "full self-consciousness we can never get beyond the shallows; the tide of feeling is far out, and there is nothing to be sounded": on the other hand, pleasure does not admit analysis,

> since whatever dwells on the uttermost borders of self-consciousness will be as wild, wandering and unruly as borderers generally are, and whatever ranges beyond its eyeshot, must have crossed the bourne of knowledge altogether.[7]

It should be noted here that, in spite of the suggestiveness of an occasional phrase, Dallas' understanding of the term "unconscious" has little, if anything, to do with its Freudian sense, but, as his illustrations clearly show, is radically ethical and Christian. The three laws of poetry grow out of one another, but all are implicit in the Law of Activity; the Law of Unconsciousness, however, is the greatest of the three. The question now arises, what kind of pleasure is poetry, the answer to which Dallas attempts in Book Second, "The Nature of Poetry."

Corresponding to the four Kantian categories of knowledge, there are four kinds of pleasure, pleasure of Spirit, Sense, Imagination, and Understanding. It is immediately plain from the first Law of Pleasure that the characteristic activity or pleasure of poetry is imaginative, and thus the first Law of Poetry is the Law of Imagination. Imagination, again, according to the Kantian psychology, is both productive and reproductive (Dallas rejects, as Ruskin had already rejected, the limited view of the eighteenth century empiricists in which the imagination was confined to its productive capacity—the invention of hippogriffs). As the mediator between the "reason" and the senses, however, imagination enters into all human thought and expression, is a quality of all pleasure; it is therefore degree of imagination, degree which "in a certain sense" constitutes a difference in kind, that characterizes poetry. All pleasures can thus become poetic by addition, and some, such as love and feeling, are

[7] *Ibid.*, p. 39.

by nature so imaginative as to be poetic in themselves. What poetry does is give pleasure "a peculiar tone." Imagination, as the most active, is the dominant power of the mind, but it is not the highest; it has no power of itself to perceive spiritual truths (the office of "reason"), but it is able to make them "more plain and palpable."

Knowledge of imagination and its workings depends on knowledge of its objects, which are treated under the second Law of Poetry, the Law of Harmony. Here Dallas takes up the problems of "realism" and "idealism," imitation and creation. The Law of Harmony states that the poetic pleasure is a concord produced by, charged with, intensified by, imagination, "the grand harmonist of life." This concord is of two kinds, imaginary or productive, and imaginative or reproductive.

> An imaginary concord is an agreement between Self and a mental representation of objective reality, as Yarrow yet unvisited was to the mind of Wordsworth. The concord is simply imaginative when our nature harmonizes with reality itself, something being added, and perhaps also something cancelled by imagination, as when Wordsworth for a summer month gazed upon the sea by Peele Castle, and beheld upon it "the light that never was on sea or land." Imagination enters wholly into the former, into the latter only in part.[8]

When Bacon says that poetry is "a creation, submitting the shows of things to the desires of the mind," he is taking account only of the imaginary concord of poetry. The same is true of Johnson when he denies the possibility of religious poesy. In fact, however, reality is composed of sense and spirit, Nature and God, and they are apprehended by distinct faculties; but "reason" and sense are bridged by the imagination in its double function, in the one case raising the realities of sense to the ideal, in the other persuading the mind to accept spiritual realities as they are. The adequate

[8] *Ibid.*, pp. 51-52.

definition of poetry must take account of both the "subjec-
tive" and the "objective" functions of imagination.

The distinction between poetry and other forms of mental
activity is made under the heading of Dallas' third Law of
Poetry, the Law of Unconsciousness: "the nobler activities
of the mind require the unconsciousness not only of those in
whom they are awakened, but also of the awakeners." By
"unconscious" here Dallas means a state in which there is
little or no conscious activity; the imagination accomplishes
its most astonishing feats, for instance, in sleep, and is out-
stripped only by the activity of spirit in trance. Imagination
revels in unconsciousness, its element of freedom, which is
also the native element of poetry. Dallas does not elaborate
his point in the *Poetics*, but will return to it later in *The Gay
Science*. The unconscious nature of poetry is further attested
by examination of the three possible states of the human
mind, which Dallas labels the poetic, the unpoetic or prosaic,
and the antipoetic or philosophic. Following Wordsworth
and Coleridge, he makes philosophy, not prose, the logical
opposite of poetry. The prosaic state of mind is passive and
indifferent to beauty and truth; philosophy, on the other
hand, is a true opposite, because every active mind is en-
gaged either in philosophizing or in poetizing, both of which
are operations of the whole mind, but differing as the poles
of the same activity.

> The mind, when philosophizing, dwells in the subjective
> or self; when poetizing, it is thrown into the objective or
> unself; as a consequence of which it is self-conscious in
> the one case, in the other self-forgetting.[9]

Later, in *The Gay Science*, Dallas points out that Coleridge's
analysis of this problem is "ragged." Coleridge had said
that the true opposite of poetry was science, not prose, and
that the immediate object of science was truth, the imme-
diate object of poetry, pleasure; but in this definition the
objects are of different orders, one objective and one sub-
jective. More accurate description shows that the subject-

[9] *Ibid.*, p. 62.

133

matter of both science and poetry is truth, while the states of mind which they induce differ, science or knowledge in the one case, pleasure in the other.

> To say that the object of art is pleasure in contrast to knowledge, is quite different from saying that it is pleasure in contrast to truth. Science gives us truth without reference to pleasure, but immediately and chiefly for the sake of knowledge; poetry gives us truth without reference to knowledge, but immediately and mainly for the sake of pleasure.[10]

Dallas is, of course, right about Coleridge; whether he is right with Augustine that poetry is *splendor verae*, against Aquinas' *splendor formae*, is quite another matter. In any case, the point in the *Poetics* is that poetry, and Dallas quotes Longinus, "always brings us to an ecstasy . . . an outgoing or outstanding."

It is not surprising that the Law of Unconsciousness exalts the lyric as "the most perfect kind of poesy," nor that self-consciousness is responsible for three (Dallas is obsessed with trinity) poetic fallacies, the didactic, the artistic, and the satiric. Here, for the first time, one learns that it "is an object with poesy to direct the mind as well as to please"[11] (before he is through Dallas will write, "The avowed object of the poet is pleasure; but he has laid in ambush other ends as mighty and as earnest as any that rule mankind";[12] his Victorian readers had no cause for alarm). Direction is of precept or example, and the didactic fallacy is the substitution of the former for the latter. In the artistic fallacy, the poet's self-consciousness invades the poem: "Wordsworth not seldom allows a glimpse behind the scenes";[13] and in

---

[10] *Op. cit.*, p. 110.   [11] *Poetics*, p. 64.   [12] *Ibid.*, p. 273.

[13] *Ibid.*, p. 67. "Wordsworth is more like Scott, and understands how to be happy, but yet cannot altogether rid himself of the sense that he is a philosopher, and ought always to be saying something wise. He has also a vague notion that nature would not be able to get on well without Wordsworth; and finds a considerable part of his pleasure in looking at himself as well as at her." John Ruskin, *Works*, v, 343.

the satiric, it contracts the mind into itself with wit and sneer.[14] It is as a sub-variety of the satiric fallacy that Dallas treats the problem of unbelief. The argument follows Coleridge, although Dallas does not quote him. The critics who insist on fiction, on the conscious recognition of the fictitiousness of poetry, as essential to the poetic experience, reduce poetry to "a mere word-game, a kind of leasing where we utter self-evident lies by way of amusement, as when we speak of rage boiling when everybody knows that it cannot boil" (Ruskin's pathetic "fallacy"!). On the contrary, "poetry is poetry only so long as we believe it," believe it unself-consciously with a faith excited under the press of imagination.

In summary, Dallas defines poetry as the "imaginative, harmonious, and unconscious activity of the soul,"[15] and supports his definition with three lines of Keats, who had a deeper insight into the nature of poetry than any critic of the century with the possible exception of Coleridge (still, Dallas did not think Keats's influence "likely to be lasting"[16]).

> A drainless shower
> Of light is poesy: 'tis the supreme of power;
> 'Tis might half-slumbering on its own right arm.

The three phrases assert the three Laws of Poetry in order. The difficulties of definition (Dallas himself was apparently dissatisfied, for he returned to it again in *The Gay Science*) lie in the unself-consciousness of imaginative activity; in the end they will yield only to some improbable "dreamy Aristotle" (who, by the way, in spite of Freud and Jung and the

---

[14] "Wit is certainly not produced where there is any depth, but the energy of the deep passes on to the shallows of the shore, and the sparkling foam which rises there floats out again to sea. Wit is among the fruits of poesy what crabs are among apples, small and often very sour, but the stock from which all have sprung. It is always very difficult to distinguish between friendly wit and poesy, or to say when an expression passes from the one to the other." *Poetics*, p. 68. Donne and Cowley are criticized (p. 271), not for their use of wit, but for addressing themselves to "the passing taste of a little circle" rather than to "feelings universal and irrepressible."

[15] *Ibid.*, p. 76. [16] *Ibid.*

rest, does not yet seem to have arrived). Two observations are perhaps worth repeating at this point: Dallas has been working towards a description of the state of mind in which poetry is felt, and his description is metaphysical rather than psychological in the modern sense of that word.

Book Third of the *Poetics* turns to the Art of Poetry. The subject is split into two parts, the Kinds of Poesy, and the Language of Poesy. The section on kinds begins with the usual division into dramatic, narrative, and lyric, which hardly ever occur as pure forms, and which derive from one another, making a trinity with drama the key term. The epic poet and his reader stand in relation of *dramatis personae*; the epic is thus the only remaining speech in a lost play; and the lyric poet, an epoist who sings the epos of his own soul.[17] The objective trio of kinds tallies with the subjective trio of laws—the dramatic with the Law of Imagination, the epic with the Law of Harmony, and the lyric with the Law of Unconsciousness. The drama is plainly characterized by action and the lyric by spontaneity. If the epic is conceived as history, the correlation of mind and fact, it is evident that narrative is characterized by harmony. The power of Dallas' laws to generate triplets, "historical," "historico-philosophical," and "philosophical" is almost without limit; one learns, for instance, that drama, epic, and lyric are Modern, Antique, Primitive; Western, Graecian, Eastern; Romantic, Classical, Divine, and so on through the arbitrary and almost meaningless list. In the end, the lyric exemplifies the concepts of Future, Unity, I, Immortality, Life, Good; this is "German criticism" with a vengeance. Of some antiquarian interest is Dallas' discussion of the terms classical and romantic, which, as far as he is concerned, mean nothing more than ancient and modern.[18] One triad deserves special mention:

[17] "But the modern critic not only permits a false practice; he absolutely prescribes false aims.—'A true allegory of the state of one's own mind in a representative history,' the Poet is told, 'is perhaps the highest thing that one can attempt in the way of poetry.'—And accordingly he attempts it. An allegory of the state of one's own mind, the highest problem of an art which imitates actions!" Matthew Arnold, *Poems*, London, 1853, p. xviii.

[18] *Ibid.*, pp. 84ff.

the "leading ideas" of the three kinds, the Beautiful, the True, and the Good respectively. All are, of course, co-present, but one dominant, in each of the kinds (the Good is a little puzzling; it seems, however, to stand for the moral end of poetry in this context). The triad itself is suspiciously reminiscent of Ruskin's "Ideas of Truth, Beauty, Relation" in *Modern Painters*, and, in fact, Dallas takes issue with Ruskin's conclusions, after conceding that he "speaks with authority" on aesthetics. The end of the formal or imitative arts, Dallas says, is beauty, not truth; but misled by his interest in historical painting, Ruskin regards the painter as a historian as well as an imitator, and thus confuses the end of a representative art, truth, with the end of an imitative art, beauty.[19] This beauty, by the way, is not moral, but formal. The distinction (itself rather confused) between imitative and representative art is made in Dallas' analysis of the ends of the various kinds.

What is the formal principle of drama, of the dramatic? Not action, in the sense of plot, as Schlegel had maintained, for we speak of a dramatic painting or piece of sculpture; but imitation. Aristotle's theory, wrong for the arts in general, is right for the drama. "All dramatic art, then, is imitative, and all imitative art is dramatic."[20] The imitative arts, painting, sculpture, and the drama, must represent their subject matter faithfully, and thus may be said to aim at truth; but truth of likeness is shared with the representative arts, and in the case of the imitative arts is merely a means to an end, "the expression of the beautiful." This end is "evident" in painting and sculpture. If it is not so evident in the drama, it is because the speeches of the drama can be abused.

For looking at dramatic speeches in their true light, as the means of imitating character and life, not as a means of as it were by slanting mirrors throwing opinions among an audience, and far less as a running commentary on the whole play, it will be seen that if they convey anything

[19] *Ibid.*, pp. 111ff.   [20] *Ibid.*, p. 122.

different in kind from what may be conveyed, however feebly, by dumb show, they swerve from dramatic fitness, or at least are more than dramatic.[21]

Dallas' use of "imitation" is literal, narrow, and unconvinc ingly formalistic. He admits that classical or epic drama expounds "the riddle of life," but "the romantic drama merely exhibits life, its beauty and its grandeur, in shine, in shade, and in shower."[22]

Dallas' "imitative arts" seem to be purely formal and in essence non-conceptual, the "representative arts" mainly thematic and conceptual. The end of the representative arts is truth. Now there are two kinds of truth, one subjective, the other objective: "We tell truth when we represent things as they appear to us; and we tell truth when we represent things as they really are."[23] All art must tell truth in the first sense; it is the distinguishing mark of the epic, which, it will be remembered, is a kind of history, that it must tell truth in both senses. Nineteenth century criticism invented a dozen different ways in which art could represent things as they really are; for Dallas, to tell truth in this sense is to show cause, to expose the inner mechanism of the outer result, to trace the inner source of the outer effect. This the narrative technique does in its comment on the action and dialogue as they develop. Author's analysis is, of course, impossible in the drama, and explanation is incompatible with the unself-conscious nature of the lyric. In the highest forms of the narrative the poet explicates not only second causes, but the First Cause Itself, a sufficient account of the divine machinery of the epic, which is essential to the genre in giving a base of reality to the fiction. The theory, it must be admitted, is ingenious but, in the end, arbitrary; Dallas cuts neither deeply nor cleanly enough.

Where the drama represents outward shows, and the epic both outward shows and inner life, the lyric represents the inner life alone. In the drama things are shown as they appear, in the epic as they appear and as they really are;

[21] *Ibid.*, pp. 131-32.   [22] *Ibid.*, p. 133.   [23] *Ibid.*, p. 138.

in the lyric "things are what they seem, a perfect lyric being the perfect expression of feeling, and more than this, a perfect expression of the singer's own feeling."[24] Again, Dallas' distinction is somewhat confusing. If the truth of the lyric would seem to be subjective, it is in reality objective; by the Law of Unconsciousness poetry throws the mind out of itself into the objective, and "we are most ourselves when we forget ourselves." The highest lyric is never imitative, never uses the highly self-conscious dramatic mask, never deals in appearance. The English, with their gift for drama and because of their dramatic impulse, have failed notably in the lyric. Tennyson, for instance, is seldom more dramatic than when he is most lyrical, and in general it may be said that the modern lyric is lyrical in form but imitative in conception—an evidence, Dallas thinks, of "the dramatism of Christian art." In contrast, the Scots, and Burns in particular, are not afraid to expose their ego, their personality, their inmost soul. A reference to Carlyle brings the argument around to familiar ground, the notion of sincerity and the morality of art. The value of the lyric as the direct expression of the poet's personality depends upon unmistakable evidence of a religious life and understanding in the poet. The lyric is not less religious in essence than the epic—its leading idea, after all, is the Good—but where the epic begins with God, the lyric ends in God. It is aspiration. Even the drinking song is aspiration for a good to come; and man's chief good is God, therefore the end of the lyric is the Good.

In attempting to evaluate Dallas' discussion of the kinds, one is struck primarily with the havoc caused by the categorizing instinct. The distinction of ends and laws is almost pure obfuscation. The assimilation of drama to the visual arts, and the general confusion of manner of treatment and genre, are not helpful; and the casual analysis of the truth and morality of art add nothing new towards the solution of difficult problems. The whole chapter, however, accurately reveals the attitudes, preoccupations, and confusions

[24] *Ibid.*, p. 146.

of the amateur metaphysical critic (Ruskin was such another) in the Early Victorian milieu.

Part Second of The Art of Poetry is called the Language of Poesy and deals with the questions of verse and imagery. In what way does the poetic imagination work, and what is its distinguishing feature in poetic expression? Dallas' position is at once a critique of schools that make one or the other, verse or imagery, exclusively essential to poesy and an attempt at a synthetic explanation of their function in terms of the Kantian imagination. Imagery and verse, says Dallas, are twin born.

> Since poetry passes through the imagination to and from the soul of man, it is perfect or imperfect according as it adapts itself more or less to the forms of that faculty. But since the imagination is a copy of sense, its forms must be those of its pattern.[25]

The Kantian forms of sense are, of course, time and space; whatever the imagination produces will be determined by these forms, and thus poesy will express time by timed or measured words, and space by imagery. And so, although all three Laws of Poetry play a part in the genesis of verse and imagery, the first law is of major importance. And since time is mainly heard, space seen, the senses of hearing and sight, as the senses which have the firmest grasp of the forms of sensuous reality, are the most important for poesy; and of these two hearing is more important, because "time is presented, space is only represented to the mind."[26]

Meter in its simplest form is time heard. This time, measured by the imagination, is subjective, and depends not only on number and length of syllables and sounds, but on order and nature of accent, which in turn is a matter of sharpness of tone.

> Their sharpness depends upon time; upon the number of their vibrations in a given time. And thus at bottom, music is sound expressing divisions and infinitesimal subdivisions of time.[27]

[25] *Ibid.*, pp. 156-57.   [26] *Ibid.*, p. 165.   [27] *Ibid.*, p. 164.

Under the Law of Harmony Dallas attempts to explain the synaesthesia of sight and sound, the way "concords" addressed chiefly to "the mind's eye" are expressed by "concords which the bodily ear alone can perceive" (*brilliant* music, *silver* sound). The answer is that light and sound are manifestations of the same physical law as formulated in modern "wave" theories. Again, under the Law of Harmony a distinction must be made between harmony and love of harmony. The former is an organic relation of mind and object, represented in verse by an agreement between sound and sense; the latter is delight in metrical patterns without particular regard to their interpretative functions.

> When by the first law of poetry, that is, by a necessity of the imagination, a timed or tuned expression is required, the nature of the concord struck between self and unself (in plain English, the sense) will determine a particular movement in the verse, and be satisfied with nothing else; but the love of harmony is pleased with any and every music, now with namby-pamby, again with the Alexandrine, and it ensures nothing, unless to insist that the connexion between the inward concord and the outward melody shall be well marked, thus only enforcing what is otherwise imperative.[28]

Dallas has a good point, however oddly it is put. Critics like Aristotle, who ascribe the use of verse to "love of melody," miss the organic relation between sound and sense, and deny the organic relation between verse and poesy. Dallas observes, in passing, that the theory of meter as obedience to, and expression of, law as law (he cites Bacon, Wordsworth, and Coleridge) is good as far as it goes, but in the end falls something short of completeness. Generally, the second law prolongs and repeats the time or tune engendered by the first law, imparting "its own self-complacency to the outward form"; it is "that *rest*, which was described as belonging to the second law of pleasure, stilling the *motion* of the first,—rest in the midst of motion." Dallas

[28] *Ibid.*, p. 168.

supplements the descriptions of Wordsworth and Coleridge with one (confessedly dependent on the larger theory of the Kantian forms) of his own. Although the poetic mind is said to work unconsciously, self-consciousness is by no means entirely extinct; in fact, the mind moves in a circle, out to the edge of consciousness and back again to the self.

> And what the effect? The centrifugal force wherewith the mind rushes forth into the objective, acting on the centripetal force of self-consciousness, generates the circling numbers, the revolving harmonies of poesy—in one word, a roundelay.[29]

One would feel a little happier if it were possible to test such statements.

Each of the laws of poetry has a specific prosodic function. The first sponsors the foot, the basic measure of time; the second, repetitions of feet or bars (Dallas would like to use the term lines, but is deterred by the "absurd practice" of writing run-on lines, particularly in blank verse); the third, larger repetitions of metrical units called staves. Foot, bar, and stave are the characteristic units of versification for the drama, the epic, and the lyric. This fine bit of systematizing turns out to be not quite as ridiculous as it sounds. Dallas points out the breakdown for conversational effect of the regularity of the pentameter line in Shakespeare's dramatic blank verse.

> In the more strictly dramatic parts, the melody of that meter, wonderful though it be, is not self-repeating, is not made up of equivalent bars; it is made up of feet.[30]

The obvious contrast is, of course, Milton's "mighty line," where the bars, if not of equal length, are at least of equal weight, and "you are made to feel of a surety that you are in among the billows of always the same great stream." The most perfect of the epic bars or lines is the hexameter, both Greek and Latin. Dallas' points, as usual, are argued ingeniously (and for the most part unconvincingly) at some length.

[29] *Ibid.*, p. 171.   [30] *Ibid.*, p. 179.

As verse expresses the imagination's grasp of sensuous reality as time, so imagery expresses the imagination's grasp of sensuous reality as space or place. By place Dallas means both locality or geographical place and shape or form—defined or figured place; his point is that imagery is not limited by definition to the comparative figures of speech.

> Wordsworth has a habit, peculiar I believe to himself and to but one other poet, of laying out the mind as so much ground; and he does this (always admirably) sometimes with and sometimes without a decided metaphor. The haunt and main region of his song is the human mind; he beholds throughout nature a presence whose dwelling is, among other *places* mentioned, the mind of man; his heart is housed within a dream; a sound carries the mountains far into the heart of the Windermere boy; nature is at the heart of Peter Bell.[31]

Dallas gives a number of illustrations. Poetry, and particularly dramatic poetry, is thus not to be judged by the number and novelty of its "happy comparisons"; the unity of the whole is not to be sacrificed to the beauty of the parts. Dallas' argument anticipates Arnold in stressing the difference between ancient and modern attitudes towards imagery, the difference between Keats ("whoever can stand out the extravagance of Keats, must have yielded very far to the third and highest law of poetry—its unconsciousness"[32]) and the "severe beauty" of Sophocles.[33] "We want a more manly poesy; rich in ornament if you will, so it help out the idea, and do not encumber the poem."[34]

[31] *Ibid.*, p. 191.　　　　　　[32] *Ibid.*, p. 197.

[33] "The poem of Isabella, then, is a perfect treasure-house of graceful and felicitous words and images: almost in every stanza there occurs one of those vivid and picturesque turns of expression, by which the object is made to flash upon the eye of the mind, and which thrill the reader with a sudden delight. This one short poem contains, perhaps, a greater number of happy single expressions which one could quote than all the extant tragedies of Sophocles. But the action, the story?" Matthew Arnold, *op. cit.*, p. xxii.

[34] *Ibid.*, p. 198. There is a brief discussion of form or structure, which Dallas calls symmetry, in *The Gay Science*, i, 287: "There

The Laws of Harmony and Unconsciousness, when applied to imagery give rise to simile and metaphor. Here Dallas feels compelled to pause and criticize Wordsworth's distinction between imagination and fancy; the distinction, he says, wants breadth. The imagination is split in two, not on the basis of any distinction in the nature of the faculty itself, but on an observed distinction in the manner in which, under varying circumstances, comparisons are made. In reality, as may be seen in doubtful, rather than extreme, examples of imagination and fancy, the distinction is merely one of degree—in Dallas' terms it depends upon a difference in the amount of consciousness evident in the comparison, imagination as its most unconscious being the strongest. Dallas returns to this argument in *The Gay Science*, where, at considerable pains, he attempts to prove that the imagination is not a special faculty but a special function, the automatic, unconscious activity of the mind; and that what is called fancy is merely the imagination as it seizes resemblances, and what is usually called imagination is the imagination as it seizes resemblances of wholes rather than of parts.[35] The Wordsworthian distinction between fancy and imagination, resuming the discussion in the *Poetics*, corresponds to a similar critical distinction between simile and metaphor, to which Dallas makes the same objection. Simile differs from metaphor, not by a turn of expression, but by the feeling which produces it; it is a virtual metaphor, not different in kind. Here again the difference is in the degree of consciousness with which a resemblance is perceived, for simile compares like with like, not forgetting that they are only like,

---

are poets who boast, or whose critics boast for them, that they seldom or never, in certain works, condescend to the weakness of metaphor; that they are sparing of what is especially called imagery—namely, images in figures of speech. But it will be found that these very writers fly to similitude of another kind—to similitude on a large scale—in one word, to symmetry. The classicism which eschews the symmetry of details produced by figures of speech, eschews them only to ensure a wholesale symmetry, as in that sort of architecture where the two sides of the edifice are alike. . . ."

[35] *The Gay Science*, I, pp. 193ff., 270ff.

and metaphor gives like for like, not doubting that they are the same.

The second law of Poetry "begets" simile, and the third, metaphor. Simile, the expression of man's love of unity, traces likenesses between man's inner and outer worlds, and metaphor is the fusion of these likenesses under the powers of unself-consciousness, of which the highest result is personification.[36] The imagistic functions of the three laws are localization, assimilation, and identification, and they are characteristic of the drama, the epic, and the lyric, respectively. Dramatic imagery is picturesque, epic imagery is illustrative, lyric imagery is creative. Needless to say, Dallas asks the reader to rely on general impressions. Shakespeare, for instance, is chiefly remarkable for his word-painting and scene-painting. The point here is, perhaps, best made by negation; the expanded similes of the epic and the flashy metaphors of the lyric are out of place in the true dramatic style. Epic poesy, on the other hand, is built on simile, because in accordance with its end, which is to express truth "substantial and phenomenal," it makes use of that form of imagery which points out the substantial agreement between things apparently disparate. Epic simile is a continual assertion that the poem is working beneath the surfaces of things and relating substantial truth; in other words, the use of the epic simile is functional, a necessary mode of illustration, and not merely ornamental. Finally, it is the object of lyrical imagery to "animate," and here metaphor, the highest type of personification, is supreme. As the lyric aspires to the Good, the Love of Life, its imagery must be creative, life-giving, personifying, or simply metaphorical.

The fourth book of the *Poetics* deals with the poet and the nature of the poetic impulse. The argument begins overtly with the problem of determinism. Is the poet possessed, or is he self-possessed? Are we to take the theory of poetic

[36] In *The Gay Science*, i, 282, Dallas says that Ruskin is wrong in using the "pathetic fallacy" as a distinguishing mark of the second order of poets. "It by no means denotes the height of art. . . ; it denotes the kind of art—it belongs to the lyrical mood."

inspiration in a literal, or a metaphorical, sense? In answer
to the first question, Dallas quotes Scripture, to gain mastery
over others man must cease to be his own master. The poet
is indeed bound by Necessity; but his bondage, a condition
of his created nature, is no derogation of his dignity. At the
same time the poet is free. "He is thus not only possessed,
but likewise self-possessed." When he gives up his self-con-
trol it is by choice, and while waiting on his impulse, he
works and gathers his materials, consciously and uncon-
sciously. In answer to the second question, the nature of
creative Necessity, Dallas observes that a metaphorical inter-
pretation of inspiration—the genius or "hero" differs in kind
from other men, and his mysterious and extraordinary powers
are "inspired"—is fashionable at the moment. But the theory,
which Carlyle loudly disclaimed, is founded on ignorance
and buttressed with conceit, for it cannot, and does not,
explain anything; and furthermore, as Wordsworth had al-
ready remarked, it exalts genius at the expense of humanity.
Opposed to this is the theory of "real" inspiration, to which
Dallas himself subscribes, and which means, quite simply,
that the knowledge of sense and spirit is immediate, that
there is a direct spiritual action of the divine upon the human
mind. The theory is intuitionist and primitivist. Instinct, in-
tuition, insight, "the simple faith of childhood," are surer
and safer guides than "mere understanding." Now, Berkeley
believed the knowledge of sense, George Fox believed the
knowledge of spirit, directly inspired by God; together they
suggest that every man in his nature is something of seer.
Greek and Christian alike affirm the reality of divine in-
spiration in general, and for verbal inspiration, who can say
that the theory of Biblical inspiration is wrong,

> until we explain how it happens that not only do
> thoughts flash unbidden on the poet's mind, but they even
> rise up fleshed in an imagery which is none of his choos-
> ing, and from which he can no more sunder them than he
> can part a soul from its body without losing both; and,
> most marvellous of all, that he finds them on his lip clothed

in words which to himself are wholly new, and which he cannot, dare not, will not, alter, we seem to be utterly unfit to pass any trustworthy judgment on this head.[37]

This theory, even if it must rest ultimately on faith, at least leaves the question of the poetic process open, whereas the theory of genius precludes all investigation by any except a genius himself. In the end, what do we know of creation? The unself-conscious nature of the process is an effective bar to complete rational understanding.

Persistent inquiry may, however, yield "some superficial knowledge of the forms assumed by the active principle in the course of its development." The expression of feeling, the relief of feeling by expression, is generally unavoidable (Newman, Keble, Mill); but communication is by no means so. This fact suggests to Dallas that the creative impulse is individual, rather than social, and that it is rooted in the instinct of self-preservation by which the human being is moved to make memorials (Plato had arrived at the same conclusion in the *Symposium*). It is essentially a longing for immortality, a longing which may take the form of love of fame, but which is actually something different.

> It is himself and all that really belongs to him, all that is his by birthright, or that he has made his own by conquest of love, his country and his times, whatever he has seen or thought or felt; not things, but his own ideas of things, that he desires and attempts to keep in memory, as on that faculty depends the assurance of his own identity.[38]

The poet thus writes first of all to please himself; his audience is an afterthought. The source of poetry is in the Ego; its natural mode of expression is lyrical, and historically it is purest in primitive societies. The conformity of Dallas' theory to the general pattern of Early Victorian criticism at this point is clear: the creative act is compulsive, medicinal, individual, lyrical, and only in a secondary sense communicative.

[37] *Op. cit.*, p. 234. [38] *Ibid.*, p. 243.

From the primitive stage of the poetic impulse, in which the Ego, desiring immortality, identifies itself with God, there is a progression to two higher stages of development. The epic poet, the Greek as opposed to the primitive Orientals, discovers that immortality is not in the Ego, but in the Non-Ego which is God, and he denies the self in order to merge his own desire for immortality in that of his race; he turns from himself to speak of the eternal realities, and he prizes immortality as the characteristic of the true, the real, and the divine. Thus the Greek or epic artist realizes the only steadfast reality in the divine ideal and he is gifted with the heart and hand to embody it.[39]

The third and highest form of the poetic impulse is the dramatic, which Dallas associates closely with Christianity. Where the lyric poet attempted to perpetuate his own existence by reproducing it in new forms, and the epic poet attempted to take possession of objective reality, to make the divine a human possession, the dramatic poet, in virtue of his sympathy, exercising itself within the terms of Christian revelation (the Greek drama, one remembers, was "epic"), "draws nearer to God, is transformed into the Divine likeness, and begins to imitate for the sake of imitating."[40] The Christian life is an imitative life and it is a life which is freely chosen. It is also true that the drama has flourished under the Christian dispensation—it is the "modern" form *par excellence*— and since the dramatic artist is free to sympathize and imitate or not (the lyric is conditioned by his emotion, the epic, as historian, by fact), the dramatic artist is free, a true creator. The view of the artist as creator, Dallas observes, is peculiarly modern. The Greek attitude, exemplified by Plato, made the artist a mere copier of the archetypal forms; but

[39] "For the ablest, the fullest, the most eloquent, and in every way the best exposition of this, the theology of art, the reader is referred to Mr. Ruskin's work on Modern Painters. It is true that he there says little or nothing directly bearing on the productions of Greek art, but the whole of his work is written from a Greek, that is, an epic or historical point of view." *Poetics*, p. 251. This statement must surely have surprised Mr. Ruskin if he ever saw it.
[40] *Ibid.*, p. 252.

modern art is not merely a mirror, it is creative. If the modern drama is said to be imitative, there is no contradiction, for to "imitate the Divine, and that in the spirit not of epic, but of dramatic art, is to create." Dramatic sympathy implies freedom; freedom carries with it the power to originate, and in freedom man shares relationship with God, a relationship which strives for expression of Beauty and Freedom in the drama. Dallas' argument, once more, is tenuous and speculative; one can credit neither his essences nor his examples, and yet mixed in with the nonsense and fantasy there is a certain amount of shrewd observation and fresh emphasis of old and persistent idea.

The final book of the *Poetics* is an old-fashioned apology for poetry, modeled more or less on Sidney and Shelley. One by one Dallas takes up the attacks which are leveled at the Beauty, Truth, and Goodness of poesy. His conclusion is a reaffirmation of the health and validity of the imagination, of the transcendental and symbolic truth of poetry, and of its influence in training, if not teaching, the mind in virtue. The influence of poetry on practice may not be great in degree, but it is the highest and best in kind.

It would be short-sighted to boggle at the obvious absurdities of Dallas' critical method, his "laws" and "trinities" and improbable analogies, and dismiss the *Poetics* altogether without grace. The book has its virtues, some of them very real and very high. In a period rather given, as he says, to writing prose poems about the nature of poetry, which is usually placed beyond the province of the rational understanding, Dallas at once sets up his theory of the unself-consciousness of the imaginative activity and affirms the powers of the philosophical mind to investigate its workings. One of the highest virtues of Dallas' criticism is his acute and constant awareness of the problems of poetry, and another is his ideal, consistently aimed at, if never realized, of a systematic theory of poetry. His analysis of the state of criticism in the middle of the century is unusually complete and perceptive, and his plan of attack was a good one, to bring the understanding of the psychological aspects of poetry up to

149

the level of contemporary semantic and historical criticism. It was not his fault that "psychology" was still very largely metaphysical in its cast; but if he failed, he failed, not because of his metaphysical approach, but because his metaphysical arguments were inexpert, because his psychology was crude and almost entirely deductive, because he isolates his psychological arguments too arbitrarily from their rhetorical counterparts, and because his knowledge of history was not historical enough. He must have felt that he had failed, for some years later, in *The Gay Science*, he returned to an "exhaustive analysis" of the imagination, which he redefined in more purely psychological terms as the automatic, unconscious activity of the mind or the Hidden Soul.[41] In the end, however, *The Gay Science* too, like the *Poetics*, is speculative, and has little, if any, bearing on practical criticism. Still, Dallas' account of the imagination, inconclusive as it is, is interesting, nor does it suffer in comparison with the other, various, ineffective accounts of the period. He is best in dealing with the nature of "poetry." His attack on the problem of definition is sound, and his Kantian approach to the problems of "realism" and "idealism," "imitation" and "creation," turns up suggestive resolutions. Sharper analysis, or less obstinate categorizing, might have made something of his triad of the beautiful, the true, and the good, as the formal and cognitive elements of art, and their moral significance, but the split between beauty and truth, the "imitative" and "representative" arts, drama and epic, is utterly unconvincing, and, in fact, the whole discussion of the "kinds" exposes the inadequacies of the concept and Dallas' critical method both. The divided emphasis on the drama on the one hand, and the lyric on the other, is curious. It is perhaps symptomatic of a basic conflict in Early Victorian theory between the impersonal and personal, the formal and moral, aspects of art, from the first of which was

[41] "Imagination, therefore, can only be defined by reference to its spontaneity, or by reference to its unconsciousness. Regarding it as automatic, we define it the Play of Thought. Regarding it as unconscious, we define it the Hidden Soul." *The Gay Science*, i, 308.

to come the theory of "art for art's sake" at the end of the century. Dallas' theory of the origin of verse and imagery (he reverses the usual weight of eye and ear) and of their organic relation to poetry is at least clever, and scattered among his remarks on these subjects are a number of shrewd individual observations. Again, in dealing with the poet, Dallas meets the problem of determinism head on, and while his argument is ultimately theological and can hardly be said to settle anything, it is not entirely nonsense. One might notice, incidentally, that Dallas' transcendentalism is set squarely in a Christian frame, and that Christian concepts from the Beatific Vision to the "dramatism" of Christian art play an important part in the theory as a whole. In the final estimate, when all allowances are made for his weaknesses and vagaries, and for his eclecticism, Dallas still stands up, with his curiously informed, inquiring, synthesizing, speculative mind, as the best abstract theorist of his period.

9. Matthew Arnold
Preface. 1853

MATTHEW ARNOLD's early criticism is most meaningful as the criticism of the practicing poet. It finds its proper place in the distinguished tradition that runs from Dryden, through Johnson, Wordsworth, Coleridge, and Keats, to T. S. Eliot. The mark of this tradition is a ruling concern with the work being done or to be done, a concern with practical ends and means; and, as a consequence, the informal criticism in this tradition is likely to deal with matters of craft, and the formal to offer commentary and rationalization in defense of practice. It is also characteristic of this tradition, since the problems of the critic are so nearly those of the poet and the problems of the poet so nearly those of the man, that the full meaning of the final critical statement can only be worked out in terms of the particular practice and the emotional and intellectual history of the man. Whether the definition holds or not, some explanation is certainly in order for the eccentric appearance of Matthew Arnold's "Preface" to the *Poems* of 1853 in the concert of Early Victorian criticism. Fortunately, we have a record of Arnold's personal and artistic development for the previous eight years in the correspondence with Arthur Hugh Clough.

The trouble is, of course, to account for what looks like, on the face of it, a classical theory of poetry in a criticism dominantly romantic. It will perhaps be helpful to get rid of the old tags at once and try some others. Specifically, the Preface is reactionary: a cold-blooded attack on modernism, individualism, subjectivism, and expressionism, and a reassertion of the values of ancient Greek art and culture—heroism, dignity, calm, sanity, detachment, and objectivity. For a theory of poetry, the Preface returns to Aristotle and the concept of poetry as essentially dramatic and epic, essentially the construction of a complete and completely objectified action involving the universal passions of men, essentially the execution of a total effect, at one and the same time aesthetic and moral, in which treatment—especially the use of imagery and versification—is strictly subordinated to the end in view. This, in brief, is Arnold's classicism, and on the surface it is unexceptionable. The tone of the Preface, however, a little too positive, a little too assured, suggests that underneath there may be something factitious. Now, the real point of departure for the Preface is Arnold's feeling about the modern situation—these "damned times," this "untoward generation." Quite simply, Arnold had come to the surely romantic conviction that the times were diseased. The diagnosis is familiar; it is the prescription, one submits, which was factitious. The patient is suffering from melancholia, and Arnold says, "Be cheerful; read cheerful poetry." Once again poetry is panacea, even in the words of Hesiod, " 'a forgetfulness of evils, and a truce from cares'."[1] More particularly, the panacea is Greek poetry, with its admirable but alien and irrecoverable view of life, which is to exorcise the demon of nineteenth century scepticism. No, Arnold was himself at bottom a "sick" romantic (the evidence is in the poems and in the Clough letters), and the Preface is his desperate—and romantic—escape from the unresolved problems of his personality and his art. If Arnold's classicism is thus a mask however, it must be admitted that he wore it reasonably well.

The spiritual biography of the years from 1845 to 1853 in the correspondence with Arthur Clough is a fascinating subject. It explains many things. "But, my dear Clough, have you a great Force of Character"? he wrote in 1845. "That is the true question." "For me, I am a reed, a very whoreson Bullrush: yet such as I am, I give satisfaction."[2] And in 1853, "I am past thirty, and three parts iced over—and my pen, it seems to me is even stiffer and more cramped than my feeling."[3] One letter begins a postscript, "Down again dressed

[1] Matthew Arnold, *Poems*, London, 1853, p. vii. Quotations from the Preface are from this edition.

[2] *The Letters of Matthew Arnold to Arthur Hugh Clough*, edited by H. F. Lowry, London, 1932, p. 56.

[3] *Ibid.*, p. 128.

for dinner—after dinner to the Prices—but thou'dst not think, Horatio, how ill it is here—"[4] Or again, "My dearest Clough these are damned times—everything is against one—the height to which knowledge is come, the spread of luxury, our physical enervation, the absence of great *natures*, the unavoidable contact with millions of small ones, newspapers, cities, light profligate friends, moral desperadoes like Carlyle, our own selves, and the sickening consciousness of our difficulties. . . ."[5] And, "A thousand things make one compose or not compose: composition seems to keep alive in me a *cheerfulness*";[6] and finally, "Goldwin Smith likes the classical ones: but they hinder females from liking the book: and Shairp urges me to speak more from myself: which I less and less have the inclination to do: or even the power."[7] But this is not the place for spiritual biography; the issue is Arnold's theory of poetry, or rather the personal setting of that theory, for which a single point must do. Arnold had to start with an impressionable sensibility, what is usually called a poetic temperament, not very strong in his case, but genuine. The early letters of the correspondence show him trying to exploit this sensibility as a sufficient reason for existence against the claims of the intellect and a restless social conscience. Gradually, Arnold becomes aware of the failure of his sensibility to generate of itself a meaningful pattern for living; as with Keats, the "multitudinousness" of experience threatens to confound his "identity," and he begins "snuffing after a moral atmosphere to respire in," after "an Idea of the world" to give shape and point to his existence. But where, in the middle of the nineteenth century, does the artist find a design for living? Is it possible at all to escape from complete subjectivism, from "the dialogue of the mind with itself"? The great Romantics, Goethe, Byron, Lamartine, and Wordsworth, had exploited their own personalities, and had already failed in universality. The Tractarians were no better than "emotees"; the Transcendentalists were "moral desperadoes." Arnold admired the ra-

4 *Ibid.*, p. 113.   5 *Ibid.*, p. 111.
6 *Ibid.*, p. 146.   7 *Ibid.*, p. 104.

tionalism of the French Enlightenment, but could be no rationalist himself. What was needed was a discipline, comparable in its objectivity and universality to logic, capable of organizing the basic drives of the individual into meaningful units. Arnold recognized this discipline in poetry, conceived, not, as in the beginning, as a more or less pure aesthetic object of delight, but as a *magister vitae*, a poetry such as that of Homer and the Greek dramatists, at once regulative, humanistic, and aesthetic. In 1848 he had written to Clough, "Or do you indeed as you suggested mean to become one of those 'misanthropical hermits who are incapable of seeing that the Muse willingly *accompanies* life but that in no wise does she understand to *guide* it.' "[8] In 1852 he writes, "modern poetry can only subsist . . . by becoming a complete *magister vitae* as the poetry of the ancients did: by including as theirs did, religion with poetry, instead of existing as poetry only, and leaving religious wants to be supplied by the Christian religion, as a power existing independent of the poetical power."[9] Here, it would seem, is the annunciation, to be made explicit in Arnold's later criticism, of the grounds for the nineteenth century religion of art.

Arnold's earliest theory of poetry appears to have been formalistic. The second of the Clough letters (*circa* 1845) refers to the "strong minded writer" who imagines himself "a Reformer, instead of an Exhibition," and speaks of keeping "pure our Aesthetics by remembering its onesidedness as doctrine."[10] The end of art is the beautiful, he tells Clough; the beautiful alone is "properly *poetical* as distinguished from rhetorical, devotional or metaphysical." The passion for truth characterizes the sciences.[11] Form, he writes again, is "the sole *necessary* of Poetry as such: whereas the greatest wealth and depth of matter is merely a superfluity in the Poet *as such*."[12] This is because the appeal of form is more universal than the appeal of content. Form of "conception" is, like form of "expression," a matter of natural talent, but

[8] *Ibid.*, p. 84. [9] *Ibid.*, p. 124. [10] *Ibid.*, p. 59.
[11] *Ibid.*, p. 66. [12] *Ibid.*, pp. 98-99.

it is more mature than the latter, which is common in minor poets who may have very little to say.

> The question is not of congruity between conception and expression: which when both are poetical, is the poet's highest result:—you say what you mean to say: but in such a way as to leave it doubtful whether your mode of expression is not quite arbitrarily adopted.[13]

Clough misunderstands the formal end of poetry; it is not the attempt "to solve the Universe." Clough's efforts "to get breast to breast with reality" are instructive and invigorating, but they are not poetry. Arnold calls him "a mere d—d depth hunter," "you poor subjective, you," and doubts whether he is an artist, for his poetry is one of direct communication, insight and report, in which form is sacrificed to content.[14] On the contrary, it is form which is regulative:

> You might write a speech in Phèdre—Phedra loquitur— but you could not write Phèdre. And when you adopt this or that form you must sacrifice much to the ensemble, and that form in return for admirable effects demands immense sacrifices and precisely in that quarter where your nature will not allow you to make them.[15]

Poetry is not the pursuit of moral and intellectual truths; it is not concerned with "going to the bottom of an object"— "Not deep the Poet sees, but wide." But neither is poetry Tennyson's "dawdling" with the "painted shell" of the universe. "Mere painting" is as fatal to the living movement of poetry as depth-hunting is to its sensuousness.[16] The true matter of the poet is *the hitherto experience of the world, and his own,* the movement and fulness of life itself."[17] The poet must organize this experience and reproduce this life and movement by "grouping" objects.[18] Arnold underlines

[13] *Ibid.*, p. 99.   [14] *Ibid.*, p. 66.   [15] *Ibid.*, p. 81.
[16] *Ibid.*, pp. 63, 99.
[17] *Ibid.*, pp. 65, 97. The poet "must life's *movement* tell" Arnold says in the "Epilogue to Lessing's Laocoon." Arnold recommends the *Laocoon* to Clough in 1848-1849.
[18] *Ibid.*, p. 99.

both "grouping" and "objects." "Grouping" is the formative process, and suggests the familiar Early Victorian analogy between poetry and sculpture or painting; and "objects" suggests the indirection and impersonality (Eliot's "objective correlative") of the poet's projection of his experience. Arnold is certain that poetry is indirect. "Shakespeare says that if imagination would apprehend some joy it comprehends some bringer of that joy"; and Arnold proposes that poetry is the attempt "to *reconstruct* the Universe." This is hardly satisfactory, for Shakespeare himself seems to contradict it— "Shakespeare, Shakespeare, you are as obscure as life is";[19] still, Arnold clings to it as his best description of the end of poetry. "For me," he writes, "you may often hear my sinews cracking under the effort to unite matter."[20] The importance of form to Arnold in 1848-1849 is most clear, perhaps, in a letter written after he had just finished reading Keats's letters on Clough's recommendation:

> What harm he has done in English Poetry. As Browning is a man with a moderate gift passionately desiring movement and fulness, and obtaining but a confused multitudinousness, so Keats with a very high gift, is yet also consumed by this desire: and cannot produce the truly living and moving, as his conscience keeps telling him. They will not be patient neither understand that they must begin with an Idea of the world in order not to be prevailed over by the world's multitudinousness: or if they cannot get that, at least with isolated ideas: and all other things shall (perhaps) be added unto them.[21]

And Arnold goes on to say, "I have had that desire of fulness without respect of the means, which may become almost maniacal: but nature had placed a bar thereto not only in the conscience (as with all men) but in a great numbness in that direction." Arnold's insistence on form in poetry is thus the reflection of his need of form in life. From another point of view, however, that of the relative value of content and expression or style, Arnold allows that fulness of content

[19] *Ibid.*, p. 63. [20] *Ibid.*, p. 65. [21] *Ibid.*, p. 97.

may atone, as in the case of German literature, for deficiency of form.[22] Over the years, the problem of poetry, particularly of the practice of poetry, was most present to Arnold as an antithesis between content and expression, and in 1852 he so far reverses his earlier stand as to say that "modern poetry can only subsist by its *contents*."[23]

In light of Arnold's concept of form in poetry, his attitude towards poetic expression and style becomes clear. Style "is the saying in the best way *what you have to say*. The *what you have to say* depends on your age."[24] The question of style is related to the content of poetry, but the relationship is in no sense an organic one, for "the best way" is determined partly by formal considerations and partly, and perhaps more impressively, by Arnold's "Idea of the world," that is, by moral and social, or quite broadly, cultural ideals. Arnold explains his point in terms of history. In the past, when the poet's experience and the experience of the world was comparatively limited, the body of that experience could be more readily compassed, and thus there was "time" to elaborate it with fine and curious style (the "Idea" here seems to be some version of "the decline of the West"). In the modern world, on the other hand, with its vast accession of new thoughts and feelings, "the immense series of cognoscenda et indagenda," there is no "time" for elaboration of expression. More important than either quantity of experience or time, however, is the matter of cultural integration. The ancients and the poets of the Renaissance found the organization of their material relatively easy because they lived in periods in which culture was more or less unified. For the modern, working in a fragmentary culture, the organization of experience is vastly more difficult because it is very largely an individual matter, and unless he adopts some principle in terms of which he can himself impose unity on that experience, he is likely to be overwhelmed by its "multitudinousness."[25] For him, style is not

[22] *Ibid.*, pp. 64-65.   [23] *Ibid.*, p. 124.   [24] *Ibid.*, p. 65.
[25] "Reflect too, as I cannot but do here more and more, in spite of all the nonsense some people talk, how deeply *unpoetical* the age and

an embellishment, but is a function of the order which the poet imposes on his materials, and in keeping with the rigors of that process, his style will be severe and unadorned. Misunderstanding of the true relation between style and content is responsible for the failure of modern poetry, in which the problem of organization is evaded or ignored, and in which the style, the elaborated style of Shakespeare, for instance, is alien to the complexity of the modern world. Keats, Browning, and Tennyson, not only fail as poets; they and "those d—d Elizabethan poets generally" constitute pernicious models: "Those who cannot read G[ree]k sh[oul]d read nothing but Milton and parts of Wordsworth: the state should see to it."[26] Arnold sums up his opinion on these matters in a letter of 1852.

> More and more I feel that the difference between a mature and a youthful age of the world compels the poetry of the former to use great plainness of speech as compared with that of the latter: and that Keats and Shelley were on a false track when they set themselves to reproduce the exuberance of expression, the charm, the richness of images, and the felicity, of the Elizabethan poets. Yet critics cannot get to learn this, because the Elizabethan poets are our greatest, and our canons of poetry are founded on their works.[27]

It is needless to remark that the Preface of 1853 was an attempt to alter the canon of English poetry.

Arnold does not say very much about the "function" of poetry in the letters, but the few remarks he does make are illuminating and point ahead to the Preface. Poetry must give pleasure, and it must do this by the presentation of the beautiful; but this pleasure is not merely aesthetic, it is moral as well. The moral pleasure of poetry Arnold attaches to style. There are two offices of poetry, he writes, "one to add to one's store of thoughts and feelings—another to com-

---

all one's surroundings are. Not unprofound, not ungrand, not unmoving:—but *unpoetical.*" *Ibid.*, p. 99.

[26] *Ibid.*, p. 97.   [27] *Ibid.*, p. 124.

pose and elevate the mind by a sustained tone, numerous allusions, and a grand style."[28] (It is remarkable how early Arnold found his characteristic vocabulary, and how consistently he clung to it.) The moral effect of poetry inheres in tone, form, or style, rather than in logical content, because style is the reflex of the poet's personality; when this personality is morally great (the familiar "moral center" of Early Victorian criticism), the impress of greatness is communicated to the reader's moral sense through style in the form of a heightened awareness of perfected and satisfying order.

What is Keats? A style and form seeker, and this with an impetuosity that heightens the effect of his style almost painfully. Nay in Sophocles what is valuable is not so much his contributions to psychology and the anatomy of sentiment, as the grand moral effects produced by *style*. For the style is the expression of the nobility of the poet's character, as the matter is the expression of the richness of his mind: but on men character produces as great an effect as mind.[29]

Arnold's distinction between mind and character, like his distinction between form and content, is tenuous at best, and he will be found very shortly assigning moral value to content as such in his idea of the "noble" subject; at the time, however, the distinction enabled him to avoid the moralistic excesses of many of the expressionists. But, as has already been observed, preoccupation with the morality of poetry as a cultural force, under the pressure of his own personal difficulties, led him to the greater moralistic excess of the theory of poetry as "a complete magister vitae." It is this quasi-religious function of poetry which ultimately determines all the elements of Arnold's poetics.

But the language, style and general proceedings of a poetry which has such an immense task to perform, must be very plain direct and severe: and it must not lose itself in parts and episodes and ornamental work, but must press forwards to the whole.[30]

[28] *Ibid.*, p. 100. [29] *Ibid.*, pp. 100-1. [30] *Ibid.*, p. 124.

The formulation and explication of his concept of the function of poetry is Arnold's most original contribution to nineteenth century theory. The letter in which it is first advanced is dated 1852, and marks the emphatic shift in his theory from his earlier and relatively pure aestheticism and formalism: now "modern poetry can only subsist by its *contents*."

The later Clough correspondence shows that by the time Arnold came to the writing of the Preface to the *Poems* of 1853 he had already fully developed his theory of poetry, and his task was merely to give his ideas the formal "articulation" of prose. The origin of the theory in Arnold's personal situation and in his practice of poetry is indicated most clearly in the sentences which occur at the end of the Preface: ". . . in the sincere endeavour to learn and practise, amid the bewildering confusion of our times, what is sound and true in poetical art, I seemed to myself to find the only sure guidance, the only solid footing, among the ancients. They, at any rate, knew what they wanted in Art, and we do not. It is this uncertainty which is disheartening, and not hostile criticism." It is no time for *dilettanti*, the emotionalist or the technical virtuoso, but "if it is impossible for us, under the circumstances amidst which we live, to think clearly, to feel nobly, and to delineate firmly: if we cannot attain to the mastery of the great artists—let us, at least, have so much respect for our Art as to prefer it to ourselves"; let us pass on the practice of poetry to posterity as regulated by its proper laws and not contaminated by "their eternal enemy, Caprice." The ideas of the cultural chaos of the nineteenth century, of the regulative norm of Greek art, and of the impersonality of poetry are all here. For the message of the Preface, as Arnold says in the advertisement to the second edition of the *Poems*, it is twofold: quite simply, "choose great actions" and "study the ancients."

The authority of Aristotle, as is right and fitting, presides over the Preface. Arnold follows Aristotle's division of his subject into four heads: 1) the nature of poetic pleasure, 2) the nature of poetical action, 3) structure and expression, and 4) the function of poetry. The arguments in every case start from Aristotle and are developed in an Aristotelian spirit; the analysis of poetic pleasure is an *explication de texte* of the relevant passages in the *Poetics*. In 1849 Arnold had written to Clough of the two offices of poetry, to add to man's store of thoughts and feelings, and to compose and elevate the mind by a sustained tone. He now goes behind this statement to Aristotle's account of the origins of poetic pleasure. We like poetry because all of us naturally take pleasure in any kind of imitation. Imitation is a kind of knowledge, and as human beings we naturally like to learn. Any representation which is consistent—which adds to our knowledge and which is "particular, precise, and firm" as opposed to "general, indeterminate, and faint"—will be interesting because it will satisfy our natural appetite for knowledge. For a representation to be poetical, however, it must do more than interest; it must "inspirit and rejoice" the reader; it must not only add to the store of man's knowledge, but it must add to his happiness. There is some question whether harmony and rhythm, which Aristotle mentions at this point of the argument in the *Poetics*, constitute a second source of poetical pleasure; Arnold probably thought they did, and by a legitimate extension made them, as form or style, the source of the delight peculiar to poetry. But even if Arnold's reference to Hesiod—"the Muses . . . were born that they might be 'a forgetfulness of evils, and a truce from cares'"—is construed in the spirit of the Aristotelian *catharsis*, his concept of poetic pleasure goes considerably beyond Aristotle and takes on a distinctly modern color. Arnold quotes Schiller, "'All Art,' says Schiller, 'is dedicated to Joy, and there is no higher and no more serious problem, than how to make men happy.'" The "serious problem" suggests some sort of equation between the pleasure of poetry and metaphysical happiness, and points straight to Arnold's theory of poetry as a counteragent to the "romantic agony" of nineteenth century culture. The concept of poetic pleasure in the Preface is basically moralistic—a fact which is made clear in Arnold's account of actions that do not give pleasure.

Now, the "eternal" objects of poetry according to Arnold

(and Aristotle) are human actions. The phrase is absolute, but the advertisement to the second edition of the *Poems* shows that Arnold was thinking about the drama and the narrative poem. Human actions, as such, are inherently interesting, and the poetical value of a representation will depend, not on treatment, but on the quality of the action represented. The poet must see to it, therefore, that he chooses a good action to begin with, by which Arnold means an action that will give pleasure. As Aristotle had observed, it is the peculiar nature of poetic pleasure to persist in the presence of tragic circumstances as they are represented in art; but certain actions, even when accurately represented, do not give pleasure; these Arnold defines as actions "in which the suffering finds no vent in action; in which a continuous state of mental distress is prolonged, unrelieved by incident, hope, or resistance; in which there is everything to be endured, nothing to be done."[31] Mere "passion," in other words, is not tragic, but as Arnold says, "morbid" and painful. The good action is one which appeals powerfully to "the great primary human affections; to those elementary feelings which subsist permanently in the race, and which are independent of time." The description suggests Aristotle's universals in Wordsworthian phrase. It is the poet's business to select such an action, and to concentrate on its construction; it must be presented as a meaningful whole and in order to achieve unity of effect, expression, the exploitation of separate thoughts and images for their own sake, must be subordinated to this end.

The function of poetry, and again Arnold is probably thinking of great tragic poetry, is to move the fundamental human passions. It aims at producing a total impression which will move the whole man, an effect which will be at

[31] "The Poet, when he is most himself, rises to a high and serene view. He will not exhibit grief, misery, horror, in isolated sharpness and for the mere sensational effect; these must lose their harsh and painful prominence, and fall into place in a large and noble circle of ideas. The merely painful always marks as inferior the work in which it is found." William Allingham, *Varieties in Prose*, London, 1893, III, "On Poetry" (1865), p. 268.

once aesthetic and moral. The formal effect Arnold describes in sculptural terms. The "terrible old mythic story" of the Greek dramatist "stood" in outline in the spectator's mind before he entered the theater;

> it stood in his memory, as a group of statuary, faintly seen, at the end of a long and dark vista: then came the Poet, embodying outlines, developing situations, not a word wasted, not a sentiment capriciously thrown in; stroke upon stroke, the drama proceeded: the light deepened upon the group; more and more it revealed itself to the rivetted gaze of the spectator: until at last, when the final words were spoken, it stood before him in broad sunlight, a model of immortal beauty.

This formal effect, joined with passionate and universal significance of subject, noble simplicity of treatment, and calm detachment of tone, constitute a total effect of unity and profoundness of moral impression which operates powerfully on the human spirit, and which is for Arnold the tragic *catharsis* of the Greeks.

Arnold set down his Aristotelian theory of poetry ostensibly in self-defense for rejecting his own dramatic narrative, "Empedocles on Etna," from his new volume of poems. The poem, he says, is not rejected because its subject was taken from "an exhausted past" and is therefore lacking in contemporary interest, but because it was based on a defective action, an action painful not tragic. "Empedocles" accurately represented the situation of a man living in an age in which calm, cheerfulness, and disinterested objectivity had disappeared, the "dialogue of the mind with itself" had begun, and "modern" problems, the doubts and discouragements of Hamlet and Faust, had presented themselves. "Empedocles" was accurate, but it was morbid; it did not inspirit and rejoice. Arnold knew the poem was accurate, at least for his own times; he virtually admits that the poem is a cultural allegory; but he must also have realized (though he could hardly acknowledge it) that the poem was also lyric as well as dramatic, and that it gave an accurate picture of his own mind and a picture that was not very cheerful. "Empedocles" not only violated Arnold's idea of what was good for the sick soul of his generation; it also violated the privacy of his own hopelessness. The fact that the subject of the poem was taken from classical story, however, allowed Arnold to reopen the quarrel of the ancients and moderns. He quotes from a contemporary critic to the effect that a modern poet must engage the attention of the public by taking his subjects "from matters of present import, and *therefore* both of interest and novelty." No advocate of "originality," Arnold cuts through this argument with his philosophic analysis of the nature of a poetic action, and shows that the nearness or remoteness in time of the action is of no essential importance. Wordsworth had been ready to welcome the modern world into poetry when the experience of it should become meaningful in terms of human emotion; Arnold too would gladly make use of modern subjects if the age were capable of supplying adequate ones. But Arnold, who could only "delight himself with the contemplation of some noble action of a *heroic* time" (the italics are not Arnold's), was convinced precisely that his own age could not supply them: "an age wanting in moral grandeur," he says, "can with difficulty supply such, and an age of spiritual discomfort with difficulty be powerfully and delightfully affected by them." In comparison with the latter books of the *Iliad*, the *Oresteia*, and the episode of Dido, the modern "domestic" epics, *Hermann and Dorothea, Childe Harold, Jocelyn*, and *The Excursion* "leave the reader cold"; the reason is simply that in the former "the action is greater, the personages nobler, the situations more intense." Arnold's conclusion is summary: "The date of an action, then, signifies nothing: the action itself, its selection and construction, this is what is all-important"; and he adds that this was understood by the Greeks and is ignored by the moderns.

The failure of modern poetry can be traced in the end to the false and pernicious theory on which modern poetry is based. This theory is, of course, Arnold's old enemy, romantic expressionism. He takes his example from a contemporary critic, " 'A true allegory of the state of one's own mind in a representative history is perhaps the highest thing that one can attempt in the way of poetry.' "[32] "An allegory of the state of one's own mind," Arnold exclaims, "the highest problem of an art which imitates actions! No assuredly, it is not, it never can be so: no great poetical work has ever been produced with such an aim." Judged as a whole and by strictly poetic standards, *Faust* itself, the work of "the greatest poet of modern times, the greatest critic of all times," is defective, and Goethe only defended the poem as " 'something incommensurable.' " Needless to say, Arnold was not prepared to deal with the incommensurable in the Preface. Great poetry for Arnold is not lyric, subjective, personal; it is above all objective and impersonal: the poet needs to be continually reminded

> to prefer his action to everything else; so to treat this, as to permit its inherent excellences to develop themselves, without interruption from the intrusion of his personal peculiarities: most fortunate when he most entirely succeeds in effacing himself, and in enabling a noble action to subsist as it did in nature.

Arnold's argument is reminiscent of Keble's, but it is much more thoroughgoing and points ahead to the Imagists and the theory of the early Eliot. The implications of the argument extend further to the nineteenth century concept of the poet, Carlyle's, for instance, or Browning's, which Arnold repudiates emphatically with the example of the ancients' "plain and simple proceedings." The ancients

> attained their grand results by penetrating themselves with some noble and significant action, not by inflating themselves with a belief in the preeminent importance and greatness of their own times. They do not talk of their mission, nor of interpreting their age, nor of the coming Poet; all this, they know, is the mere delirium of vanity;

[32] "A *perfect Poem is the perfect expression of a Perfect Human Mind.*" Sidney Dobell, *Thoughts on Art, Philosophy, and Religion*, London, 1876, "Lecture on Poetry" (1857), p. 7.

their business is not to praise their age, but to afford to the men who live in it the highest pleasure which they are capable of feeling.

False theory and pernicious models are both responsible for the modern failure to understand the true relation between form and expression. Modern critics take the concept of "total-impression" as a mere commonplace of "metaphysical criticism," conceive the essence of a poem to lie in fine writing, in its isolated thoughts and images, in "language about the action," not in the complete structure of the action itself; they permit the poet "to leave their poetical sense ungratified, provided that he gratifies their rhetorical sense and their curiosity." Such was not so with the ancients who insisted on careful construction of the action, and a strictly functional use of expression. The trouble has been that in an age of confused critical standards young writers in search of guidance have chosen the wrong models. For the English writer Shakespeare is the first of these; but Arnold, like his successor, T. S. Eliot, is by no means convinced that he is the best. Shakespeare, indeed, chose poetical actions, and he took them where he found them, in the present or in the past; but he was also gifted with a "happy, abundant, and ingenious expression" which has thrown his other virtues into the shade. Shakespeare's chief virtue *as a poet* is his *architectonice*, "that power of execution, which creates, forms, and constitutes: not the profoundness of single thoughts, not the richness of imagery, not the abundance of illustration." But the moderns have ignored Shakespeare's actions, and devoted themselves exclusively to imitating his expression, with the result that the detail alone of modern poems is valuable, the composition worthless. Arnold uses Keats's *Isabella* to make his point; it is "a treasure-house of graceful and felicitous words and images"; it contains more "happy single expressions" than all the extant tragedies of Sophocles.[33] "But the action, the story?" The story is good

[33] "On the contrary, some of our makers fall into the gross error of writing not a poem, but a book of beauties, stringing their pearls almost at random, in the vain hope that they may give up the unity

but so feebly constructed as to produce no effect whatso-
ever.

In contrast to Shakespeare and the Elizabethans the an-
cients have much to teach the young writer as models; they
have three things in particular to teach, three things which
Arnold has stressed from the first page of his essay: "the all-
importance of the choice of a subject; the necessity of accu-
rate construction; and the subordinate character of ex-
pression." From the ancients the young poet will learn the
superiority of a single moral impression to the most brilliant
isolated image or thought, and he will learn the value of
simplicity and permanence in the work of art addressed
to the simple and permanent feelings of men. Furthermore,
there are the personal and cultural advantages of familiarity
with the ancients.

> I do not know how it is, but their commerce with the
> ancients appears to me to produce, in those who con-
> stantly practise it, a steadying and composing effect upon
> their judgment, not of literary works only, but of men and
> events in general. They are like persons who have had a
> very weighty and impressive experience: they are more
> truly than others under the empire of facts, and more in-
> dependent of the language current among those with
> whom they live.

The Preface of 1853, which, by the way, implicitly or
explicitly, contains most of the important ideas of his mature
criticism, has its points of agreement with nineteenth century
criticism. Arnold had read his Wordsworth closely—there are
verbal echoes of the Preface of 1800 in the Preface of 1853—
where he might have found, among other things, an account

---

of the whole for the exceeding beauty of the parts. And the remark
of Lord Jeffrey, that there can be no better test of a man's liking for
poetry than his liking for John Keats, has often been wrested into an
approval of this manner: whereas, it only means that whoever can
stand out the extravagance of Keats, must have yielded very far to
the third and highest law of poetry—its unconsciousness. On the other
hand, one shows a taste for good poesy, who can enjoy the severe
beauty of Sophocles, a style the most opposite of any to that of Keats."
E. S. Dallas, *Poetics*, London, 1852, p. 197.

of the depravity of contemporary taste, an insistence on the importance of subject-matter, a definition of that subject-matter as the great and permanent passions of men, a plea for accurate rendering and a censure of capricious embellishment, a doctrine of the plain and naked style, and an endorsement of pleasure, a moral pleasure, to be sure, as the end of poetry. Arnold had also read Carlyle's diatribes against the *Zeitgeist*, and, like Carlyle, had found his century lacking in heroism. Keble, before Arnold, had pointed to the virtues, if not the same virtues, of the classical writers, and had maintained, furthermore, that poetry was not the direct expression of personality; and Dallas, the year before the Preface, had presented an extreme, formalistic theory of the drama. The theory of poetry as one kind of panacea or another was almost universal in the period, and Arnold himself remarks that the theory of the total-impression was a commonplace of criticism. If the Preface is thus related in various of its ideas to earlier and to contemporary criticism, it is probably due to the persistence of fragments of the Aristotelian theory in the nineteenth century. What makes the Preface unique, and turns it ultimately against the main line of march of that criticism, is the completeness and consistency with which it restates Aristotle. Arnold is virtually the only critic in the Early Victorian period who was seriously concerned with the problem of form in poetry, and who gave anything like an adequate weight to it in his theory. This may account for the fact that,.of the various critical essays of the period, the Preface is likely to be the only one familiar to the general reader, which is merely another way of saying that Arnold is the most modern of the Early Victorian critics.

Matthew Arnold's feeling and understanding of the cultural crisis of the nineteenth century, ultimately a crisis of intelligence, appears to have a strong attraction for the twentieth, which has itself experienced with growing intensity "the dialogue of the mind with itself" and the doubts and discouragements, not only of Hamlet and Faust, but of the innumerable protagonists of the serious literature of the time. Arnold's account of the failure of nineteenth century poetry, at once a failure in significance and a failure in significant form, is, again, in general valid for the failure of twentieth century poetry; and if his theory of poetry ignored the possibilities for development of the lyric or reflective mode, it was still right in broad principle. But it is in the aspect of his larger theory in which he is perhaps most modern that Arnold is most misleading and most inadequate, the aspect of his theory which proposed that poetry take over and perform the function of religion. Arnold never completely understood the religious experience, particularly its formal and intellectual elements; and through their common but sharply distinct interests in morals Arnold succeeded in confusing religion and art. As a counteraction to the scepticism and materialism of his generation, Arnold offered his humanistic theory of great poetry as effective and saving myth. Since Arnold's time humanism has been fighting for its life against naturalism, and all belief has become myth, even the belief in science; but Arnold can be held partially responsible at least for any persistence of the myth of art (it was more evident, perhaps, at the turn of the century), and thus for the irrelevant and intolerable burden which, until very recent times, in theory, the art of poetry has been trying to carry. This is no derogation of Arnold's personal humanism which was admirable, and if it seems impossible today to make his synthesis of complementary parts of the Greek and Hebrew cultures, without the religious commitments of either, a living force of integration for our own culture, this in turn does not vitiate Arnold's basic demands for a literature of classical significance and proportion.

10. John Ruskin

Modern Painters, III. 1856

THE most controversial figure in Early Victorian criticism
was not a belle-lettrist at all, but a critic of the fine arts,
John Ruskin. The evidence for this statement is found every-
where after the publication of the third volume of *Modern
Painters* in 1856—in the clamorous comment of the maga-
zines, in the renewed interest in theorizing about art on all
sides, and in the actual practice of creative artists. No critic
had ever provoked such a response; no critic had ever made
himself felt so directly as a force to be reckoned with in all
the fields of criticism. John Ruskin, as one writer put it,
was an institution like the House of Lords or the National
Gallery.[1] "Three interpretations, or keys of interpretation,"
another claimed, "may be said to have been given by man
to man. The first was for the interpretation of the human
soul, and the world of mind, given by Plato; the second, for
the interpretation of nature, was given by Bacon; the third
is now furnished for the interpretation of art, by Ruskin."[2]
What more could be said? There were hostile critics, of
course, who were quick to point out the flaws in his reason-
ing, his shifting emphases and self-contradictions, his dog-
matic style of presentation; but even in their hostility they
acknowledged the force of his argument.

Although the early Ruskin is primarily an aesthetician and
critic of art, he belongs to the study of Early Victorian
poetic theory for a number of reasons. His theory of art,
like that of Sir Joshua Reynolds in the *Discourses*, assumes
the sisterhood of poetry and painting, and the terms poet
and painter are used throughout *Modern Painters* inter-
changeably. "Painting," according to Ruskin, "is properly
to be opposed to *speaking* or *writing*, but not to *poetry*. Both
painting and speaking are methods of expression. Poetry is

[1] Sir John Skelton ("Shirley"), "What Are the Functions of the
Artist?" *Fraser's Magazine*, LV, 1857, p. 619.
[2] *The London Quarterly*, XV, 1861, pp. 110-11.

the employment of either for the noblest purposes."[3] Again, Ruskin's approach to painting itself is literary. The ultimate values which he found on wall or canvas are more often than not conceptual values, as well and sometimes better expressed in his own recreations of the pictures in prose. Many of his arguments, for instance, his analyses of Imagination and fancy and of the pathetic fallacy, are conceived in literary terms and illustrated from poets and dramatists.[4] Then, too, Ruskin's readers applied his principles to the criticism of poetry, and there were some, like Rossetti and Coventry Patmore, who took from him suggestions for poetic theories of their own. Without question Ruskin is of the first importance in the history of criticism.[5]

The most characteristic statement of Ruskin's theory of poetry is contained in the third volume of *Modern Painters*, his compendious and persistent defense of the English painter and water-colorist, J. M. W. Turner. This volume, published in 1856, was separated by ten years from its predecessor and represents in many ways a fresh approach to his subject. The highly schematized analysis of the "Ideas of Truth, Beauty, and Relation" carried through the first two volumes is abruptly cast aside, and the new volume is labeled frankly "Of Many Things." Ruskin described its contents in a letter to Mrs. Carlyle, "various remarks on German Metaphysics, on Poetry, on Political Economy, Cookery, Music, Geology, Dress, Agriculture, Horticulture, and Navi-

[3] *The Works of John Ruskin*, edited by E. T. Cook and A. Wedderburn, London, 1904, v, *Modern Painters*, III, 31. Quotations will be made from this edition.

[4] "Il est lui-même comme le dernier mot de l'esprit littéraire appliqué aux choses de l'art. Tous ses efforts . . . n'ont tendu qu'à renouveler la peinture en assimilant entièrement les tableaux aux livres." J. Milsand, "De L'Influence Littéraire dans les Beaux Arts. M. John Ruskin et ses Idées sur la Peinture," *Revue des Deux Mondes*, XXXIV, 1861, p. 871.

[5] George Saintsbury thought otherwise. "We reach, however, as every one will have anticipated, the furthest point of our 'eccentric' in Mr. Ruskin." His exquisite unreason "very often, generally indeed, is committed in admiration of the right things; it is always delightful literature itself. But it never has the judicial quality, and therefore it is never Criticism." *A History of English Criticism*, pp. 492-93.

gation."[6] More to the point, he now develops the implications of his "naturalist" aesthetics, outlined earlier in the chapter "On the Nature of Gothic" in *The Stones of Venice* (1853), and he informs the reader that during the ten year interval he has had occasion "to collect materials for the complete examination of the canons of art received among us."[7] It is in this volume that Ruskin specifically proposes his definition of poetry and the book is studded with observations on particular poets ancient and modern. All of these reasons lend weight to the choice of the third volume of *Modern Painters* as the focal point for a study of Ruskin's theory of poetry. A word of warning, however, should stand at the beginning of any essay on *Modern Painters*; Ruskin is notoriously elusive, unsystematic, and self-contradictory, and as one of his early reviewers caustically noted, it takes something of a Ruskin to catch a Ruskin.[8] From volume to volume and sometimes from chapter to chapter emphases shift and change as Ruskin tries to reconcile idealism and naturalism, the twin bases of his aesthetic. In spite of these difficulties a certain amount of reasonably clear explication seems possible if one can resist the tendency to haggle over Ruskin's partial statements and keep a firm grasp on the position as a whole.

The most important single fact for an understanding of Ruskin's criticism is that for Ruskin criticism is part of a much larger "world-view," a world-view which is basically and radically Christian—Protestant, nonsectarian, supernaturalist, and above all moralistic. Man's end is salvation, the means is the imitation of Christ, and all human activity is judged and evaluated in immediate relation to this means and this end. Religion then for Ruskin comes first, and his aesthetic and his practical criticism are conceived and applied within a religious frame. In one sense *Modern Painters* from beginning to end is a relentless attack on the growth of secularism from the Renaissance to his own times. This

[6] *Modern Painters*, Vol. III, v, xlix
[7] *Ibid.*, p. 4.
[8] *The Quarterly Review*, XCVIII, 1856, p. 386.

position also very probably had much to do with Ruskin's running battle with the "busy metaphysicians" who "are always entangling *good* and *active* people, and weaving cobwebs among the finest wheels of the world's business," and more particularly with the German idealists.[9] He admits ingenuously that he has "strong inclination" to metaphysics "which would, indeed, have led me far astray long ago, if I had not learned also some use of my hands, eyes, and feet."[10] He makes his real point, however, in an appendix to the third volume of *Modern Painters* where he remarks that he has been "brought continually into collision with certain extravagances of the German mind, by my own steady pursuit of Naturalism as opposed to Idealism."[11] Ruskin's "naturalism," needless to say, is not to be taken in any twentieth century sense; philosophically it seems to represent roughly the position of moderate realism with overtones of a nature mysticism which owes at least something to Wordsworth and Carlyle.[12] Another appendix to the book repudiates all charges of plagiarism from "the interesting and powerful poems of Emerson."[13] In Ruskin's use of the term, naturalism is defined quite simply as "the love of natural objects for their own sake, and the effort to represent them frankly, unconstrained by artistical laws."[14] The philosophical implications of Ruskin's criticism (and for that matter, the theological) are not treated systematically in the third volume—the world-view and the position are implicit—and it is enough to remember that Ruskin is attacking what seemed to him the egocentric aberrations of subjective idealism.

A word or two is perhaps needful at the outset on the deep and pervasive moral ground of all of Ruskin's writing about art. Life is always greater than art for Ruskin, and art is always an integral part, but only a part, of life; action is

[9] *Modern Painters*, Vol. III, v, 334.
[10] *Ibid.*, p. 334n.   [11] *Ibid.*, p. 424.
[12] In the chapter "On the Moral of Landscape" in the third volume of *Modern Painters* Ruskin is bold enough to dispute the mode of the experience of nature with Wordsworth!
[13] *Op. cit.*, p. 427.
[14] *The Stones of Venice*, Vol. II, x, 251.

greater than passion; character and moral habit dominate sense and sensibility.[15] There can be then no facile separation between moral and aesthetic values whatever the difference, which Ruskin carefully marks, between moral perception and moral practice. This position is familiar enough in Early Victorian criticism; however, Ruskin pushes it at least one step further; as most of his contemporary reviewers pointed out, Ruskin is first and foremost a reformer. The most important question for his aesthetic is the use of art, and Ruskin hammers away at his answer in terms of his general cultural ideals, but again and again a bleak pessimism will have its say: art has contributed nothing to the development of religion; it is doubtful whether art has or can contribute anything to human happiness. This feeling, together with the facts of Ruskin's subsequent career as a social critic and worker, offers a striking similarity to those of Carlyle and Arnold. Still, it would be a mistake to overemphasize Ruskin's pessimism, and it is even possible to see how unwittingly his insistence on certain purely artistic aspects of his problem point towards the aestheticism of the end of the century.

At the end of *Modern Painters*, III, Ruskin lists the names of the men by whom he has been most powerfully influenced, Wordsworth, Carlyle, and Helps, and "in olden time," Dante and George Herbert. Of these he owes most perhaps to Carlyle, he says, and surely the voice of Carlyle speaks throughout *Modern Painters*; but in Ruskin's poetic theory the more interesting debt is to his master in "naturalism," Wordsworth, who supplies the epigraph to the whole undertaking:

> Accuse me not
> Of arrogance, ...
> If, having walked with Nature,
> And offered, far as frailty would allow,
> My heart a daily sacrifice to Truth,
> I now affirm of Nature and of Truth,

[15] Ruskin recommends, among other books, the Bible and Plato to his earnest reader.

Whom I have served, that their Divinity
Revolts, offended at the ways of men,
Philosophers, who, though the human soul
Be of a thousand faculties composed,
And twice ten thousand interests, do yet prize
This soul, and the transcendent universe,
No more than as a mirror that reflects
To proud Self-love her own intelligence.

There is almost certainly an allusion to Wordsworth, as well as to the Pre-Raphaelites, in Ruskin's mention of "other forms of Art . . . partly developed among us, which do not pretend to be high, but rather to be strong, healthy, and humble,"[16] the art, that is, which serves as the basis of Ruskin's attack on the eighteenth century concept of the "Grand Style," and which generates the central problem of his poetic, the problem of imitation. The whipping boy is Sir Joshua Reynolds in his paper for the *Idler* of October 20, 1759, written, Ruskin pointedly notes, "under the immediate sanction of Johnson." Reynolds' argument is typical, the distinction between poetry and history in terms of the Italian and Dutch schools of painting:

> The Italian attends only to the invariable, the great and general ideas which are fixed and inherent in universal Nature; the Dutch, on the contrary, to literal truth and minute exactness in the detail, as I may say, of Nature modified by accident.[17]

The realistic imitation of nature, however, is for Reynolds "merely mechanical," and according to this principle, painting, which claims kindred to poetry "by its power over the imagination," must "lose its rank, and be no longer considered as a liberal art, and sister to Poetry."[18] Poetry, then, is the imaginative representation of the invariables in nature, history the literal reproduction of nature with all of its accidental detail. This position Ruskin sets out to refute by an examination of the actual difference between a poetical and

[16] *Op. cit.*, p. 19.   [17] *Ibid.*, pp. 23-24.   [18] *Ibid.*, p. 21.

a historical statement, using as his example a stanza from "The Prisoner of Chillon." Ruskin's conclusion is also typical: a poetical statement differs from a merely historical statement, "not by being more vague, but more specific"; the whole power of poetry consists "in the clear expression of what is singular and particular."[19] Plainly the poet relies on detail, but it is also true that the mere elaboration of detail in a historical statement may only make the statement more prosaic.

It thus appears that it is not the multiplication of details which constitutes poetry; nor their subtraction which constitutes history, but that there must be something either in the nature of the details themselves, or the method of using them, which invests them with poetical power or historical propriety.[20]

What then is poetry? Ruskin asks, remarking rather naively that he does not "recollect hearing the question often asked," and he concludes "after some embarrassment" that poetry "is the suggestion, by the imagination, of noble grounds for the noble emotions." Ruskin, like Newman in his own case, later acknowledged that his definition left out rhythm, but what is important is that he is attempting to define poetry rather than the poetical. He goes on to say that the grounds of the emotions must be suggested by the imagination, because poetical feeling or noble emotion pure and simple is not poetry. It is the peculiar power of the poet to assemble, "by *the help of the imagination,* such images as will excite these feelings."[21] Allowing for the moral bias, this is not bad. The poet is thus literally a maker and poetry is something invented or made. It will be necessary to hold firmly to the fictional nature of poetry in Ruskin's basic definition later on when he begins to talk about "fact." Now, since the aim of the poet is to excite the noble emotions, the detail he will use is strictly determined by this aim; the details as such ought not to, and never do, possess any definite character.

[19] *Ibid.,* p. 27.   [20] *Ibid.,* pp. 27-28.   [21] *Ibid.,* p. 29.

Generally speaking, poetry runs into finer and more delicate details than prose; but the details are not poetical because they are more delicate, but because they are employed so as to bring out an affecting result.

A particular poem is to be evaluated, "not according to the kind of details which it represents, but according to the uses for which it employs them."[22]

The real trouble with Reynolds' theory of poetry is the relativistic concept of beauty upon which it is based. Idealism (or aesthetic relativism) has, since the Renaissance, distorted nature in art in accordance with false, because subjective, notions of shifting standards of taste, and has persistently sacrificed truth to beauty. The formal end of art, however, is not beauty, but truth. In a patient footnote, Ruskin warns against the popular fallacy that "beauty is truth" and "truth is beauty": truth is a property of statements, beauty of objects. In the criticism of art, the terms true and false are correctly used only when "the picture is considered as a statement of fact." Ruskin here takes the representation of form as an assertion; if the painter's representation is not accurate, one may speak of false line or false color in the sense that they misrepresent the actual form; the lines and colors are not, of course, false in themselves, and their beauty is independent of any assertion. A picture can be realistic and ugly, or beautiful and unrealistic—but not necessarily false—if no assertion of fact is intended.

If this were not so, it would be impossible to sacrifice truth to beauty; for to attain the one would always be to attain the other. But, unfortunately, this sacrifice is exceedingly possible, and it is chiefly this which characterizes the false schools of high art, so far as high art consists in the pursuit of beauty. For although truth and beauty are independent of each other, it does not follow that we are at liberty to pursue whichever we please. They are indeed separable, but it is wrong to separate them; they are to be sought together in the order of their worthi-

[22] *Ibid.*, p. 31.

ness; that is to say, truth first, and beauty afterwards. High art differs from low art in possessing an excess of beauty in addition to its truth, not in possessing an excess of beauty inconsistent with truth.[23]

Ruskin's stand bristles with difficulties and his moralism is not even subtle; but the position, after all, goes back at least as far as Plato's in the *Republic*, and Ruskin makes the best of it. Since art deals with "the aspects of things," as distinguished from science which deals with their essence, artistic truth is first of all truth of sense impression. Arguing from Locke's analysis of the primary and secondary qualities of objects, Ruskin fastens on form as the distinctive quality of objects and the source of specific truth in painting. He rejects, of course, Reynolds' doctrine of "central forms" with its corollary of "general truth" and proposes in their stead a doctrine of particular forms as they actually exist in nature and its corollary of "characteristic truth." The rationale for this aesthetic is Ruskin's attitude towards nature. Nature is imperfect; good and evil, beauty and ugliness, are in actuality inextricably mixed, and reverence for God's creation demands that the artist accept it as it is. Art

will not deny the facts of ugliness or decrepitude, or relative inferiority and superiority of feature as necessarily manifested in a crowd, but it will, so far as it is in its power, seek for and dwell upon the fairest forms, and in all things insist on the beauty that is in them, not on the ugliness.[24]

Caliban is set beside Miranda, Autolycus beside Perdita. "It is only by the habit of representing faithfully all things, that we can truly learn what is beautiful, and what is not."[25] The artist who arrogates "the right of rejection" produces the monstrous, the morbid, the dark, and the fatuous.

Art, then, must always give facts. Ruskin comes back to this point over and over again. For instance, he plays with the idea of an imitative art (a historical motion picture with

[23] *Ibid.*, pp. 55-56.   [24] *Ibid.*, p. 56.   [25] *Ibid.*, p. 58.

sound and color?) capable of complete illusion, "the true
and perfect image of life indeed." He observes that his stand-
ards of judgment have always been consistent: "I have
always said, he who is closest to Nature is best. All rules are
useless, all genius is useless, all labour is useless, if you do
not give facts; the more facts you give, the greater you are;
and there is no fact so unimportant as to be prudently
despised, if it be possible to represent it."[26] Furthermore, he
remarks in his Wordsworthian vein, no fact is too mean or
vulgar to the great man; Shakespeare can use the word
whelp to flatter, and Dante introduces "Straw Street" in Paris
into the "Paradiso."[27] Ruskin's emphasis on fact ultimately
resolves Reynolds' false antithesis of historical and poetical
painting, for obviously all great painting must be both. There
is a distinction between historical and poetical art, but it is
not to be accounted for by Reynolds' canons.

If it be said that Shakspere wrote perfect historical
plays on subjects belonging to the preceding centuries, I
answer that they *are* perfect plays just because there is
no care about centuries in them, but a life which all men
recognize for the human life of all time; and this it is, not
because Shakspere sought to give universal truth, but
because, painting honestly and completely from the men
about him, he painted that human nature which is indeed
constant enough,—a rogue in the fifteenth century being,
at heart, what a rogue is in the nineteenth and was in the
twelfth; and an honest or a knightly man being, in like
manner, very similar to other such at any other time. And
the work of these great idealists is, therefore, always uni-
versal; not because it is *not portrait*, but because it is
complete portrait down to the heart, which is the same in
all ages; and the work of the mean idealists is *not* uni-
versal, not because it is portrait, but because it is *half*
portrait,—of the outside, the manners and the dress, not
of the heart.[28]

[26] *Ibid.*, p. 173. [27] *Ibid.*, pp. 115-17.
[28] *Ibid.*, pp. 127-28. Dante's power of striking a likeness had already
been praised by Carlyle.

Now, although it "is one of the signs of the highest power in a writer . . . to keep his eyes fixed firmly on the *pure fact*";[29] and although art must represent facts, represent them as they are, no better and no worse, and represent them truthfully, the requirement that it represent the heart raises the problem of expression.

An "art of simple transcript from nature," such as that of the Pre-Raphaelite Brotherhood, is "wholesome, happy, and noble," but it is not the "noblest." Great art must be expressive; it must add "the great imaginative element to all its faithfulness in transcript";[30] it must, as does Hunt's "Light of the World," manifest "expressional purpose with technical power."[31] Remembered phrases from Carlyle's essay on "The Hero as Poet" sound through Ruskin's praise of Dante's "deep and harmonious" significance;[32] and he goes on to point up the symbolism in Dante's description of rock in the "Inferno":

> It is, indeed, with his usual undertone of symbolic meaning that he describes the great broken stones, and the fall of the shattered mountain, as the entrance to the circle appointed for the punishment of the violent; meaning that the violent and cruel, notwithstanding all their iron hardness of heart, have no true strength, but, either by earthquake, or want of support, fall at last into desolate ruin, naked, loose, and shaking under the tread.[33]

All great and thoughtful artists, we learn, "delight in symbolism" and employ it fearlessly.[34] Having firmly established the artistic (and at the same time moral) value of faithful representation, Ruskin is now prepared to allow that the greatest advantage of art over reality is its capacity for expression "of the power and intelligence of a companionable human soul."[35] The means by which art becomes expressive, by which the artist reaches to the heart of his subject, is "vision," or more precisely, imagination.

[29] *Ibid.*, p. 211. [30] *Ibid.*, p. 188. [31] *Ibid.*, p. 52.
[32] *Ibid.*, p. 291. [33] *Ibid.*, p. 307. [34] *Ibid.*, p. 135.
[35] *Ibid.*, p. 187.

The concept of the poet as seer is an old and familiar one; Ruskin, however, draws primarily on Wordsworth and Carlyle for his own interpretation of the idea, but gives it an original cast as he fits it into the context of his naturalist aesthetic. The key phrase is perhaps, ". . . the greatest thing a human soul ever does in this world is to *see* something, and tell what it *saw* in a plain way . . . To see clearly is poetry, prophecy, and religion,—all in one."[36] "Vision," the power of insight of the whole personality, because of its moral implications is a more inclusive term than imagination, although they are sometimes used synonymously. Strictly, imagination is the organ of vision; it has two functions, one cognitive and one creative.

> Now, observe, while as it penetrates into the nature of things, the imagination is pre-eminently a beholder of things *as* they *are*, it is, in its creative function, an eminent beholder of things *when* and *where* they are NOT; a seer, that is, in the prophetic sense, calling "the things that are not as though they were," and forever delighting to dwell on that which is not tangibly present.[37]

The "Work of Imagination" in the actual production of the poem or painting is called in Ruskin's poetic by the somewhat old-fashioned word invention. Poetry, it will be remembered, is something invented or made, the suggestion by the imagination of the grounds of the noble emotions. He uses the term invention, then, advisedly, for, in the first place, "all imagination must deal with the knowledge it has before accumulated; it never produces anything but by combination or contemplation. Creation, in the full sense, is impossible to it";[38] and in the second place, the pattern or arrangement of the parts to form a whole, which constitutes the work of imagination in the artistic process, is at its best literally "found" in nature itself.[39]

A comprehensive analysis of the nature and function of the imagination had already appeared in the second volume

[36] *Ibid.*, p. 333.   [37] *Ibid.*, p. 181.   [38] *Ibid.*, p. 65.
[39] *Ibid.*, pp. 111ff.

of *Modern Painters* in 1846. There the perceptive or intuitive imagination, as the organ of artistic truth, is sharply distinguished from neoclassical and psychological concepts of imagination based on the assumption "that its operation is to exhibit things as they are *not*, and that in doing so it mends the work of God."[40] Imagination is not a special manner of associating ideas under the control of judgment and taste as Alison and Stewart had claimed; nor is it the image-making faculty of Walter Taylor as Wordsworth had shown in 1815: these men confused imagination with fancy. With help from Wordsworth and Leigh Hunt (there is no evidence that he had read Coleridge's criticism at this time), Ruskin set out to formulate a theory of imagination of his own. The theory has no metaphysical bearings; in fact Ruskin considers the working of imagination to be utterly mysterious and inexplicable, "the highest intellectual power of man."[41] It can be recognized, however, in its results, and by analyzing these Ruskin reveals its modes of operation and the signs of its presence in any given work of art. He contends, he says, not for nomenclature, "but only for distinction between two mental faculties, by whatever name they be called; one the source of all that is great in the poetic arts; the other merely decorative and entertaining."[42]

The imagination is active in three ways, in combining, in penetrating, and in regarding, from which it is called Associative, Penetrative, or Contemplative. Fancy, also, in corresponding but subordinate way, combines, penetrates, and regards. Imagination differs from fancy, however, "in complexity, in the reality of its effect and in the importance of its emotional power."[43] Composition in the academic sense, the

[40] Quoted, Henry Ladd, *The Victorian Morality of Art*, New York, 1932, p. 204.

[41] "We have our little *theory* on all human and divine things. Poetry, the workings of genius itself, which in all times, with one or another meaning, has been called Inspiration, and held to be mysterious and inscrutable, is no longer without its scientific exposition." Carlyle, *Works*, xxvii, 76.

[42] *Modern Painters*, Vol. ii, iv, 224.

[43] Ladd, p. 207.

mere selection and arrangement of memory-images, is not imaginative at all, although the rapid association of images necessary in composition may be made by the fancy. Imagination has nothing to do with the association of images.

The lowest form of imagination (or from another point of view, the highest mechanical function of the intellect), is the associative. It is the "Inventor of Wholes," more specifically "the corelative conception of imperfect component parts." It associates ideas according to a formal principle of unity. The powerful imaginative mind here

> seizes and combines at the same instant, not only two, but all the important ideas of its poem or picture; and while it works with any one of them, it is at the same instant working with and modifying all in their relations to it, never losing sight of their bearings on each other; as the motion of a snake's body goes through all parts at once, and its volition acts at the same instant in coils that go contrary ways.[44]

"Imagination Associative" is the unifying force of the mind, recognized in art as the source of all organic unity. The fancy in this connection merely calls up or associates images quickly.

But imagination must also deal with and arrange separate conceptions; it must apprehend the materials from which eventually it will select. This is the function of "Imagination Penetrative," the highest of the imaginative faculties. The penetrative imagination gets at the root of things; it holds them by the heart, and lays bare their utmost truth, life, and principle. It works intuitively and from within, and "never stops at crusts or ashes, or outward images of any kind." Dante's imagery by this criterion is far more imaginative than Milton's which is too "detailed and deals too much with externals." Ruskin's theory of the penetrative imagination allows him to emphasize "the absolute truth of statement of the central fact as it was," and at the same time

[44] *Modern Painters*, Vol. ii, iv, 235-36.

admit the originality of art.[45] The artist discovers the "springs of things" and by working from within and giving them an imaginative organization, he directs the minds of his readers or beholders and has power over their feelings.[46] Where the imagination here perceives the "characteristic truth" of natural objects, the penetrative fancy merely sees their outsides; it gives a portrait of things, clear, brilliant, and detailed. Fancy is never serious; it is quite unfeeling and restless, and it expresses itself in the accumulation of details—in all of this the very opposite of imagination. As an example of the difference in mode of operation Ruskin marks the well-known flower-passage from Lycidas.

Bring the rathe primrose, that forsaken dies,	*Imagination*
The tufted crow-toe and pale jessamine,	*Nugatory*
The white pink, and the pansy freaked with jet,	*Fancy*
The glowing violet,	*Imagination*
The musk rose, and the well-attired woodbine,	*Fancy*, vulgar
With cowslips wan, that hang the pensive head,	*Imagination*
And every flower that sad embroidery wears.	*Mixed* [47]

It is impossible better to illustrate the capriciousness of Ruskin's actual use of these theories.

[45] This, according to Bosanquet, is the solution of the idealistic aesthetic. *A History of Aesthetic,* p. 186n.

[46] "Among the attributes of the inspired writings is to be noted the power with which they bring home to us high truths, not by a didactic process, but in brief, luminous narrative, flashing forth the truth of the idea, as if by electric torch, from the truth of fact, which is commonly at once its shrine and its veil. So it is with Song—that lower form of inspiration which yields us the poetic rather than the spiritual interpretation of Nature. But it is not to the common eye that Nature reveals this lore. She offers it, indeed, to all; but it is only 'a gift of genuine *insight*' which can penetrate her meanings." Aubrey De Vere, *Essays Chiefly on Poetry,* 2 vols., London, 1887, ii, 80.

[47] *Modern Painters,* Vol. ii, iv, 255.

The combining and penetrating acts of imagination, which are not stages in a process nor separate faculties but modes of operation, complete the definition of this function of the mind. There is still a third mode of operation, however, in which the mind delights, but which is not strictly a power of the mind. This is "Imagination Contemplative," in reality, though Ruskin does not say so, the "idealizing force" of imagination. Contemplative imagination strips objects of material and bodily shape, and regarding only those of their qualities which it chooses for a particular purpose, forges them into new groups and forms, and gives these abstractions consistency and reality by embodying them in images belonging to other matter.

> Thus, in the description of Satan . . . "And like a comet burned," the bodily shape of the angel is destroyed, the inflaming of the formless spirit is alone regarded; and this, and his power of evil associated in one fearful and abstract conception, are stamped to give them distinctness and permanence with the image of the comet.[48]

For other examples of this particular imaginative process Ruskin refers his readers to Wordsworth's "Preface." The subordinate operation of the contemplative fancy is the highest of which it is capable, rising to and merging with the imagination. Contemplative fancy regards its object seriously, and for the time being believes in its creations; at its best it spiritualizes its objects. An example, according to Ruskin, is the stanza of Wordsworth's address to the daisy beginning, "A Nun demure—of lowly port; Or sprightly maiden of Love's court." In art this category of the contemplative imagination is the source of all literary, religious, and philosophical ideas. In poetry it is equally important as it is responsible for the imaginative representation of such things as the horror of Milton's Death. More generally, it is through the "Contemplative Power" of the imagination that the fact "is made emotionally (or morally) significant."[49]

[48] *Ibid.*, pp. 291-92.
[49] Ladd, p. 222. The problem of allegorical figures in poetry in rela-

Ruskin's theory of imagination is central to his aesthetic and it is developed in the third volume of *Modern Painters* in a number of different contexts. For instance, the theory of the penetrative imagination explains the true relationship of art and nature. The power of a natural object, and therefore the power of images of natural objects, depends, when analyzed, upon the understanding of it—"that penetrating, possession-taking power of the imagination, which has been . . . defined as the very life of the man, considered as a *seeing* creature."[50] The imagination is "noble" when it conceives the truth; experience proves, however, that active minds are moved to private imaginings by slight or even deceptive suggestions, and for this reason it becomes the "duty of an artist . . . not only to address and awaken, but to *guide* the imagination; and there is no safe guidance but that of simple concurrence with fact."[51] It is because the chief function of imagination is to deal with absent objects rather than present reality, because the imagination is quickly exhausted by the infinite, unevaluated detail of nature, that art has certain precious advantages over life. Thus there is a "dangerous realism" which frustrates the imagination and is the denial of art.

> So far from striving to convince the beholder that what he [the artist] sees is substance, his mind should be to what he paints as the fire to the body on the pile, burning away the ashes, leaving the unconquerable shade—an immortal dream.[52]

Ruskin is elaborating, not repudiating, his theory of truth in art; it now reads "truth so presented, that it will need the help of the imagination to make it real."[53] He remarks on

---

tion to the theory of imitation is discussed by Masson in the *North British Review*, XIX, 1853, p. 162. His argument is particularly apposite because he refers to the Pre-Raphaelite painters who were attempting to put Ruskin's "naturalist" ideal into practice. It must be remembered, however, that Ruskin's account of the imagination contemplative is in his most idealistic vein.

[50] *Op. cit.*, p. 177. [51] *Ibid.*, p. 179.
[52] *Ibid.*, p. 185. [53] *Ibid.*

the charm of "imperfect sketches, engravings, outlines, rude sculptures, and other forms of abstraction," and contends that artistic perfection consists in the maximum truth consonant with an appearance of unreality.[54]

Ruskin's psychology of the imagination, which again recalls both Wordsworth and Carlyle, determines his attitude towards the rules and towards artistic form. The work of the imagination is instinctive; vision is essentially passive:

> All the great men *see* what they paint before they paint it,—see it in a perfectly passive manner,—cannot help seeing it if they would; whether in their mind's eye, or in bodily fact, does not matter; very often the mental vision is, I believe, in men of imagination, clearer than the bodily one; but vision it is, of one kind or another,—the whole scene, character, or incident passing before them as in second sight, whether they will or no, and requiring them to paint it as they see it; they not daring, under the might of its presence, to alter one jot or tittle of it as they write it down or paint it down. . . .[55]

With the "awful, . . . inspired unconsciousness" of the masterworker,[56] unteachable and not to be gained,[57] rules, forms, composition, "effects," have nothing to do. The nobility of the end and the integrity of the insight imbue and so justify the means. This is possible because the selection, arrangement, and form of the work of art is "given" together with the vision, and the artist becomes "simply a scribe."[58] The genuine artist will know little of rules,

> not despising them, but simply feeling that between him and them there is nothing in common,—that dreams cannot be ruled—that as they come, so they must be caught, and they cannot be caught in any other shape than that they come in; and that he might as well attempt to rule a rainbow into rectitude, or cut notches in a moth's wing to hold it by, as in any wise attempt to modify, by rule, the forms of the involuntary vision.[59]

[54] *Ibid.*, p. 186. [55] *Ibid.*, p. 114. [56] *Ibid.*, p. 122.
[57] *Ibid.*, p. 189. [58] *Ibid.*, p. 118. [59] *Ibid.*, p. 119.

Nor does it follow, as Coleridge in describing his own theory of organic form earlier had pointed out, that the work of art can be contrary to the rules.

> It may be contrary to certain principles, supposed in ignorance to be general; but every great composition is in perfect harmony with all true rules, and involves thousands too delicate for ear, or eye, or thought, to trace. . . .[60]

The penetrative imagination, it might be observed, is in Ruskin's definition faultless.[61] Ruskin allows the "pleasure and profit" in reasoning about principles after the work is done, as we reason about the way the bee builds its comb; but the point is that neither the bee nor the artist knows anything of these matters. It is curious to find Ruskin retreating in the end to the characteristic Early Victorian position of lyricism; he quotes approvingly from Stendhal's "Lives of Haydn, Mozart, and Metastasio":

> Counterpoint is related to mathematics: a fool, with patience, becomes a respectable savant in that; but for the part of genius, melody, it has no rules. No art is so utterly deprived of precepts for the production of the beautiful. So much the better for it and for us.[62]

Ruskin's final position is also typical: great art is *"the expression of a mind of a God-made great man"*; surely we have here the "naturalist" as "idealist."[63]

But Ruskin is by no means prepared to accept the imagination of genius at face value, for there is "a strange connection between the reinless play of the imagination, and a sense of the presence of evil."[64] At times Ruskin makes imagination virtually dependent on moral feeling:

> it is observable, generally, that all true and deep emotion is imaginative, both in conception and expression; and . . . the mental sight becomes sharper with every full beat of the heart; and, therefore, all egotism, and selfish care, or regard, are, in proportion to their constancy, destructive

[60] *Ibid.*, p. 121.   [61] *Ibid.*, p. 146.   [62] *Ibid.*, p. 120.
[63] *Ibid.*, p. 189.   [64] *Ibid.*, p. 103.

of imagination: whose play and power depend altogether on our being able to forget ourselves and enter like possessing spirits into the bodies of things about us.[65]

More often, and in keeping with contemporary critical theory, the moral check is placed on the character of the artist. Given the instinctive nature of invention, how is it to be made to serve the ends of art, Ruskin asks?

> Simply by the sense and self-control of the whole man; not by control of the particular fancy or vision. He who habituates himself, in his daily life, to seek for the stern facts in whatever he hears or sees, will have these facts again brought before him by the involuntary imaginative power in their noblest associations; and he who seeks for frivolities and fallacies, will have frivolities and fallacies again presented to him in his dreams.[66]

To the narrow aestheticist Ruskin's answer, no doubt, begs the question; it seemed right to his own audience, and it may still seem right in substance to the modern humanist.

The moral implications of Ruskin's poetic, however, go far beyond his account of the imagination, although he gives a concise list of its legitimate uses and two chapters on its abuses; the latter constitute "false idealism," religious and profane, quite simply the pursuit of beauty without regard to truth, in one case leading to the secularization of religious art, in the other to the exploitation of sensualism. In the end, "the habit of disdaining ordinary truth, and seeking to alter it so as to fit the fancy of the beholder, gradually infects the mind in all its other operations," and the problem of nineteenth century literature becomes a problem of nineteenth century morality.[67] Among other signs of decadence Ruskin mentions

> the giddy reveries of insatiable self-exaltation; the discontented dreams of what might have been or should be,

[65] *Modern Painters*, Vol. II, IV, 287. Cf. also pp. 357-58. Dallas' theory of the unconsciousness of the imaginative activity undoubtedly owes something to Ruskin here.
[66] *Modern Painters*, Vol. III, v, 123-24.
[67] *Ibid.*, p. 100.

instead of the thankful understanding of what is; the casting about for sources of interest in senseless fiction, instead of the real human histories of the people round us; the prolongation from age to age of romantic historical deceptions instead of sifted truth; the pleasures taken in fanciful portraits of rural or romantic life in poetry and on the stage, without the smallest effort to rescue the living rural population of the world from its ignorance or misery. . . .[68]

This is the Carlylean vein, and willy-nilly, Ruskin is well on his way from contemplation to action. If art is to justify itself in this kind of world, it must teach—delight to teach, but teach. The "first work" of the imagination is "to wake" the spectator, "then to teach him."[69] The great man is sent to earth "for some special human teaching."[70] Ruskin complains of a certain "idealist" painter that his sketches not only lacked "the higher elements of beauty," but were "wholly unavailable for instruction of any kind beyond that which exists in pleasureableness of pure emotion."

> And considering what cost of labour was devoted to the series of drawings, it could not but be matter for grave blame, as well as for partial contempt, that a man of amiable feeling and considerable intellectual power should thus expend his life in the declaration of his own petty pieties and pleasant reveries, leaving the burden of human sorrow unwitnessed, and the power of God's judgments unconfessed; and, while poor Italy lay wounded and moaning at his feet, pass by, in priestly calm, lest the whiteness of his decent vesture should be spotted with unhallowed blood.[71]

It seems clear that in spite of all Ruskin's shifts and qualifications he stands guilty of the "moral fallacy." No other explanation can account for his extravagant admiration for "The Light of the World."

The matter of greatness in art was especially meaningful to the Early Victorian critics. Ruskin, like his contempo-

[68] *Ibid.*, pp. 100-1.   [69] *Ibid.*, p. 181.   [70] *Ibid.*, p. 191.
[71] *Ibid.*, pp. 107-8.

raries, attacked it with moral weapons. His repudiation of the eighteenth century concept of the "Grand Style" on aesthetic grounds has already been summarized. There are three points at issue. Ruskin agrees (but in Wordsworthian phrase!) with Reynolds that "it is produced by men in a state of enthusiasm." He maintains against Reynolds, however, that it does not exclude "common nature" nor careful elaboration of detail.[72] But framing the aesthetic argument is a moral argument which goes back to the first volume of *Modern Painters* where Ruskin had defined great art as that which contains "the greatest number of the greatest ideas."[73] He now expands his notion of "the greatest ideas." Great art is distinguished from lesser manifestations, not in methods of handling, in stylistic manner or choice of subject, but in the "nobleness" of the end which the artist proposes; the poet "is great if, by any of these means, he has laid open noble truths, or aroused noble emotions."[74] Since greatness is a composite term, however, it can be analyzed into its component parts; arguing from an ideal "sum total" of the powers of the human soul, Ruskin sets down four elements of greatness in rising order of importance: choice of subject (!), which involves right moral choice; love of beauty, which involves right admiration; sincerity or the grasp of truth, which implies strength of sense and judgment, and honesty of purpose; and invention, the poetical power which includes accuracy of historical memory. All of these standards had been advanced before in Victorian criticism with varying emphasis and in various combination, and the tendency to categorize might almost be called chronic. Ruskin's characteristic touch is his insistence that great art is "literally" great—because it contains "the greatest number of the greatest ideas." Great ideas, however, are only accessible to genius born; so in the end, as with Carlyle and Browning, the quality of greatness belongs to the poet, and great art is "preeminently and finally the expression of the spirits of great men."[75]

[72] *Ibid.*, pp. 32-3.   [73] *Modern Painters*, Vol. I, III, 92.
[74] *Op. cit.*, p. 42.   [75] *Ibid.*, p. 69.

Moral and aesthetic judgments are again inextricably in-
volved in Ruskin's analysis of the modes or styles of art. He
distinguishes a true and a false idealism. The latter is marked
by the pursuit of effects instead of facts, and in religious art
it produces emotionalism, academic realism, and sentimen-
talism; in secular art, sensualism. Of true idealism there are
three modes, differentiated according to the action of the
(moral) imagination as it fronts reality: the "Purist" rejects
the evil in nature, and its virtue is its loving enthusiasm; it
must be instinctive, and it is always primitive, childish, and
incomplete. The "Naturalist," "that central and highest
branch of ideal art which concerns itself simply with things
as they ARE, and accepts, in all of them, alike the evil and
the good,"[76] represents the "inventive skill" in its display of
the world; and the "Grotesque" is fascinated by evil as its
playful energy exercises in the impossible. The naturalist
ideal, "naturalist, because studied from nature, and ideal,
because it is mentally arranged in a certain manner,"[77] has
already been glanced at in connection with Ruskin's theory
of the ·imagination. It is essentially "the plain narration of
something the painter or writer saw."[78] The naturalist ac-
cepts the imperfection of nature and makes the evil serve
"both for teaching and for contrast."[79] The key word for this
style might be "portrait" in a full sense.

And the greater the master of the ideal, the more per-
fectly true in *portraiture* will his individual figures be
always found, the more subtle and bold his arts of har-
mony and contrast. This is a universal principle, common
to all great art. Consider, in Shakspere, how Prince Henry
is opposed to Falstaff, Falstaff to Shallow, Titania to Bot-
tom, Cordelia to Regan, Imogen to Cloten, and so on;
while all the meaner idealists disdain the naturalism, and
are shocked at the contrasts. The fact is, a man who can
see truth at all, sees it wholly, and neither desires nor
dares to mutilate it.[80]

[76] *Ibid.*, p. 111.   [77] *Ibid.*, p. 113.   [78] *Ibid.*, p. 114.
[79] *Ibid.*, p. 112.   [80] *Ibid.*, pp. 112-13.

Ruskin's naturalism comes out of Wordsworth and Scott, is embodied in the Pre-Raphaelites, and goes on, in spirit, into George Eliot and Trollope. It finds beauty "by gathering together, without altering, the finest forms, and marking them by gentle emphasis."[81]

Curiously, the implications of the "Grotesque" are rather more interesting for Ruskin's theory of poetry than the "Naturalist." The grotesque is radically subjective, expressionistic, and symbolic; as a pole to naturalism, it exerts a strong pull on Ruskin's admiration, so much so at times that he seems to consider it even greater than his "central branch." In fact, on the basis of certain work of Turner, Watts, and Rossetti (and Browning?), he announces "the dawn of a new era of art, in a true unison of the grotesque with the realistic power."[82] There are three forms of the grotesque, derived from three distinct but related acts of the imagination: its irrational play produces Ariel and Titania; its preoccupation with the terrible, the bitter or wicked jest of Holbein and Durer; its confusion by the power of truths it cannot grasp, "nearly the whole range of symbolical and allegorical art and poetry." The last Ruskin defines in a paragraph:

> A fine grotesque is the expression, in a moment, by a series of symbols thrown together in bold and fearless connection, of truths which it would have taken a long time to express in any verbal way, and of which the connection is left for the beholder to work out for himself; the gaps, left or overleaped by the haste of the imagination, forming the grotesque character.[83]

Ruskin illustrates his point with Spenser's picture of Envy from the First Book of the *Faerie Queene*. It is by means of the grotesque that "the most appalling and eventful truth" has been communicated, from Divine Revelation, oracles, and dreams, to "ordinary poetry," and wit and satire of everyday speech.[84]

[81] *Ibid.*, p. 102.
[82] *Ibid.*, p. 137. Cf. Bosanquet, *A History of Aesthetic*, p. 458.
[83] *Ibid.*, p. 132.   [84] *Ibid.*, pp. 134ff.

The systematic analysis of the modes of the creative mind takes Ruskin into an historical account of the changes in sensibility in Western culture from the Greeks to the moderns as studied in their attitudes towards nature or more precisely, landscape. Several interesting points come up in the course of the discussion which covers more than half of the book. Art, for instance, from the early Middle Ages to Ruskin's own times, splits into two great blocks, one on either side of the year 1500; the first is symbolic, the second imitative and realistic. The notes of change are skepticism for faith, utilitarianism for esteem of beauty, pacifism for heroism, and scientific naturalism for humanism. Ruskin leaves no doubt about his stand on the matter of poetry and belief which has troubled later critics. He feels that his "are much *sadder* ages than the early ones; not sadder in a noble and deep way, but in a dim wearied way,—the way of ennui, and jaded intellect, and uncomfortableness of soul and body"; and the "profoundest reason," he believes, is "our want of faith."[85] The ground of belief was sapped by the collusion of aestheticism and the technique of realism in the Renaissance.

In early times *art was employed for the display of religious facts; now, religious facts were employed for the display of art.* The transition, though imperceptible, was consummate; it involved the entire destiny of painting. It was passing from the paths of life to the paths of death.[86]

The result is the "mere mythic absurdity" of Raphael's "Charge to Peter." The modern situation is reflected in Ruskin's observation of an intimate connection between our pleasure in "unnatural" landscapes and "our habit of regarding the New Testament as a beautiful poem, instead of a statement of plain facts." The believer has a right to expect "real olive copse behind real Madonna, and no sentimental absurdities in either."[87] Ruskin is, of course, confusing different senses of the word real, and he has forgotten for the moment the multiple capacities of symbolism, but he has a

[85] *Ibid.*, pp. 321-22.   [86] *Ibid.*, p. 77.   [87] *Ibid.*, pp. 393-94.

point. The worship of false gods has stamped modern art with its mark.

Assuredly, much of the love of mystery in our romances, our poetry, our art, and, above all, in our metaphysics, must come under that definition so long ago given by the great Greek, "speaking ingeniously concerning smoke." And much of the instinct, which, partially developed in painting, may be now seen throughout every mode of exertion of mind,—the easily encouraged doubt, easily excited curiosity, habitual agitation, and delight in the changing and the marvellous, as opposed to the old quiet serenity of social custom and religious faith,—is again deeply defined in those few words, the "dethroning of Jupiter," the "coronation of the whirlwind."[88]

The theme is an old and unpopular one, and after the middle of the century few would want, or be able, to state it; but it appears again in later dress in Paul Elmer More and in T. S. Eliot's "After Strange Gods."

Ruskin also has something to say about poetry and science. His view recalls Wordsworth's and is similar to the later Arnold's. In its relation to art, science works for good or ill according to the moral ends for which it is used. It has made "knowledge fruitful in accumulation and exquisite in accuracy,"[89] and in so far as it has raised men "from the first state of inactive reverie to the second of useful thought," it is to be praised.[90] On the other hand, as it has tended to identify happiness with materialistic and utilitarian values alone, it has gone wrong. There is really no quarrel between the "science of aspects" and the "science of essence"; "it is as much a fact to be noted" in the constitution of objects "that they produce such and such an effect upon the eye or heart (as, for instance, that minor scales of sound cause melancholy), as that they are made up of certain atoms or vibrations of matter."[91] The magnificent metaphors into which the Biblical writers translate their experience of nature represent "the view of nature which is taken by the unin-

[88] *Ibid.*, p. 318.   [89] *Ibid.*, p. 326.   [90] *Ibid.*, p. 386.
[91] *Ibid.*, p. 387. Cf. *supra*, p. 69, n.10.

vestigation affection of a humble, but powerful mind"; they have nothing to do with science, and are therefore not invalidated by science; they represent a childlike and at the same time profound expression of sympathy with the infinite mystery of God's creation.[92] Granting Ruskin's basic assumptions, it is at least possible to say that his whole account is consistent and persuasively argued; he avoids, of course, the problems raised by more "modern" frames of reference.

In the modern period, however, from the "fatal seventeenth century" on, it is the "dissectors," not the "dreamers," who have been the most useful members of society. Judging on the basis of delight in natural objects, Ruskin decides that the modern poet belongs to the second order of intellect, and is characterized by unusual sensibility, "brilliant imagination, quick sympathy, and undefined religious principle," and "strong and ill-governed passions."[93] Some of the elements of Ruskin's description of the ideal poet have already been given. The poet is first of all the "seer," the poet-prophet, the heaven-sent teacher of his fellowmen. The source of his power, insight or vision, is native genius, perfected by education, circumstance, resolution and industry. This genius is God-given and is accurately covered by the word "inspiration"; in the work of genius,

> all this choice, arrangement, penetrative sight, and kindly guidance, we recognize a supernatural operation, and perceive, not merely the landscape or incident as in a mirror; but, besides, the presence of what, after all, may perhaps be the most wonderful piece of divine work in the whole matter—the great human spirit through which it is manifested to us.[94]

Ruskin is no doubt right in thinking that, as human beings, we are rather more interested in persons than in things; in company with his contemporaries, however, he has a strong tendency to regard art as a superior sort of biography. He could define greatness as nothing, in the end, but "the expression of a mind of a God-made man." Like Carlyle, and

[92] *Ibid.*, pp. 384-86.   [93] *Ibid.*, p. 360.   [94] *Ibid.*, p. 187.

on the basis of a similar questionable biology, Ruskin makes the highest manifestation of his hero a mouthpiece not only of the "Zeitgeist" but of a national culture.[95] This interpretation of the function of the poet is made possible by the passive or unconscious nature of the creative process which has been touched upon before. In keeping with Early Victorian theory, the term "unconscious" here is heavily, if not exclusively, weighted towards the meaning of "unselfconscious." The great idealist, in other words, can never be egoistic.

> The whole of his power depends upon his losing sight and feeling of his own existence, and becoming a mere witness and mirror of truth, and a scribe of visions,— always passive in sight, passive in utterance,—lamenting continually that he cannot completely reflect nor clearly utter all he has seen. . . .[96]

Both Wordsworth and Goethe are finally barred from the ranks of the really great on the grounds of their egoism. It follows from the principle of unconsciousness that the expression of the poet is "impersonal": "So, in the higher or expressive part of the work, the whole virtue of it depends on his being able to quit his own personality, and enter successively into the hearts and thoughts of each person. . . ."[97] The ideal is that of Browning's "objective" poet, the narrator or the dramatist; opposed to this ideal is on the one hand the "unsubstantial vision" of the Purist, and on the other the morbid introspection of the Sentimentalist:

> The true Seer always feels as intensely as any one else; but he does not much describe his feelings. He tells you

---

[95] *Ibid.*, p. 344.

[96] *Ibid.*, p. 125. Ruskin goes on to say, "But the man who has no invention is always setting things in order, and putting the world to rights, and mending, and beautifying, and pluming himself on his doings as supreme in all ways." Ruskin's editors reprint his comment on this passage from *Frondes Agrestes* (1875): "I am now a comic illustration of this sentence myself. I have not a ray of invention in all my brains; but am intensely rational and orderly, and have resolutely begun to set the world to rights."

[97] *Ibid.*, pp. 124-25.

whom he met, and what they said; leaves you to make out, from that, what they feel, and what he feels, but goes into little detail. And, generally speaking, pathetic writing and careful explanation of passion are quite easy, compared with this plain recording of what people said and did, or with the right invention of what they are likely to say and do; for this reason, that to invent a story, or admirably and thoroughly tell any part of a story, it is necessary to grasp the entire mind of every personage concerned in it, and know precisely how they would be affected by what happens; which to do requires a colossal intellect; but to describe a separate emotion delicately, it is only needed that one should feel it oneself. . . .[98]

But, while Ruskin (with Aristotle) praises the mimetic sympathy of the poet and, further, insists that the poet's vision includes its own artistic principles or rules, he is (with Plato, and the Early Victorians generally) profoundly suspicious of the amoral "alterability" of the poetic temperament. For this reason, greatness in the poet is made ultimately to depend upon moral character, habit, "the magnificence of tone in the perfect mind."[99]

The several elements of Ruskin's theory of poetry come together in the famous chapter of the third volume of *Modern Painters* on the "Pathetic Fallacy." This chapter deals ostensibly with "the difference between the ordinary, proper, and true appearances of things to us; and the extraordinary, or false appearances, when we are under the influence of

[98] *Ibid.*, pp. 334-35. "The epic artist beholding something divine, say, in a flower, if he be a painter, endeavours with his pencil to imitate its shape and hues; but this, only that he may appropriate the divine something as by a bond or deed of security. On the other hand, the dramatist, when he sees the godly existence of a plant, puts himself into the position of a plant, becomes in some sense a flower, thus appropriates by a profound fellow-feeling its divine life, and with pencil and palette projects upon the canvass what is now a reflection as much of himself as of the flower. In so doing, he is virtually an historiographer; but he is not such an historian as Mr. Ruskin describes in his pamphlet on the Pre-Raphaelites. His object is not history, although in a manner more or less historical he gives expression to his sympathy." Dallas, *Poetics*, pp. 252-53.

[99] *Ibid.*, p. 187.

emotion."[100] One recognizes immediately the tension be-
tween the naturalist and the grotesque ideals, but Ruskin's
interpretation of Western culture in the modern period is
equally relevant. He notices elsewhere that, "as the admira-
tion of mankind is found, in our times, to have in great part
passed from men to mountains, and from human emotion
to natural phenomena, we may anticipate that the great
strength of art will also be warped in this direction";[101] and
further that, "exactly in proportion as the idea of definite
spiritual presence in material nature was lost, the mysterious
sense of *unaccountable* life in the things themselves would
be increased, and the mind would instantly be laid open to
all those currents of fallacious, but pensive and pathetic
sympathy, which we have seen to be characteristic of modern
times."[102] The pathetic fallacy, then, is modern, secularist,
idealist, and sentimental; neither Homer nor Dante, typical
artists of the ancient and medieval periods, indulged it.
When the poet writes,

> The spendthrift crocus, bursting through the mould
> Naked and shivering, with his cup of gold,

he writes what is beautiful but untrue, for the crocus is in
fact a plant and its cup is saffron, not gold (!). Here is a
case in which the mind takes pleasure in a fallacy. This fal-
lacy takes two forms, one of wilful fancy, when (the crocus)
there is no expectation of belief, the other of emotional ex-
citement, when for the moment the mind is more or less
unbalanced. The second of these is the "pathetic" fallacy.
Ruskin's example illustrates the personification of the sea
by a mind overpowered with grief:

> They rowed her in across the rolling foam—
> The cruel, crawling foam.

[100] *Ibid.*, p. 204.
[101] *Ibid.*, pp. 329-30.
[102] *Ibid.*, p. 252. One of Ruskin's reviewers remarks that Homer
could not use the pathetic fallacy because he did not believe in ani-
mated nature, and for this reason is not a case in point. Cf. "Ruskin
on the Ancient and Modern Painters," *Fraser's Magazine*, LIII, 1856,
p. 651.

If the feeling is true, the pathetic fallacy is pardoned and even enjoyed; Kingsley's lines please, "not because they fallaciously describe foam, but because they faithfully describe sorrow."[103] The capital sin against art, however, is to use such metaphorical expressions in cold blood. The conceit in Pope's lines,

O, say, what angry power Elpenor led
To glide in shades, and wander with the dead?
How could thy soul, by realms and seas disjoined,
Outfly the nimble sail, and leave the lagging wind?

is not a pathetic fallacy at all, because it is placed "into the mouth of the wrong passion—a passion which never could possibly have spoken them—agonized curiosity."[104] If Ruskin is trying to make a point about dramatic propriety at all, he quickly moralizes it, for while bad writing is known by the use of such expressions as current coin, the worst is their use by a master "skillful in handling, yet insincere, deliberately wrought out with chill and studied fancy."[105]

The implications of Ruskin's fallacy are basically moral

[103] *Ibid.*, p. 210. " 'His hand the good man fastens on the skies, And bids earth roll, nor feels her idle whirl.' Pause for a moment to realise the image, and the monstrous absurdity of a man's grasping the skies and hanging habitually suspended there, while he contemptuously bids the earth roll, warns you that no genuine feeling could have suggested so unnatural a conception." Quoted by G. H. Lewes (*The Principles of Success in Literature*, ed. by T. S. Knowlson, London, 1899, p. 63) from George Eliot's article "Worldliness and Other-Worldliness" in the *Westminster Review*, LXVII, 1857.

[104] *Ibid.*, p. 207.

[105] *Ibid.*, p. 216. Ruskin's tone recalls the "Preface to *Lyrical Ballads.*" Ruskin's emphasis on accuracy of factual detail in the description of natural phenomena was taken over into the poetic criticism of his younger disciples. "In this extract, for example, which is of much more than Mr. Smith's average precision, we find several glaring inaccuracies,—in a matter, too, of merely external nature, where accuracy is comparatively easy. The lark and the hedges white with May are in the worst possible keeping with the sea-shore, where the verses are supposed to be said; and the pretty lines about the sea do not in any way assist the description of a peculiarly fine summer's day, to which the remaining portion of the passage is intended to be an antithesis." Coventry Patmore, "New Poets," *The Edinburgh Review*, CIV, 1856, p. 353.

and therefore make sense only in terms of his peculiar assumptions; he confuses the matter even further, however, when he appears to identify the great "naturalist ideal" with the use of simile as opposed to metaphor (metaphor would presumably become the province of the grotesque?):

> Thus, when Dante describes the spirits falling from the banks of Acheron "as dead leaves flutter from a bough," he gives the most perfect image possible of their utter lightness, feebleness, passiveness, and scattering agony of despair, without, however, for an instant losing his own clear perception that *these* are souls, and *those* are leaves; he makes no confusion of one with the other.[106]

On the other hand, in Coleridge's

> The one red leaf, the last of its clan,
> That dances as often as dance it can,

the poet shows "a morbid, that is to say, a so far false, idea about the leaf; he fancies a life in it, and will, which there are not; confuses powerlessness with choice, its fading death with merriment, and the wind that shakes it with music."[107] Ruskin's literalism is stubborn here, but he is insisting on fact, and Wordsworth's "simple" style is not very far in the background. In this connection it is not surprising that Ruskin demands distinctness in his art; he precedes Mr. T. S. Eliot in finding Milton's "vagueness" unimaginative.[108]

[106] *Ibid.*, p. 206. "Dante's unshaken self-possession in the midst of the marvels around him, is itself a proof that his vision was true; for had it been false, that artificial excitement, which alone could have sustained the illusion, would have swept him into the vortices of splendour and motion which he describes; and he would have written with an unsteady hand as his imitators have ever done." Aubrey De Vere, "Taylor's *Eve of Conquest*," *The Edinburgh Review*, LXXXIX, 1849, p. 379.

[107] *Ibid.*, pp. 206-7. "Hence the conceits that astonish us in the gravest, and even subtlest thinkers, whose taste is not proportionate to their mental perceptions: men like Donne, for instance; who apart from accidental personal impressions, seem to look at nothing as it really is, but only as to what may be thought of it." Leigh Hunt, *Imagination and Fancy*, New York, 1845, p. 66.

[108] *Ibid.*, p. 271.

Use of the pathetic fallacy marks the second—"Reflective" or "Perceptive"—order of poets, of whom Wordsworth, Keats, and Tennyson, are examples; the first, the "Creative" poets such as Homer, Dante, and Shakespeare, seldom use it. These two classes differ in range, not in quality, and there is no third class; with "poetry second rate in quality no one ought to be allowed to trouble mankind."[109] The temperament which indulges the pathetic fallacy is always in some degree morbid and weak, and so is carried away by emotion. In the "Creative" temperament, "the intellect also rises, till it is strong enough to assert its rule against, or together with, the utmost efforts of the passions."[110] Greatness is thus a matter both of powerful emotion and "government" of it. There are, however, "some subjects which *ought*" to throw a man off balance, and the prophets in all their human strength, "submitted to influences stronger than they, . . . see in a sort untruly, because what they see is inconceivably above them."[111] These various types of temperament blend into one another and are even at different times the state of a single mind; but the difference between the greater and the less "is, on the whole, chiefly in this point of *alterability*."[112] The great man's "mind is made up; his thoughts have an accustomed current; his ways are steadfast; it is not this or that new sight which will at once unbalance him."[113] Such a man is Dante in contrast to Keats, who "with the same degree of sensibility, is at once carried off his feet" and who "wants to do something he did not want to do before; he views all the universe in a new light through his tears; he is gay or enthusiastic, melancholy or passionate, as things come and go to him."[114]

[109] *Ibid.*, pp. 205-6n.   [110] *Ibid.*, p. 208.   [111] *Ibid.*, p. 209.
[112] *Ibid.*, pp. 209-10.   [113] *Ibid.*, p. 210.

[114] *Ibid.* Ruskin's attitude towards the "Sentimental" poets may owe something ultimately to Schiller. "The treatise on naive and sentimental poetry soon produced its effect. In 1797 there appeared Fr. Schlegel's Essays on the Study of Greek Poetry, with a preface, which, referring to Schiller's treatise, declared that the principles of objective beauty could not be held to apply to modern poetic art. For, in defiance of the maxim that beauty must give a disinterested pleasure, the poet now relies on subjective fascination, poetic 'effect,' and an

In the chapter "Of Modern Landscape" Ruskin picks Scott over Wordsworth and Tennyson, Balzac and Goethe, as "the great representative of the mind of the age in literature." He is aware of the eccentricity of his choice, but he finds in Scott more of the characteristic strengths and weaknesses of the modern artist than in any of the others. Scott's strong points are four: humility with self-confidence, lack of affectation, facile execution, and the power of seeing something and telling what he saw in a plain way. The last, the characteristic of the seer, places him above the masters of "self-examining" verse, Byron, Tennyson, and Keats, although they may be perfect in their own sphere. Scott's weaknesses are also typical: lack of faith or belief,[115] the "habit of looking back, in a romantic and passionate idleness, to the past ages,"[116] ignorance of art, and the mixture of levity and

---

interest in the existence of the idea; these are his essentially 'sentimental' characters. It will at once be seen that Kant's abstraction from positive content, by which he set down a relation to the ideal as impurity in aesthetic judgment, here recoils on the theory of the beautiful with destructive effect. Schlegel further points out that the sentimental mood becomes poetry only through the characteristic, that is, through the representation of what is individual. Otherwise, I presume he must mean, it can have no plastic or structural form adequate to the depth of individual emotion which is its material." Bosanquet, *A History of Aesthetic*, p. 300.

[115] "Hence, nearly all our powerful men in this age of the world are unbelievers; the best of them in doubt and misery; the worst in reckless defiance; the plurality, in plodding hesitation, doing, as well as they can, what practical work lies ready to their hands. Most of our scientific men are in this last class: our popular authors either set themselves definitely against all religious form, pleading for simple truth and benevolence, (Thackeray, Dickens,) or give themselves up to bitter and fruitless statement of facts, (De Balzac,) or surface painting, (Scott,) or careless blasphemy, sad or smiling, (Byron, Beranger). Our earnest poets and deepest thinkers are doubtful and indignant, (Tennyson, Carlyle); one or two, anchored, indeed, but anxious or weeping, (Wordsworth, Mrs. Browning); and of these two, the first is not so sure of his anchor, but that now and then it drags with him, even to make him cry out,—

> Great God, I had rather be
> A Pagan suckled in some creed outworn;
> So might I, standing on this pleasant lea,
> Have glimpses that would make me less forlorn."

Modern Painters, Vol. III, v, 322-23.

[116] *Ibid.*, p. 336.

melancholy resulting from lack of purpose. Scott does not show the pathetic fallacy, however, his is a "pure passion for nature in its abstract being,"[117] and it differs fundamentally from that of his contemporaries.

Tennyson goes out on a furzy common, and sees it is calm autumn sunshine, but it gives him no pleasure. He only remembers that it is

> "Dead calm in that noble breast
> Which heaves but with the heaving deep."

He sees a thundercloud in the evening, and *would* have "doted and pored" on it, but cannot, for fear it should bring the ship bad weather. Keats drinks the beauty of nature violently; but has no more real sympathy with her than he has with a bottle of claret. His palate is fine; but he "bursts joy's grape against it," gets nothing but misery, and a bitter taste of dregs, out of his desperate draught.

Byron and Shelley are nearly the same, only with less truth of perception, and even more troublesome selfishness. Wordsworth is more like Scott, and understands how to be happy, but yet cannot altogether rid himself of the sense that he is a philosopher, and ought always to be saying something wise. He has also a vague notion that Nature would not be able to get on well without Wordsworth; and finds a considerable part of his pleasure in looking at himself as well as at her. But with Scott the love is entirely humble and unselfish.[118]

Ruskin's Pre-Raphaelite reading of Scott goes on to point out his sense of color, his "finish" in the portraiture of animals and birds "down to the minutest speckling of breast," and his habit of "drawing a slight *moral* from every scene," inseparable from the scene itself. Judgment of Ruskin's remarks about the Romantics must take account of the fact that he is talking about them immediately as nature poets;

[117] *Ibid.*, p. 343.
[118] *Ibid.* One reviewer signing himself "J. O. S." wrote a caustic review of Ruskin in defence of Tennyson. "Ruskin on the Ancient and Modern Painters," *Fraser's Magazine*, LIII, 1856, p. 648.

the moral approach is nonetheless typical, and within the
bounds of that approach some real acuteness of perception.

Perhaps the best word for Ruskin's criticism is humanistic.
He loved poetry and painting and architecture and he knew
a good bit about all of them, but it was inconceivable to him
that they could have any great value apart from the world
of moral choice and action in which they have their being.
In theory at least, he held that it is wrong to overemphasize
either technique or expression, but while he had no mean
capacity for technical and even semantic analysis, he never
regarded technique as anything more than a means, and
he returns again and again in his criticism to the larger
meanings of his particular subject. He is especially hard to
read today. His interests, his problems, his solutions seem
strangely remote, and his position, to put it mildly, unsym-
pathetic. His critical personality is not ingratiating, and if
he suffers justly from his dogmatism, his moralism, and his
absolutism, he is also betrayed, perhaps somewhat unjustly,
by prejudice against his Victorian vocabulary. It is true that
his aesthetic is conceptualist and leads him into undue stress
on content and sincerity when it does not lead him into un-
tenable and even absurd corners, but a little sympathy can
find a number of things to put in the balance—his sensitivity
on single points and his keen powers of analysis, his many
sharp observations on the relations between art and culture,
between culture and the artist, and between the artist and
his art.

From a simple historical perspective Ruskin looks very
big indeed. Because his direct contribution to poetic theory
has seemed, and may be, small, it has been possible to
overlook his powerful and pervasive influence on the criti-
cism of his own time; but even a cursory examination of
the critical documents and a glance at the periodicals ought
to vindicate his position as the most important critical force
in the middle of the century. He was, for instance, virtually
the only critic of art who was read by everyone. Newman,
Mill, Browning, even the early Arnold, had little or no
audience, and in most cases the theoretical writing of the

critics still remembered was hardly known to their fellow-theorists; Ruskin, on the other hand, was talked about and quoted at large. Undoubtedly his eccentricity and his virtuousity with words helped to provoke discussion, but it was rather his formulation of definite, if often arbitrary, rules and standards for art that aroused the passions of his friends and enemies. In any case, it is certain that Ruskin gave a renewed interest to speculation about aesthetics and poetic theory; he provided principles for and directed the practice of the Pre-Raphaelite painters; he sent his readers to buildings and walls and books, and back to nature itself, with a fresh eye for their effects; and he offered useful suggestions to literary theorists like Dallas, Patmore,[119] De Vere, and Bagehot, which later found their way into the general stream of criticism. More specifically, with his doctrine of naturalism in art, the representation of reality exactly as it is, no better and no worse, Ruskin was at the center of the trend towards realism in England (and even in France?); he developed the idea of the penetrative imagination in order to show how art could be at once imitative and expressive; and finally, he founded a "theology of art" that not only exerted a wide positive influence in his own time, but which eventually helped to bring about through reaction the dominant modern theory of art, art for art's sake.

[119] Cf., for example, "The Ethics of Art" in the *British Quarterly Review*, x, 1849, in which Patmore discusses "the practical result of art upon the moral and religious condition of men and nations." The article begins with a specific reference to the close of *Modern Painters*, III.

11. The Substance of English Poetic Theory, 1825-1865

WHEN Matthew Arnold came to define the function of criticism in 1865, it seemed to him that the main effort of the mind of Europe had already been, for many years, critical: "in all branches of knowledge, theology, philosophy, history, art, science, to see the object as in itself it really is." Now, there are suggestions in the Clough letters that Arnold from the beginning entertained, probably unconsciously, a rather romantic notion of creativity. Some such notion would seem to underlie the dubious historical analogy by which in retrospect he allowed himself to think of the French Revolution as in some sense abortive because it did not produce an art comparable to that of Greece or the Renaissance; and it is undoubtedly an exalted notion of creative activity which leaves Arnold dissatisfied with the achievement of English romanticism and which leads him to ignore the development of the nineteenth century novel. Was Arnold really looking for a whole crop of Goethes? In any case, he observed the very genuine access of critical activity and what he took to be failure in creativity, and he went on to propose a startlingly new idea—the idea of creative criticism. The creative artist works with ideas, the best ideas of his culture; but there are times when his culture does not provide him readily with these ideas. At such times it becomes the function of the critic to make available to the artist not only a fresh current of the best ideas but an intellectual order in which the artist can find himself and so create. Arnold almost seems to say that it is the critic's job to create an artificial culture for the artist. Furthermore, the critical act itself, in Arnold's description, is rather more than simple judgment; it is the communication of fresh knowledge in which judgment is insensibly and concomitantly passed, and as such is allied to, and gives the sense of, creative activity.

Arnold's essay on "The Function of Criticism" probably represents a turning-point in the self-consciousness of criticism, perhaps even the beginning of the "art" of criticism, and therefore belongs to modern history rather than to this book; but its perspective may help to suggest certain generalizations about Early Victorian criticism and poetic theory. In the first place, the same wave of creativity carried the poetic theorists and the Arnold of "The Function of Criticism"; if Arnold in 1865 failed to acknowledge it at its own value, the theorists for the most part seem to have taken it for granted. They do not seem to have questioned the creativity of the first quarter of the century, nor the possibility of genuine creation in their own circumstances. The theorists were all aware in differing degrees of their troublous times; their discussion of poetry invariably starts and ends in a cultural context; and they canvassed thoroughly the individual, social, and cultural functions of art to the limits of their vision. Their solutions cover art as integration (myth), art as explanation (symbol), art as morals (cultivation of emotion, value), art as catharsis, and psychotherapy (expression). They believed, perhaps too fondly, perhaps anachronistically, in the power of poetry as feeling or imagination to effect a material change in their own culture, or even more accurately, in the power of the poet as the man of feeling or insight to lead them out of the wilderness. As a matter of fact, Arnold's creative critic looks suspiciously like the poet-prophet of the formularies, the same magician patched with new stars. If Arnold could see no immediate progeny for Goethe, the seer of the theorists, he could, and did, call attention to Goethe, the critic, and assimilating something of the quality of the former, modeled his hero as man of letters on the latter. Whether the genealogy is right or not, the critic still seems to be another manifestation of the nineteenth century hero, and in that world of rising industrialism and democracy seems equally illusionary with his more conventional counterpart.

Arnold's serious attempts to appreciate the romantic poets in print all belong to a later date, although it is true that he had used them as examples of false theory and practice in 1853. In general, however, romantic poetry and romantic

209

theory constituted the very impulse and stuff of the Early
Victorian critics. The romantic movement is now more than
a hundred years old, and we see its great figures through
a long perspective of criticism, criticism of which the Early
Victorians began the elaboration. Their attitude towards
Wordsworth and Keats and the others is admiring but unawed;
sometimes to the modern it seems disarmingly casual. They
examined the poetry in the light of already moderated prin-
ciples and when they found it wanting they did not hesitate
to say so. The strength of the new poetry was found in the
simplicities and subtleties of its emotional responses, in its
interpretations of the world of natural objects and in the
intimations of immortality and of morality revealed through
the gifted soul; the weaknesses, not so much in the poetry
as in the individual lives and characters of the poets them-
selves. There is a strange ambivalence in the Early Victorian
judgment: it sanctioned prophecy and revelation but re-
quired that they conform to law and fact; it applauded in-
dividual expression but was likely to label the personal
statement eccentric; its affinities were all subjectivist but it
longed for objectivity; and while its prime test was feeling,
it was quick to point out absence of idea and moral.

Of the several English poets Wordsworth is rightly the
most influential, but he is also far and away the most influen-
tial of the English critics. Coleridge now so completely covers
the critical horizon of the nineteenth century that it is easy
to forget he came into his reputation late. German criticism
counted directly with individual critics such as Carlyle and
Dallas, but more generally it operated through Words-
worth's treatment of the imagination as that generated fur-
ther elaborations in the native tradition. It was Wordsworth
who publicly announced the definitive break with eighteenth
century poetic principles and laid down the strategic plan
of attack at the same time he was engaging in certain tactical
skirmishes of his own. It is perhaps worth observing that
the issue was by no means settled in 1825, and that towards
the end of our period Ruskin is still fighting a major battle
with Reynolds. In its simplest form the issue was between

form and content, execution and conception, technique and expression; the problem is, of course, perennial, and as long as the pairs are regarded as antithetical, probably insoluble. It seems to be a fact that the eighteenth century leaned towards the first and the nineteenth towards the second term of each pair. One indication of the shift in emphasis is the almost universal disparagement of rhetoric—Carlyle's "grammar"—and the rhetorical aspect of poetry in Early Victorian theory. Another indication is the Early Victorian rejection of mechanistic doctrines of association for a dynamic and transcendental theory of the imagination in line with Coleridge. It is perhaps here that we can locate the most characteristic ambiguity of Early Victorian poetics— the dual role of science.

The nineteenth century watched the mushroom growth of experimental and practical science. In so far as science could be identified with mechanism and materialism, and especially with utilitarianism, it seemed to the Early Victorian critics, following once again in the steps of the romantics, not only the logical opposite of poetry but its active enemy. The main reason for this attitude was undoubtedly the view of science as a dangerous competitor in interpreting the nature of ultimate "reality." Revulsion against eighteenth century rationalism, resulting in skepticism, sensationalism, and subjective idealism, had successfully prejudiced the status of the human reason, and had led to the extravagant claims of romantic theory for the epistemological powers of "imagination." Poetry professed to discover the "real" and the "true." Meanwhile the empirical methods of science were discovering a world, also advertised as "real" and "true," but which looked very different from the world of the poets. One difference was crucial; there seemed to be no room for "spirit" in the world of the scientists, nor consequently any validity for the poet's intimations of reality. The unfortunate analysis of the problem in Wordsworth's Preface is at the back of the countless discussions of the relations between poetry and science in Early Victorian criticism, and with one or two exceptions, misled that criticism to the end. There are still no really adequate treatments of the subject in the period in spite of all the attempts.

On the other hand, the pressures, encroachments, and successes of the scientific method provoked or invited the critics to emulation. The spirit of fresh discovery, the enthusiasm of the march of mind, took all but the bitterest opponent, and the effects begin to appear everywhere, in the revived interest in the history of poetics, in the attempt to explain the psychology of the imagination, in the determination to give a systematic account of the nature of poetry, and in the careful induction and comparison of instances. More important yet, perhaps, were the efforts of the critics to account for the value of poetry in a society rapidly taking over a scientific way of looking at the world. In this context the theorists are most likely to stand on the individualistic and subjective qualities of poetry, the expression of emotion, or the exercise of the feelings; but poetry, as sympathetic imagination or imaginative sympathy, is also conceived as a binding social and political force, as well as a powerful moral agent. Once at least it is proposed to incorporate the discoveries of science into the subject matter of poetry itself where, as Wordsworth had granted conditionally they might, they would be sources of integration and adaptation. The relationship between early nineteenth century science and poetic theory is not easy to define with any certainty, but it does appear that the spate of theorizing in the Early Victorian period came about very largely through a simultaneous attraction and repulsion.

The nine chief justices of Early Victorian poetic theory can be grouped in a variety of patterns. Carlyle, Dallas, Hunt, and Ruskin are the professional critics, although Dallas is the only one of the nine whose activities were primarily, if not exclusively, devoted to literary criticism. Keble might be called a professional critic by appointment, but his Oxford Lectureship really stands outside his career and he persisted in regarding himself as an amateur. Dallas and Ruskin pair again in their larger concern with the theory of art as a systematic ground for their poetic. Hunt, Browning, and

Arnold are the professional poets of the group. It is worthy of remark, however, that Newman and Keble published volumes of verse; Carlyle and Ruskin both indulged in "prose-poetry"; and Ruskin sketched and painted. Only Mill and Dallas, so far as one can see, give no signs of poetic talent. Newman, Keble, Dallas and Ruskin all write from a pervasive Christian position, and the first two, of course, were theologians by vocation. Eight of the nine, the exception is Hunt, show at least a general training in philosophy; Mill might be called a professional philosopher and Carlyle perhaps an amateur. The same eight are also, at least in some degree, cultural historians with Carlyle the professional here. What such groupings bring out in the last analysis is the staggering multiplicity of talents in these Early Victorian men of letters; they are theologians, philosophers, political and economic theorists, historians, biographers, editors, aestheticians, poets, and last but not least, critics and poetic theorists. It is perhaps futile to attempt to distinguish between the qualities of already distinguished minds; Mill's is probably the best as mind, followed by Newman's; but this does not mean that Mill and Newman are the best poetic theorists. Mill seems to have been deficient in imagination and Newman in understanding. Hunt, Arnold, and Ruskin, in different ways, seem to have the best combination of qualities for literary criticism—Hunt and Ruskin in their power of generalizing from accurate and sensitive perception of particular effects, Arnold in his power of applying general principles to the analysis of given cases. Dallas, who knew more about the history of poetics than any of his contemporaries, is fertile and ingenious, but his mind lacks originality. In spite of the many virtues and successes of the Early Victorian theorists, it still seems to be true that no one of the nine deserves to rank with Coleridge, or even Wordsworth, in the lists of English criticism.

Of the virtues of Early Victorian poetic theory the first is surely its breadth of perspective. The nine all come to the problems of definition by a considered humanistic approach, and they look at poetry and art as not unrelated to man's

other and varied activities. Furthermore, they had studied
the Greeks and the Romans; they had read sensitively, if
not exhaustively, in modern European literatures, and they
had been profoundly moved by their own literature of the
romantic period. In this view it seemed to them quite simply
that poetry was important in the economy of the good life,
especially important in their own uncertain time. It was a
value which had long been tried and proved, and which
could be tried and proved on the common pulse. They be-
lieved with Wordsworth that poetry, as primal, communal
feeling, as sympathy, as imaginative compassion, could, and
would be, of the various powers at work in society, the
effective unifying, generating, and regenerating force. Their
poetic theory is thus conceived, and for the most part de-
veloped, in large and general terms. This very fact is likely
to prove a stumbling block to the twentieth century reader,
expert in the countless special theories of the last thirty
years; but it is salutary to be reminded that poetry does not
have to be either pure or propaganda, or ambiguous or ironic,
but may be all of these together and much else besides. A
second virtue might be that all nine were radically impli-
cated in the new way of looking at things which we call
romanticism, and yet again and again they managed to
transcend their involvement at particular points and achieve
a certain independence. The best witness to their independ-
ence is probably the censure of the idiosyncratic lapses of
the romantics without prejudice to the central insight of
romantic experimentalism and the recognition of moral
stability as the precondition of a mature poetry.

If one had to choose, one would probably say that modern
criticism is characterized by its interest in the poem as a
self-contained structure of meaning, in form in other words,
and in the techniques by which forms are produced. It is
understatement to say that this interest, particularly in so
far as it is exclusive, is quite foreign to Early Victorian
poetics. Mill may talk of poetry as presenting "objects" for
contemplation, Carlyle may mention the "architecture" of
the *Divine Comedy*, or the "harmony" of meanings in poetry,

and there are scattered references throughout Early Victorian theory to "total impression"; but as Arnold observed, the principle of "total impression" is little more than critical commonplace, and the primary stress on the "structure" of the poetic action in his own theory is virtually unique in the period, even though Hunt, indeed, attaches importance to the successful resolution of formal difficulties as a sign of the poet's technical mastery of his impulse, and Keble, in keeping with his theory of poetry as "medicinal," points in passing to the cathartic effect of the poet's struggle with the formal exigencies of his medium. Two or three of the nine had no mean hand for technical analysis (Ruskin, the most "moral" of them all, does as pretty a piece of semantic analysis as one could want on two lines in his chapter on the "Pathetic Fallacy"); but on the whole technical criticism seemed to them of very minor importance. Going on the assumption that in essence poetry was a matter of "feeling" or of "imagination" or of "expression," they tended to regard the particular poem rather as a sign and instrument, a simple medium of qualities in the poet or effects in the reader, than anything of final value in and for itself. For this reason Early Victorian criticism virtually ignores the matter of form in its preoccupation with what may conveniently be called the psychological and moral aspects of poetic theory. Whatever general success we may credit to the nine will necessarily lie in their observations on the relations between art and the artist, between art and the audience, and between art and society. In this connection it is perhaps worth noting that the tone of Early Victorian theory is more often than not apologetic and defensive (it may be that the tone is chronic), and that again and again the rather formal apology or defense, revived in the English Renaissance and enshrined in the romantic period by Shelley, is usually made a part of Early Victorian essays on poetry.

In the very broadest view the main topics of Early Victorian poetics are four: genius, imagination, expression, and teaching. Since they constitute four parts of a single general theory, they would probably be regarded by most of the

nine as equally important, but if one were to hazard a guess
as to their relative weight in the ideal Early Victorian theory,
genius would be the generating concept and the others
would follow in rough descending order. The topics cover
the poetic agent, the poetic faculty in the agent and in the
audience, the poetic means, and the poetic object or effect.

Most of the Early Victorian poetic theories are theories
of the poet. The typical poet, who can probably be fathered
on romantic hero-worship in general and on Carlyle in par-
ticular, is the God-gifted, heaven-sent, divinely inspired
seer, the interpreter of man and nature, the living breath of
his time and place, and the prophet of eternal verities and
of things to come. He is Shelley's (not Samuel Johnson's !)
"legislator of the world," the leader and the great teacher;
he is also the creator, the revealer, the originator, the maker.
He is born and not made, but since he is born late he will
not scorn the advantages of Victorian education and culture.
With all of his special graces and privileges, however, he is
still a man speaking to men as Wordsworth had insisted;
he differs from his fellow-men in degree, not in kind. His
prime virtue (a virtue, by the way, in which the least of his
readers could share if so disposed) is sincerity; he is in
earnest with the world. The highest function of art in Early
Victorian theory is to facilitate the intimate knowledge of
the moral and spiritual qualities of great men, knowledge
of the finest patterns of thinking and feeling, character and
personality. The description of the typical poet is, of course,
plainly immoderate; but the elements all actually appear,
often in heavy concentration, and one is forced to the con-
clusion that, in fact, there was something a little monstrous
in the Early Victorians' wishful fantasy of the poet. Matthew
Arnold raised more than one impatient protest against the
exaggerated ideals indulged by his compeers, but at best
the critics were thinking of Homer and Aeschylus and Soph-
ocles, of Dante and Shakespeare, Milton and Wordsworth
and Goethe, and they were right without the slightest doubt
(although it is perhaps unfashionable now to say so) that
high converse with the distinguished living and the mighty

dead is one, if not the chief nor the only one, of the abiding values of art.

Characteristic of the Early Victorian theory of the poet are the various classifications according to nature and kind. Dallas gives an elaborate account of the traditional classification according to kind—narrative, dramatic, and lyric— farced with historical and metaphysical distinctions in the manner of "German" criticism. Of some theoretical interest, perhaps, is Dallas' suggestion that the modern poet *par excellence* is essentially dramatic. Equally popular is the classification according to nature into poets of "impulse" and poets of "will" of which Mill's version, poets of nature and poets of culture, is representative. Keble calls the first "creative" and will admit the second only on sufferance, while Mill actually prefers the latter. A third classification which combines nature and kind is that of the poets of the "inner," and poets of the "outer," life. Carlyle uses this, and Browning develops it in his contrast of seer and fashioner, the subjective and the objective poet. The first and the third distinctions play a part in Ruskin's classification of "creative" and "perceptive"; most of the romantics and all of the Early Victorians, incidentally, seem to fall into the second category. To categorize is human, and these groupings are no doubt of some service to the critical understanding; if they no longer seem particularly significant, it may be because the early Victorian theorists have told us all we need to know on the subject.

The poetic faculty may also be regarded as constitutive, and for the Early Victorians, as for the romantics, this faculty was the imagination, with its many synonyms, vision, insight, inspiration, intuition, intellect, originality, power. More often than not, poetry, in the sense of the poetic, is identified with any manifestation of the imagination, and the poem is valued primarily as a sign of the fact or quality of imagination in the poet. There are two broad attitudes towards the psychology of imagination in our nine critics: one considers the problem beyond analysis—the imagination is the highest power of the human mind, mysterious, superrational, and incomprehensible; the other, proceeding from analysis of its manifestations, distinguishes the two familiar modes of romantic criticism, imagination and fancy, and within these, various types, classes, and subcategories. Whether imagination and fancy differ in kind or only in degree is still very much a matter of open debate in the period. It might be observed that none of the Early Victorian theories of the imagination seems to have anything like the metaphysical significance nor the psychological subtlety of Coleridge's earlier speculations on the subject. The chief characteristic of imagination is its "given" nature, which then may be described variously and even simultaneously as "active" and "passive." The passive aspect is further defined as unconscious, generally in the sense of unself-conscious; more simply, imagination is preeminently feeling and instinct. There is some disagreement as to whether the imagination, considered as "inspiration," is to be understood literally or metaphorically; in general the transcendentalists lean towards a literal interpretation in keeping with the doctrine of a direct action of the Divine upon the human intellect. In any case, with the exception of Mill, who is an associationist, the Early Victorian critics all attribute a dynamic power to the imagination. The Kantian distinction between the productive and the reproductive imagination is quite common in the period, sometimes in forms which show no trace of systematic origin, and, as might be expected, the reproductive— the naturalistic, representational—function of the imagination receives a characteristic stress. The work of the imagination is to provide images of absent objects, to associate in various manners such images, to mirror and even intuit the true essence of reality, material and spiritual. Furthermore, it is peculiarly fitted to do this, as Wordsworth had pointed out, by connatural affinity. It is also characteristic of the imagination that it seizes its object as particular type or form, and similarly in the large, supplies the form with the essence of its subject-matter in the more intricate relations of images which constitute the poem or work of art. Any signs of self-conscious preoccupation with conventional or rhetorical patterns will very likely be interpreted as a failure in imagination.

For all the Early Victorians' interest in the faculty of imagination, they add very little to what had already been observed by Wordsworth and Coleridge. The modifications introduced by Hunt in Wordsworth's classification of types of imagination have little, if any, practical bearing, and the same is true of most of Ruskin's proliferation of the subject. Ruskin did, however, in his formulation of the penetrative function of the imagination, hit upon a happy description of the realistic validity of imaginative perception which is ordinarily only feebly suggested by the language of romantic and Early Victorian criticism in general. Heavy stress on the realistic, reproductive power of the imagination allows for the typical Early Victorian ideal of "portraiture" in art, and probably underlies Ruskin's naturalistic argument against the pathetic fallacy. Newman, Keble, Mill, Browning, and Arnold, have very little to say about the imagination as such; they are more interested in other aspects of poetic theory. As insight or vision, it is central to Carlyle's position where it functions as the Kantian "reason," but Carlyle scorns all faculty psychology and deliberately refuses to analyze the imagination which he prefers to regard as indefinable. It is Dallas, perhaps, who makes the most suggestive use of German ideas on the imagination with his insistence on the imaginative quality of all knowledge and with his distinction between imaginary (subjective) and imaginative (objective) concords by which he attempts to reconcile the extremes of the theories of creation and imitation, representation and expression. Also of some speculative interest is his use of the Kantian categories of space and time as they affect the imagination to account for the functions of rhythm and imagery in poetry.

The typical Early Victorian theory of poetry has been described as a theory of the genius whose virtue is imagination. In keeping with this theory the characteristic means is expression and what is expressed is feeling. Some theories, Newman's and Keble's for example, hardly go very far beyond this principle; they are consequently preoccupied with an essence, "the poetic," and show no concern whatever for the art or the object, the poem. Expression—common alternatives are effusion, utterance, contemplation, self-communion—is always spontaneous and is regularly described as passive or unconscious, and is closely associated with imagination and inspiration. Further, it is by definition subjective and lyric, and in extreme formulations it denies not only form and matter but communication as well. Typically, the theory also sanctions obscurity, since the poet's intuitions, especially of the universe of feeling and spirit, cannot always be expected to be clear, and since the poet's primary allegiance is to his vision, and only secondarily and indirectly to his audience. Some modification of this principle will, of course, be found in certain theories, such as Ruskin's, which stress accuracy of representation, but the apology for obscurity is widespread. The theory has one signal advantage: it stresses one important fact about poetry and at the same time obviates many of the vexing problems of aesthetics, such as the apparent antithesis between creation and imitation; but it has one devastating disadvantage, for it must explain why the direct, physiological or simply personal expression of emotion is not poetry. Some theorists, in the line of Wordsworth's sensational realism, will allow that in fact it can be, but usually the answer is categorical: the problem is referred to the poetic faculty. Imagination is feeling, but it is also a special quality of feeling, partially abstracted, mediated, refined, and therefore some principle of indirection is implied, if not explicitly defined, in most Early Victorian theory. Indirection is also induced as a mode of generalizing individual feeling, and it takes on a moral function when it is used to eliminate the "egoistic" or "immodest" expression. Thus in the typical form of the Early Victorian expressionist theory poetry becomes the indirect or imaginative expression of emotion, takes on characteristics of "impersonality" and symbolism, even in some systems of a certain "objectivity," and so modified, the theory becomes tenable at least. Even at best, however, the theory is reductive, and fails notably to account for the facts of conventions and skills, representational and mimetic values in poetry, and particularly communicative and rhetorical purposes.

Expressionistic principles, for example, account for Newman's rejection of the Aristotelian action or plot as central to the Greek drama (a word, for Newman, can be as "poetic" as a whole play); for Keble's remark that Vergil had no real interest in any of the epic machinery of the *Aeneid*; for Mill's argument that all poetry tends to the condition of the lyric. They are seen at work in Hunt's selection and analysis of passages, rather than poems, to illustrate "Imagination and Fancy" (although he does affirm in theory the necessity of "continuity" in poetry); and they can be seen perhaps in a limited way in Ruskin's preoccupation with detail in so many of the poems and paintings he deals with. The genius theories of Carlyle and Browning, heavily saturated with Platonism, are expressionistic to a fault in spite of some recognition of the representative values of symbolism. Ruskin, with his "naturalist ideal," made a brave and persistent attempt to dress the balance of contemporary theory on this point, but it was Matthew Arnold who conspicuously challenged expressionism from the stronghold of Aristotelian poetics. Arnold stressed the deliberate choice of meaningful subject, the constructive aspect of the poetic process, and the ultimate importance of total impression in the work of art. Arnold's stringency on the sacrifice of form to the brilliant image or the telling figure in romantic and contemporary poetry alike is a measure of the force of expressionist principles in Early Victorian theory.

So far, in discussing the fundamental parts of Early Victorian poetics, genius, imagination, and expression, the whole question of value has been very largely taken for granted. On the subject of the end of poetry there was general (and conventional) agreement: the end of poetry is to teach and delight. All nine are aligned on this point. Some divergence in emphasis there is, of course,—the chief in the order of importance of the two functions; it is generally allowed, however, that the pleasure of poetry is instrumental to the purpose of instructing or enlightening. Now, the formal end of poetry in seven of the nine theories is truth—beauty, which is sometimes placed before or with truth is in these theories either synonymous, or like pleasure in the final end, a means; two of the theories appear to be genuinely formalistic, but one of these at least seems to shift ground on occasion. Theoretically genius, imagination, and expression are neutral terms, but actually in Early Victorian criticism all three take on solid color from a moral conception of the formal and the final ends. Poetry must instruct; the matter of instruction is truth; truth is a moral good: then the moral acceptability of the poetic statement determines the poet's right to his title. But the theory is still more complicated by the possibility of insincerity. Since moral attitudes may be feigned, it becomes necessary to have recourse to the poet's biography in order to be sure of his "moral center," the true character of his imagination, and the spontaneity of his expression. Sincerity is the ultimate test of value in all Early Victorian criticism, and the morality of art is placed squarely, in theory at least, in the character of the poet—which, by the way, is probably where it belongs. The omnipresent discussions of moral centers and tones, of dominant and master feelings, are an integral part of the Early Victorians' genuine and valid interest in the men who make poems, and in what they still took to be an effective power in poetry to operate on culture through a large audience (there are plenty of indications that the critics were uncomfortably aware of the alienation between artist and audience which was actually going on, but Early Victorian theories seem to ignore the fact for the ideal). Furthermore, individual critics so modified the general stand as to alleviate the worst effects of the didactic fallacy: poetry teaches by indirection, by example not precept, by tone not theme; and in the poet morality is after all a matter of degree so that some good can be salvaged from anything short of the completely depraved. Practically all of the Early Victorian theorists describe the effect of poetry as some sort of catharsis of emotion; the

222

definitions run all the way from the release of repressions, through character training, to the induction of spiritual exaltation. In general there is very little that is new in these accounts, but it might be observed that the theory of catharsis is not uncommonly applied to the poet in the period with interesting adumbrations in one case of the Freudian theory of art. It is surprising how often in Early Victorian criticism the function of poetry is regarded as "consolatory"; one wonders if in fact this is not the characteristic mark of Early Victorian theories of the end. Perhaps Arnold was right, and in a world of crumbling values only the ideal world of the imagination held the kind of promise in which the otherwise disillusioned could put anything like their whole trust; but the Early Victorians hardly lived to see the issue of their faith, in the art for art's sake creed of the later nineteenth century, nor for the matter of that, have we in the twentieth. The Early Victorian theorists inherited from the late seventeenth and eighteenth centuries what seems like, in view of practical considerations after the Renaissance, an exaggerated and ineffectual admiration of the "great forms" of poetry, and one notes that the serious burden with which Early Victorian theory of the end loaded poetry, led to a distinctive preoccupation with problems of greatness in art, and by inversion, to the neglect of lesser and lighter possibilities of the art of verse.

Newman, Mill, Hunt, Dallas, and Arnold all treat catharsis in greater or less detail, but by far the most interesting treatment is Keble's. Keble makes the "medicinal" power of poetry the central principle of his whole theory. Poetry is defined as the release, through expression, of feelings and desires which for temperamental, moral, or social reasons are normally repressed. The condition of the poet, who differs from ordinary men only in degree, is regarded as in some sense diseased; if denied relief, the poet suffers and may even become insane. Poetry provides relief; and similarly and vicariously poetry provides relief for the troubled reader. Keble's theory is somewhat implicated by the subterfuge or indirection which the poet uses to disguise his condition, and so comes even closer to Freud's theory of wish-fulfill-ment by means of fantasy. Arnold and Ruskin both give good accounts of the place of moral judgment in the anal-ysis of the poem (a matter of tone or style according to Ar-nold) and in the analysis of the artistic character (a matter of *habitus* according to Ruskin); Newman, Keble, and Ruskin give three analogous accounts of moral centers and master feelings (Keble derives his master feelings from close examina-tion of recurrent images in an anticipation of the manner of some modern image analysis); but Newman has perhaps the best answer to the question of the relation between beauty and morality in general: the problem is not a matter of subject or of moral practice in the poet; the beauty of poetry is in propor-tion to whatever virtue is in the man; right moral feeling cen-ters the whole man and validates, from this point of view, the work. Keble's theory of "parody," by which certain expres-sions of an "impious" author can be altered by the reader to conform to his own conviction of truth, is an ingenious as well as ingenuous attempt to get around the similar vexing problem of poetry and belief. There is no balking the fact that Early Victorian poetic theory is erroneously and ob-noxiously moralistic, but granting this, two comments may be made: the critics' insights were sometimes better than their systems, and if they sinned, they sinned on the side of the lesser evil. Poetry quite simply deals with moral values, not, to be sure, in the manner of ethics or politics; if we pre-sume to have any idea what moral values are, and if they mean anything to us, we cannot abrogate the responsibility of passing final judgment in the context of whatever princi-ple we may hold. Morals come before art, as the Early Vic-torians in general knew, and rightly understood, art is an aspect of morality.

One of our keenest contemporary theoreticians remarked recently in print that poetics is even now probably the messi-est discipline of the mind. It might be well to keep this state-ment in front of us as we attempt to evaluate the achieve-ment of Early Victorian poetic theory. The critical scene would appear to have been radically altered during the last hundred years. In the largest sense, what is sometimes called the breakdown of the Graeco-Christian synthesis, or from a converse position, the trial of secularism, is upon us with immediacy. Practically all traditional values are in question, and we are now testing the possibility of ordering a society on some new combination of naturalistic and rationalistic ideals based on history, the natural sciences, and the pseudo-sciences of anthropology, psychology, and sociology. The status of the artist, especially the poet, for half a century has been, to say the least, equivocal; his alienation from society, already manifest in the romantics, has become progressively more acute. As a consequence, the typical modern artist has turned in upon himself, and located his ultimate values in his art, identifying reality and his own particular vision; or skeptical even of his own vision, he has given himself up to exploitation of means as an end in itself, and squandered himself on technique and effect: both of these consequences imply as a ground the theory of art for art's sake, and an aesthetic of expressionism in the one case, and formalism in the other.

It is not surprising, if this account is not grossly incorrect, that modern poetics too is radically altered in its bearings and interests. The newer theory has developed in intimate relation to modern philosophical idealism and pragmatism and with the systematic aesthetics which have been highly articulated from both of these positions; in relation to Freudian and post-Freudian psychologies; in relation to a revived interest in rhetoric, and especially in relation to the comparatively recently isolated "science" of semantics. Formalistic poetics seems to be primarily concerned with establishing the autonomy of poetry as a mode of discourse, and with the poem as a self-contained pattern or complex of meanings with a unique effect; it prefers to deal almost exclusively with matters of technique. The formalist usually refuses to consider any questions having to do with the nature of the poet or with the psychology of composition. Expressionistic poetics is more difficult to define succinctly; it is primarily concerned with states of feeling, and is therefore sometimes hostile to both form and theory; and it tends to regard the poem chiefly as a means, the most immediate, of communicating emotion. Expressionistic theory may show an absorbing interest in technique, but it also shows a strong predisposition for psychological analysis and biographical and even sociological treatment of the poet. The whole stress of the theory is individualistic—it is a "genius" theory, even though its exponents may not wish to accept the historical implications of the term—and in its more extreme formulations is deliberately grounded in aversion from convention, tradition, and society. Furthermore, the theory emphasizes the unconscious nature of the poetic process and commonly takes the life of the subconscious as its matter; its characteristic artistic means is therefore distortion, symbolic of revolt against the logic and order of reason, and its characteristic form, the nonprescriptive, nonrational, aperiodic patterns of emotion itself.

While it is clear that Early Victorian poetic theory is in the most general sense a direct ancestor of contemporary expressionism, it is equally clear that the ancestry is remote, and that Early Victorian theory has very little to do with either of the dominant modern theories. Neither formalism nor expressionism, however, in their typical formulations gives an adequate account of poetry; the best modern theorists do not attempt to hold "pure" positions of either kind, and the most recent speculation has been trying to reconcile the valid principles in each in a more satisfactory synthesis. Both theories are reductive and exclusive, formalism perhaps more so than expressionism; both fail to exploit the full range of possibilities as we know that range in the long and richly varied history of poetry. Both theories are weak in attempting to deal with the problem of the relation between art and society and with the problem of the relation between society and the artist. Formalism fails especially to take account of the artistic value of subject-matter—Aristotle's actions, Wordsworth's general passions, thoughts, and feelings of men; expressionism, in turn, fails to engage the intellect and violates its demands for order and proportion, while in its eccentricity, it, too, rejects all responsibility towards the general life of society. It is perfectly plain that no theory, however accurate and complete, can effect a cure for the ills of poetry, if indeed poetry is sick at all in the twentieth century, any more than a social or political theory, as theory, can solve for once and for all the social and political problems of the race. Still, a man can mend his ways if he can be made to see that they are wrong, and if he can be shown something better; and understanding and intelligence will no doubt help in the demonstration. For all the inadequacy and error and diverse interest of Early Victorian poetic theory, it may nevertheless offer one or two suggestions from which the modern critic in humility may profit.

Early Victorian theory first of all posits the responsibility of the poet, immediately to his own insight, but mediately to the fullness of the world around him, the world of things, and particularly the world of men, their acts, their thinking and feeling, and their aspiration. The Early Victorians pushed their theory of the poet too far, but the *fuehrerprinzip* is by no means a necessary corollary of human responsibility. In its central emphasis on the full role of imagination, productive and reproductive, in poetry, Early Victorian theory further recognizes the relation between poetry and an inclusive experience of life in which neither the "inner" nor the "outer" is sacrificed to principle. It is true that the doctrine of poetry as expression is inadequate where it is not misleading altogether, but at least it commanded a wide, human base, a representative and communicable experience, for what was expressed; the theory did not, in other words, sanction a break out of hand with the general life of men, with convention and tradition, merely because they were conventional and traditional. Finally, Early Victorian theory insists firmly and rightly on the relevance, the meaning, the value, the "morality" of poetry. It is not a question here of the moralistic excesses of the theory; they exist and cannot be defended. What is in point is the conviction of the Early Victorian critics that poetry is not only a genuine source of human pleasure but that it is also, because it is the most

comprehensive, the most valuable source of human knowl-
edge and understanding. Early Victorian poetic theory is
quite simply humanistic, and it is precisely the humanistic
values of poetry which in the twentieth century are most
in need of reaffirmation together with the truths of form and
expression against the perverted aestheticism both of con-
temporary theory and contemporary practice.

Bibliography

Part I of the bibliography is a chronological table of books and essays on the theory of poetry between 1825 and 1865. The documents which are discussed in detail in the text are marked with an asterisk. More complete bibliographical information on all the documents listed in the table will be found in Part II, which also contains a selection of books dealing with aesthetics, criticism, and poetic theory.

Part I

1825	Keble, John. "Sacred Poetry."
	Procter, B. W. "On English Poetry."
1828	Procter, B. W. "A Defence of Poetry."
1829	*Newman, J. H. "Poetry, with Reference to Aristotle's Poetics."
1832-41	*Keble, John. *De Poeticae Vi Medica*.
1833	*Mill, J. S. "What is Poetry?"
	*Mill, J. S. "The Two Kinds of Poetry."
	Montgomery, James. *Lectures on Poetry*.
1834	Taylor, Sir Henry. *Philip Van Artevelde*.
1839	Moir, George. *Treatises on Poetry, Modern Romance, and Rhetoric; being the Articles under those Heads, Contributed to the Encyclopaedia Britannica, Seventh Edition*.
1841	*Carlyle, Thomas. *On Heroes, Hero-Worship and the Heroic in History*.
1842	Lewes, G. H. "Hegel's Aesthetics. Philosophy of Art."
1844	*Hunt, Leigh. *Imagination and Fancy . . . with . . . an essay in answer to the question, "What is Poetry?"*
1846	Ruskin, John. *Modern Painters*. Vol. II.
1848	De Quincey, Thomas. "The Poetry of Pope."
1849	De Vere, Aubrey. "Taylor's *Eve of the Conquest*."
	De Vere, Aubrey. "Tennyson's *Princess*."
	Patmore, Coventry. "The Ethics of Art."

1850   Elliott, Ebenezer. "A Lecture on the Principle that Poetry is Self-Communion."

Mackay, Charles. "An Inquiry into the Alleged Anti-Poetical Tendencies of the Age."

1852   *Browning, Robert. *Letters of Percy Bysshe Shelley, with an Introductory Essay by Robert Browning.*

*Dallas, E. S. *Poetics: an Essay on Poetry.*

1853   *Arnold, Matthew. *Poems. A New Edition.*

Masson, David. "Theories of Poetry and a New Poet."

1854   Aytoun, W. E. *Firmilian.*

1855   Brimley, George. "Verse Books of 1854."

1856   Patmore, Coventry. "New Poets."

*Ruskin, John. *Modern Painters.* Vol. III.

1857   Dobell, Sydney. Lecture on the "Nature of Poetry."

Patmore, Coventry. "English Metrical Critics."

1858   Arnold, Matthew. *Merope.*

1864   Bagehot, Walter. "Wordsworth, Tennyson, and Browning: or Pure, Ornate, and Grotesque Art in English Poetry."

1865   Allingham, William. "On Poetry."

Lewes, G. H. "The Principles of Success in Literature."

Part II

Abercrombie, Lascelles. *The Theory of Poetry.* 1924.

Allingham, William. *Varieties in Prose.* London, 1893.

Arnold, Matthew. *Poems. A New Edition.* London, 1852.

Arnold, Matthew. *Merope.* London, 1858.

Arnold, Matthew. *Essays in Criticism.* London, 1865.

Arnold, Matthew. *Letters.* Edited by G. W. E. Russell, 1896.

Arnold, Matthew. *The Letters of Matthew Arnold to Arthur Hugh Clough.* Edited by H. F. Lowry, 1932.

Aytoun, W. E. *Firmilian.* Edinburgh, 1854.

Bagehot, Walter. "Wordsworth, Tennyson, and Browning: or Pure, Ornate, and Grotesque Art in English Poetry." *The National Review,* XIX, 1864. (Reprinted in *Literary Studies.* London, 1879.)

Bailey, P. J. *Festus.* Thirtieth Edition, London, 1866.

Bosker, Aisso. *Criticism in the Age of Johnson.* 1930.

Bosanquet, Bernard. *A History of Aesthetic.* 1934.

Brimley, George. "Verse Books of 1854." *Fraser's Magazine,* LI, 1855. (Reprinted in *Essays.* London, 1858.)

Browning, Robert. *Letters of Percy Bysshe Shelley, with an Introductory Essay by Robert Browning.* London, 1852. (Reprinted: *On the Poet Objective and Subjective; on the Latter's Aim; on Shelley as Man and Poet. The Browning Society Papers,* Part I, London, 1881.)

Butcher, S. H. *Aristotle's Theory of Poetry and Fine Art.* 1895.

Bywater, Ingram. *Aristotle on the Art of Poetry.* 1909.

Carlyle, Thomas. *On Heroes, Hero-Worship and the Heroic in History.* London, 1841.

Carlyle, Thomas. *Works.* Centenary Edition, 1896-1899.

Clough, A. H. *Poems and Prose Remains.* London, 1869.

Coleridge, S. T. *Biographia Literaria.* Edited by J. Shaw-cross, 1907.

Cowl, R. P. *The Theory of Poetry in England.* 1914.

Dallas, E. S. *Poetics: an Essay on Poetry.* London, 1852.

Dallas, E. S. *The Gay Science.* London, 1866.

De Quincey, Thomas. "The Poetry of Pope." *The North British Review,* x, 1848. (Reprinted in *The Collected Writings of Thomas De Quincey,* edited by D. Masson. Edinburgh, 1890.)

De Quincey, Thomas. *Lessing's Laocoon. Works,* XII, Edinburgh, 1863.

De Vere, Aubrey. "Taylor's *Eve of the Conquest.*" *The Edinburgh Review,* LXXXIX, 1849. (Reprinted in *Essays Chiefly on Poetry.* London, 1887, II, "Henry Taylor's Poetry: Minor Poems.")

De Vere, Aubrey. "Tennyson's Princess." *The Edinburgh Review,* XC, 1849. (Reprinted in *Essays Chiefly on Poetry.* London, 1887, II, "The Two Chief Schools of English Poetry.")

Dobell, Sydney. *Thoughts on Art, Philosophy, and Religion.* London, 1876.

Drinkwater, John. *The Eighteen-Sixties.* 1932.

Eliot, T. S. *The Use of Poetry and the Use of Criticism.* 1933.

Elliott, Ebenezer. *More Verse and Prose by the Cornlaw Rhymer.* London, 1850.

Fry, Roger. *The Artist and Psycho-Analysis.* 1924.

Gayley, C. M. and Young, C. C. *The Principles and Progress of English Poetry.* 1904.

Gayley, C. M. and Scott, F. N. *A Guide to the Literature of Aesthetics.* 1890.

The Germ. 1850.

Gilbert, K. E. and Kuhn, Helmut. *A History of Aesthetics.* 1939.

Gilfillan, George. *Critical Studies in Great Authors.* 1851.

Graham, Walter. *English Literary Periodicals.* 1930.

Gummere, F. B. *A Handbook of Poetics.* 1885.

Hainds, J. R. *J. S. Mill's Views on Art.* Unpublished dissertation, Northwestern University, 1939.

Hazlitt, William. *Collected Works.* Edited by A. R. Waller and Arnold Glover, 1904.

Herrick, M. H. *The Poetics of Aristotle in England.* 1930.

Horne, R. H. *A New Spirit of the Age.* 1844.

Hunt, Leigh. *Imagination and Fancy ... with ... an essay in answer to the question, "What is Poetry?"* London, 1844. (Reprinted: *An Answer to the Question "What is Poetry?"* Edited by A. S. Cook, Boston, 1893.)

Hunt, Leigh. *Autobiography.* The World's Classics, 1928.

Keats, John. *Letters,* Edited by M. B. Forman, 1935.

Keble, John. "Sacred Poetry." *The Quarterly Review,* xxxii, 1925.

Keble, John. *De Poeticae Vi Medica. Praelectiones Academicae Oxonii Habitae, Annis MDCCCXXXII ... MDCCCXLI.* Oxford, 1844. (Translated by E. K. Francis: *Keble's Lectures on Poetry.* Oxford, 1912.)

Ladd, Henry. *The Victorian Morality of Art.* 1932.

Landre, Louis. *Leigh Hunt.* 1936.

Lewes, G. H. "Hegel's Aesthetics. Philosophy of Art." *The British and Foreign Review,* xiii, 1842. (Reprinted in *The*

Principles of Success in Literature. Edited by T. S. Knowlson, London, 1899, "The Inner Life of Art.")

Lewes, G. H. "The Principles of Success in Literature." *The Fortnightly Review,* i and ii, 1865. (Reprinted in *The Principles of Success in Literature.* Edited by T. S. Knowlson, London, 1899.)

Lichtenstein, V. E. *Leigh Hunt's Theory of Poetry.* Unpublished dissertation, University of Iowa, 1939.

Liddell, M. H. *An Introduction to the Scientific Study of English Poetry.* 1902.

Lucas, F. L. *The Decline and Fall of the Romantic Ideal.* 1936.

Mackay, Charles. *Egeria.* London, 1850.

Masson, David. "Theories of Poetry and a New Poet." *The North British Review,* xix, 1853. (Reprinted in *Essays Biographical and Critical: Chiefly on English Poets.* Cambridge, 1856, "Theories of Poetry.")

Mill, J. S. "What is Poetry?" *The Monthly Repository,* vii, 1833. (Reprinted in *Dissertations and Discussions.* London, 1859, "Thoughts on Poetry and Its Varieties.")

Mill, J. S. "The Two Kinds of Poetry." *The Monthly Repository,* vii, 1833. (Reprinted in *Dissertations and Discussions.* London, 1859, "Thoughts on Poetry and Its Varieties.")

Mill, J. S. *Autobiography.* The World's Classics, 1935.

Mill, J. S. *Letters.* Edited by H. S. R. Elliott. 1910.

Moir, D. M. *Sketches of the Poetical Literature of the Past Half Century.* 1851.

Moir, George. *Treatises on Poetry, Modern Romance, and Rhetoric; being the Articles under those Heads, Contributed to the Encyclopaedia Britannica, Seventh Edition.* Edinburgh, 1839.

Montgomery, James. *Lectures on Poetry.* London, 1833.

Neff, Emery. *Carlyle and Mill.* 1926.

Newman, J. H. "Poetry, with Reference to Aristotle's Poetics." *The London Review,* i, 1829. (Reprinted with corrections in *Essays Critical and Historical.* London, 1871. Reprinted: *Poetry, with Reference to Aristotle's Poetics.* Edited by A. S. Cook, Boston, 1891.)

Ogden, C. K., Richards, I. A., and Wood, James. *Foundations of Aesthetics*. 1925.

Olivero, Federico. *La Teoria Poetica del Newman*. 1930.

Patmore, Coventry. "The Ethics of Art." *The British Quarterly Review*, x, 1849.

Patmore, Coventry. "New Poets." *The Edinburgh Review*, c, 1856.

Patmore, Coventry. "English Metrical Critics." *The North British Review*, xxvii, 1857.

Powell, A. E. *The Romantic Theory of Poetry*. 1926.

Powell, Thomas. *Pictures of the Living Authors of Britain*. 1851.

Procter, B. W. "On English Poetry." *The Edinburgh Review*, xlii, 1825. (Reprinted in *Essays and Tales in Prose by Barry Cornwall*. Boston, 1853.)

Procter, B. W. "A Defence of Poetry." *The Edinburgh Review*, xlviii, 1828. (Reprinted in *Essays and Tales in Prose by Barry Cornwall*. Boston, 1853.)

Raysor, T. M. "Coleridge's Criticism of Wordsworth." *PMLA*, liv, 1939.

Richards, I. A. *Coleridge on Imagination*. 1935.

Roe, F. W. *Thomas Carlyle as a Critic of Art*. 1910.

Roellinger, F. X. *E. S. Dallas. A Study in Victorian Criticism*. Unpublished dissertation, University of Michigan, 1938.

Rossetti, W. M. *Preraphaelite Diaries and Letters*. 1900.

Ruskin, John. *Modern Painters*. Vol. ii, London, 1846.

Ruskin, John. *The Stones of Venice*. London, 1851, 1853.

Ruskin, John. *Modern Painters*. Vol. iii, London, 1856.

Saintsbury, George. *A History of English Criticism*. n.d.

Selkirk, J. B. *Ethics and Aesthetics of Modern Poetry*. 1878.

Shelley, P. B. *A Defense of Poetry*. Edited by A. S. Cook, n.d.

Sherwood, Margaret. *Undercurrents of Influence in English Romantic Poetry*. 1934.

Stedman, E. C. *The Nature and Elements of Poetry*. 1893.

Taylor, Sir Henry. *Philip Van Artevelde*. London, 1834.

Taylor, Sir Henry. *Critical Essays on Poetry*. 1878.

Thorpe, C. D. "The Imagination: Coleridge vs. Wordsworth." *PQ*, xviii, 1939.

Trilling, Lionel. *Matthew Arnold*. 1939.
Watts-Dunton, Theodore. *Poetry and the Renascence of Wonder*. 1884.
Wordsworth, William. *Literary Criticism*. Edited by N. C. Smith, 1905.
Zabel, M. D. *The Romantic Idealism of Art, 1800-1848*. 1938.

I. Index of Main Topics

2 3 7

II. Index of Authors

Aeschylus, 57, 60, 216

Alison, Archibald, 51, 183

Allingham, William, 22-23, 31, 163n

Aquinas, St. Thomas, 134

Aristotle, 5, 11-14, 15, 25, 28, 36-39, 41, 42, 45, 47, 51, 55, 59, 71, 127, 129, 135, 137, 141, 152, 161-62, 163, 169, 199, 221, 226

Arnold, Matthew, 3, 4, 21, 22, 23, 25, 33, 34, 37, 41, 42, 43, 45, 46, 54, 56, 58, 65, 76, 90, 122, 136n, 143n, *152-70*, 175, 196, 206, 208-9, 213, 215, 216, 219, 221, 223, 224

Augustine, St., 134

Bacon, Sir Francis, 5, 12-14, 15, 39, 62, 89, 102, 129, 132, 141, 171

Bagehot, Walter, 12, 17

Balzac, Honoré de, 204, 204n

Beethoven, Ludwig van, 74

Bentham, Jeremy, 66, 69

Béranger, Pierre Jean de, 204n

Berkeley, George, 146

Bosanquet, Bernard, 113n, 185n, 194n, 204n

Boswell, James, 79

Brimley, George, 11, 30, 33

Browning, Elizabeth Barrett, 204n

Browning, Robert, 21, 24, 56, 89n, *111-25*, 157, 159, 166, 194, 198, 206, 212, 217, 219, 221

Burke, Edmund, 5

Burns, Robert, 55, 79, 84, 139

Byron, George Gordon, Lord, 3, 6, 40, 55, 67, 84, 93, 104, 114n, 154, 165, 177, 204, 204n, 205

Carlyle, Jane Welsh, 172

Carlyle, Thomas, 4, 14, 19, 21, 22, 23, 24, 31, 32, 39, 43, 68, 71, 73, 77, 78, 79-92, 93, 94, 109, 110n, 111-12, 116, 117, 122, 123, 124n, 129, 139, 146, 154, 166, 169, 174, 175, 180n, 181, 182, 183n, 191, 192, 197, 204n, 211, 212, 213, 214, 216, 217, 219, 221

Chaucer, Geoffrey, 102

Cicero, 42, 47, 58, 70

Clough, Arthur Hugh, 22, 152-62, 208

Coleridge, Samuel Taylor, 3, 5, 6, 8, 9, 11, 16, 18, 19, 22, 26, 32, 39, 43, 44, 47-48, 61, 66, 68, 74, 75, 78, 86, 89, 93-94, 96, 97, 98, 103, 104n, 105, 106, 108, 109, 110, 113, 129, 130, 133-34, 135, 141, 142, 152, 163, 183, 186, 188, 189, 202, 210, 211, 213, 218, 219

Cowley, Abraham, 135

Cowper, William, 40

Crabbe, George, 130

Croce, Benedetto, 49